WE WON'T BUDGE

Also by Manthia Diawara

Black Genius
(With Walter Mosley,
Clyde Taylor, and Regina Austin)

In Search of Africa

African Cinema

WE WON'T BUDGE

A Malaria Memoir

MANTHIA DIAWARA

A Member of the
Perseus Books Group

Basic *Civitas* Books,
A Member of the Perseus Books Group

Library of Congress Cataloging-in-Publication Data
Diawara, Manthia, 1953–
  We won't budge : a malaria memoir / Manthia Diawara.
    p.   cm.
  ISBN 0-465-01709-6 (hard cover)
  1. Diawara, Manthia, 1953– 2. Malians—New York (State)—New
York—Biography. 3. Immigrants—New York (State)—New York—
Biography. 4. Malians—France—Paris—Biography. 5. New York (N.Y.)—
Biography. 6. Paris (France)—Biography. 7. Bamako (Mali)—Biography.
I. Title.

E184.M33D53 2003
974.7'10049606623—dc21   2003006955

03 04 05 / 10 9 8 7 6 5 4 3 2 1

CONTENTS

I dedicate this book to the memory of my father,

Mody DIAWARA

Preface

The idea for this book came from a deep frustration I felt on the death of Amadou Diallo, who was violently killed by New York City police. He was on his way back to his apartment, after a long day's labor, when they gunned him down.

I was saddened and angry because I felt that his short life in America mirrored my own beginning here, and that his American dream was betrayed by a violent and senseless killing. My frustration came partly from the fact that there are still no opportunities for young people like Amadou Diallo in their home countries in Africa. Not much has changed since 1974, when I, myself, had left Bamako, Mali—with other young people of my generation—to go to Europe and America. Still, today, the youth are fighting to get out of Africa, to run away from abject poverty, unemployment, civil and tribal wars, religious persecution, corruption, and government oppression. Another part of my profound disappointment with the world stemmed from a realization that Amadou Diallo was shot in New York because he was a black man. If he were white, he would still be alive today. He was killed because he fit a biased description, a racial profiling.

Amadou Diallo's death left a sour taste in my mouth. Just as my success story in America could have been his, the tragedy that had befallen him could be mine, as a black man in America—albeit an African. I remember writing an editorial about that which no newspaper wanted to publish. It went as follows:

Homeboy Cosmopolitan

Amadou Diallo was a "homeboy cosmopolitan," dressed in his down jacket, baseball cap, and tennis shoes. He hustled videos outside of a storefront in Manhattan and counted his money at the end of the day, with his mind full of every immigrant's dream of making it in this land of unlimited opportunities. Culturally, Amadou Diallo, not unlike most immigrants to this country, was different from African Americans, and perhaps even prejudiced against them. But Amadou Diallo was also a black man, and that visual sign is enough to get an African or Caribbean mistaken for an African American in the streets of New York.

Amadou Diallo's generation of Francophone Africans has just discovered America. In the 1960s and 1970s, it was radical for those of my generation from the former French colonies of Cote d'Ivoire, Guinea, Mali, and Senegal to use America as a dream space for emigration. We dreamed of going to France—the land of Liberty, Equality, and Fraternity—in order to rise above what we considered our miserable condition in Africa. We hoped to prove ourselves there, and to participate in the universal humanism as it was promulgated by the République. But as soon as our numbers grew large, the National Front and other racists raised their ugly heads against immigration and homeboy cosmopolitanism as threats to public safety and as a danger to French culture.

Amadou Diallo's generation turned to America because of its new image as the winner of the cold war and as the champion of globalization and democratization. The gains of the Civil Rights movement also opened the doors to many more Africans and Caribbeans, even if these groups do not always live in solidarity with their indigenous counterparts. Amadou Diallo's generation arrived in America, full of hope and life and dressed like homeboys. They took advantage of the space created by the civil rights struggles and America's superficial consumption of African-American popular culture. They rented apartments in black communities in Harlem, Brooklyn, and the Bronx. But, like most immigrants, they lived separately in their own cultures.

Little do the Amadou Diallos of the world know that the black man in America bears the curse of Cain, and that in America they, too, are considered black men, not Fulanis, Mandingos, or Wolofs. In America, no taxi will stop to pick them up; putting a price on their heads elects politicians; and the police will hunt them down.

They cut Amadou Diallo down like a black American, even though he belonged to the Fulani tribe in his native Guinea. There is a lesson here for all of us to learn. The tragedies of Abner Louima (a Haitian-American brutally raped by members of the New York Police Department) and Amadou Diallo—two immigrants submitted to the ritualistic white violence generally reserved for African Americans— should finally suffice as a political awakening for Africans and Caribbeans to the issues of race in America.

Ironically, the killing of Amadou Diallo has elevated him to the level of a martyr whose initial identification with homeboys, and subsequent ritualistic execution by the police, should serve primarily as another landmark of injustice for African Americans. It is only when new immigrants of African descent, and immigrants from Asia and Europe, realize that their opportunities are linked to the oppression of African Americans that the sacrifice of Amadou Diallo, this homeboy cosmopolitan, will influence the improvement of race relations in America.

But *We Won't Budge* is not about the death of Amadou Diallo, even if there are parallels between his life and the stories I tell here. The book is about the developed world—that is, the former colonizers of the African continent—that is now closing its doors to Africans and Arabs; it is about human rights violations and racism against people of color. I am sadder than I have ever been before because the more they say the world is globalized, the more they marginalize Africans and endanger our lives. As the Western media monopolizes control of the communication channels, our voices are unheard in Europe, America, and even in Africa. I am now unhappy wherever I go in the world. I cannot stand the stereotypes Europeans have of Americans or Africans, and vice versa. I cannot discuss Israel with Europeans, or Palestine with Americans. How did the world decide that we Africans have nothing meaningful to say about these important issues facing us: democracy and human rights. Lest our oppressors forget, we Africans have eyes to see, ears to hear, heads to analyze, and mouths to judge. And this book shows the way one African sees the world.

In *We Won't Budge*, I want to give a human face to African immigration in today's global world. As I describe the reasons that lead many Africans to leave the continent—poverty, persecution, and lack of opportunities—I try to make visible their predicament in Europe and America, where they are caught between tradition and modernity, and hindered by their attachment to the past and the resurgence of racism and police brutality against them in the countries of immigration.

Bedridden with malaria, I take the reader back to the time when I first emigrated to Paris and then to Washington, D.C. Some of the stories I tell here come straight out of the hallucinations caused by the malaria fever—which is capable of making one who suffers from it feel a pain as acute as a racist insult. I can best characterize the other stories in the book as romantic memoirs which are laced with rock & roll nostalgia, the freedom generated by African independences, and the euphoria of the Civil Rights movement in Washington, D.C.

I begin with my own stories of immigration and the experiences of my friends and relatives to show how recent immigrations have brought race relations to the forefront in Europe and how the American dream has become the primary lure for Africans who are locked out of the old continent. But one also wonders, with the Amadou Diallo shooting, if racism and xenophobia do not constitute the main obstacle to the integration and assimilation of immigrants and their attempt to achieve the American dream.

My memoirs are interlaced with immigrant experiences in the present. I go back and forth, moving between my immigration in the 1970s during the cold war and nowadays with globalization, the clash of civilizations, and immigration as a security issue not only in France and other European countries, but also in the United States. By making the past speak to the present in this manner and using literary techniques to write the history of African immigrations, I hope to go beyond anthropology and sociology, while continuing the discussion with these academic disciplines. I call my approach reverse anthropology, or neo-anthropology, or simply cultural studies. That is, I study African immigrants in Europe and America by using, whenever appropriate, the tools of anthro-

pology, sociology, literature, memoirs, the epistolary form,
and travel narratives.

My depiction, in the present tense, of the conditions in
which my friends and relatives live in Paris today is intended to
reveal the new divisions in French society. The African ghettoes
are a sober reminder of how France is becoming like America—
a society divided between black and white, rich and poor, and
European and others. As I travel between continents, I see
myself and people like me singled out at airports because of
our national origins and the color of our skin. Despite all the
education I have received in America, the fat professor's salary,
and all the titles, I wonder if I have become the cosmopolitan
individual of my dreams, or if I am still trapped in a racial or
ethnic group.

We Won't Budge is a literary tribute to a song, "Nous Pas
Bouger," by the Malian singer Salif Keita. He sang it in defense
against the exclusion and the human rights violations of
Africans in the global world. I intend my book to continue
the dissemination of Salif Keita's ideas and to contribute to
making the lives of African immigrants better. It is a book about
Africans in Europe and how their presence influences European
politics. It is also a comparative study of two social systems: race
relations in America and France; identity politics and communitarianism on the one hand, and individualism and universal
rights on the other. I hope, therefore, that the book will provide
a more complex and nuanced take on globalization.

The most recent books related to my subjects—i.e., immigration, globalization, the politics of recognition, unemployment and racism—that inspired me include *Les misères du
monde* (*The Weight of the World*) by Pierre Bourdieu et al., and
Tahar Ben Jelloun's *Le racisme expliqué à ma fille* (*Racism
Explained to My Daughter*). While Ben Jelloun's book is about

racism against North Africans in France, Bourdieu and his colleagues address the issues of class and the dislocation of the
welfare system in France. Paul Stoller, an American scholar, also
has published a fascinating book entitled *Money Has No Smell*,
about West African immigrants in North America. It is an
ethnographic study of African vendors in places like New York
and Atlanta. I hope that *We Won't Budge* will add more fuel to
the findings in these books, and that it will contribute to the
betterment of the conditions of immigrants everywhere in the
world.

Acknowledgments

A book like *We Won't Budge* is a collective effort that is infused with the voices and ideas of many people. To write it, I had to travel to different places to enlist the support of relatives, friends, and even passers-by. I am grateful to all of them. I was well served by the generous collaboration of my cousins: Bintou, Aicha, Kadia, Rokia, and Buba Diawara. The weekends at their apartment at Créteil never failed to quench my thirst for home. I especially want to thank them for the excellent Mafé, the Cheb, the Fonio, and the tea. I also want to express my deep gratitude for the moments spent in the company of my nephew Komakan Kamissoko, my buddy Diafode Sacko, and the circle of our friends at La Rotonde, Le Petit Farafina, and the Foyers in Montreuil and St. Dénis.

I enjoyed my sabbatical in Paris, largely because of the generous hospitality extended to me by the late Professor Pierre Bourdieu and his colleagues at the Collège de France and EHESS. In Bamako, Mali, I benefited from the generosity of my childhood friends, The Rockers. As Johnny Taylor used to say, "They've Got Soul." I thank them for keeping the energy flowing. This book also owes a great deal to the enduring memory of my Washington, D.C. days and my friends—Elvis, Américain, Blanc, Diaouné, and Chuck Larson.

Finally, a special acknowledgment goes to my institution, New York University, my colleagues—Clyde Taylor, Awam Amkpa, Christopher Winks, and Bob Stam—and the staff of Africana Studies and the Institute of African American Affairs—Ramona Knepp, Laura Rice, Linda Morgan, Iris Coffield, and Ted Sammons. They deserve a big and warm applaud for going all the way with me. Walter Mosley proved to be a friend and an inspiration. Danny Glover was always there for me, like a brother.

An author needs people to believe in his work in order to keep on writing, particularly in the most difficult times, as after 9/11. These people, for me, are Gloria Loomis, my agent, and Liz Maguire, my editor. I cannot thank them enough for their understanding and support. And lastly, there is my family: Regina, Mansita, and Daman. Thank you for once again putting up with me.

Back to Bamako

EVERY TIME I AM READY to leave Bamako, I feel as if I am on the run. I begin to tire of the social roles expected of me, I run out of cash to give to relatives and friends, and I miss the cafés and the freedom my anonymity affords me in New York and Paris. It is funny how I had never thought that New York and Paris could ever stand between Bamako and myself. Before, I had thought of them as places where I had had to go in order to get an education and to work so that I could return triumphantly to Bamako. Now here I am, like a thief in the night, waiting for the plane to Paris, avoiding people's eyes, and clutching my passport and plane ticket as if they were the most important things to me at this moment.

At times like these, I question my undying love for Bamako. After all, why keep coming back to my home only to get bored after one week? It must be that Bamako is in my blood, something I cannot get rid of. No sooner am I in New York than I start missing it again. I think of it when something makes me sad, and I think of it when I am happy. But once I am in Bamako, my love for it begins to dissipate. It is especially hard now, after all these years of coming and going, for my love for any particular thing in the city to last longer. I blame that on the fact that many of my childhood friends live abroad, as I do, and that some unfortunate ones, like Aboli, have died. Never again can we have a full reunion of all my childhood friends.

Bamako has changed, and yet it is still the same. When I visit my friends who stayed at home, all we have in common is the past, which is now some thirty years old. We talk about our teenage years in the sixties, and when we come to the present, we see everything differently. They scare me with their strong religious views, which for me block their entry into the modern world, and which they never tire of forcing on me. Perhaps it is because everyone wants to convert me, as a sign of his or her love for me, that I easily tire of Bamako. I guess I had also expected the misery and squalor that had enveloped our childhoods to go away after all these years. But the same poverty that had pushed my generation and prior generations to emigrate to Europe and America is still here, as powerful as ever. It has now made me a stranger to my home.

In a funny way, I think I am sore at Bamako because I am not a celebrity here. No one knows me outside of my extended family members and the small group of my childhood friends. Dressed in jeans, a T-shirt, and tennis shoes, I go from my hotel to my uncle's house without being recognized. Even on the street in front of my uncle's compound where I grew up, nobody remembers me. My uncle, who now has memory lapses, only knows me by my name, but does not recognize me physically. When Nana, my aunt, informs him, "It's Manthia," he always asks, "Which Manthia?" "The one in America, of course," she says, rolling her eyes and smiling at me. Only then does he shake my hand, pull me down to sit next to him, and start rubbing my hair and my shoulders, as if I were still a little boy.

This scene is always followed by the arrival a group of people filing into my aunt's room to greet me. Some of them, who are from our village, have come to Bamako with the prospect of finding a plane ticket and a visa to go to France or America. Others have come to the city because the rains were scant and there was no food in the village. In my uncle's compound, there are many children who were born during my exile and women whose husbands left them behind when they went to France or America. My uncle is responsible for feeding all these mouths, paying their medical bills when they are sick, and clothing the children. The situation has not changed from the time I was a little boy with my own mother, so like these women waiting for their husbands in my uncle's compound.

For that brief moment, I become everyone's hope. After all, I am the émigré who has returned from America, and I owe it to the group to help some people get there. Somebody must have helped me in the past to get out of Bamako, and now it is time for me to pay back that debt. Complete strangers are asking me to sponsor them in order to get a visa to go to America. They assure me that once they are there, they will work to reimburse me every cent of my money. They take my uncle and everyone present as witnesses, and they allude to our extended-family blood ties to show me my obligation to them.

But how can I tell them that my years in exile have made me see the negative side of the extended-family system? That it locks people into conformity, saps the individual's energies and resources, and prevents the person from having a private life or accumulating the fortunes necessary for the development of societies and industries? Exile has made me a different person indeed. But how can I stop myself from feeling guilty about having different values from the people from whom I have come? I was once like all those little boys and girls who are now hiding behind their mothers, trying to take a peek at me and claim me as one of their own. They look dirty, barefoot, and naked with their stomachs bulging and mucus caking their nostrils. The way they cling to their mothers, with their shining brown eyes, fills me with emotion and inspires me to change everything around me and give them the same chances afforded children in America and France.

Surely, my impotence to change the situation—to get immediate results and transform the images that remind me of the poverty of my childhood—adds to the thinning of my patience with Bamako. During this trip, I realized that I have created a new way of relating to the people in my extended family. Given my lack of power to change their situation into a modern one, and my unwillingness to act for them as an authentic son who has returned home to support their way of life, I have become inadequate, a bastard of Africa and America, one who has been lost to modernity.

I have also found out that as long as I occupied this position of inadequacy in relation to them, they tolerated me. I have become the one who has mislearned the culture through a long stay in America. Even though I am the age of some of the elders today, my vocabulary in our language remains primary, like a child's. I do not dress according to tradition, in embroidered boubous befitting someone with my age and diplomas. People do not see me at the mosque during prayer time. These are misbehaviors for which only children and people who are mentally ill, strangers, or criminals can be excused. But I have found that this inadequacy is the price I pay for being accepted by my people. In fact, the same thing is true in America as well, where everyone relates to immigrants as children.

As I sit here in the VIP lounge in the airport, waiting for Air Afrique (late again), I cannot focus my mind on one single thing. The man at the check-in counter who took my passport into the back to verify its authenticity did not even look twice at the papers of the white people in line with me. I looked at the crowd for a recognizable face, but I knew nobody and no one recognized me. It's the same story everywhere I go in Bamako. All my childhood friends have either left the country or have not stayed in school long enough to do the kinds of clerical and office work that would situate them in Bamako.

The VIP room is like most such rooms at international airports—or at least it appears that way. There is a desk at the door, with a woman who checks tickets or membership cards, then the bar, a television in the background, and comfortable couches that give the place an air of luxury. The newspaper rack sits against the wall, and a newly installed air conditioner under the window makes more noise than cool air. Since the *International Herald Tribune* is at least two weeks old, I take a seat near the TV because of the loud noise emitted by the air conditioner. *CNN Headline News* is repeating itself, parrot-like, on a breakthrough peace accord between Ehud Barak and Yasser Arafat that President Bill Clinton has designed. No one wants peace in that region, and yet that's all the press talks about.

Looking around me, I see mostly white faces, except for the black women in front of the door and at the bar who look after us. It is already like being in Europe, where you never see an African in a fancy restaurant, except in the kitchen. People around me are drinking champagne, perhaps to celebrate their departure. I ask the woman at the bar for a glass of red wine. She looks at me with surprise; perhaps she knows that I am from Bamako. But I say to myself, "That's her business. I am free to do as I please." Walking back to my seat, I can feel her condemnatory gaze on my back; she must think the worst of me now. Mali is a republic. That is, the citizens are protected against religious laws such as the Muslim ban on alcohol. But the citizens themselves stigmatize alcohol, and anybody who touches it has fallen from grace in their eyes. She now thinks she's better than I. People caught drinking here are considered to be worse than thieves and are removed from the community of Muslim brotherhood, which comprises the majority of Bamako's population. Those who continue to drink—there are plenty of them in Bamako—and do not want criticism from the Muslim community go to dark places at night to drink. They also frequent the bars of international hotels, where they mix with foreigners, or visit the discotheques, where alcohol and prostitution go hand in hand. You should see those same guys—for they are mostly men who leave their wives at home—in the daytime, dressed as if they had just come from the Holy Land in Saudi Arabia, bragging about the greatness of the God who saves them from sin. Some people think that because they know something about you, they are better than you.

This makes returning home difficult, if not impossible. I am still under the shock of what I saw last night. Around midnight, I was at the Akwaba, an outdoor jazz club on the south side of the city, when two people I knew back in the 1970s in Washington, D.C., walked in. I was immediately elated to see people I knew and who would recognize me in a place like this, which was mostly frequented by foreigners in search of Malian culture and the elite of Bamako (TV personalities, civil servants, and businessmen). Everybody was either with a girlfriend or looking for one. People in West Africa rarely go out at night with their wives; that was why the lights were sufficiently dimmed so that it would not be easy to recognize the customers.

The first guy was accompanied by another man and two young women who looked to be around twenty-five, or half the men's age. After exchanging greetings, my friend introduced me to his companion, also an expatriate Malian who had been living in Sweden for more than thirty years. He worked there as a mechanical engineer and had come to Bamako to pay his condolences after his father's passing away. I had invited them to join me at my table because I was alone and tired of observing the scene. I had also wanted to hear about what my friend from Washington was doing now and to get some news of other Washington friends I knew in the 1970s. He told me that he had now completely resettled in Bamako and that he had an import/export business license to bring computers and other electronic equipment into Mali. He and his friend from Sweden, who worked with Erikson Electronics, had applied for the cellular telephone market in Mali. If their bid were to come through, his friend would also be relocated to Bamako. And what was I doing with myself? Was I still in California? He had heard from mutual friends that I was a teacher somewhere there.

"Well," I replied, "I was once a professor at the University of California at Santa Barbara. But that was a long time ago. I teach at NYU now."

"Oh yeah," he said. "I know NYU; it's in Greenwich Village, right?"

"Don't believe a word he says," interrupted a baritone voice behind us. "He be telling lies! He don't know nothing but lies. Mark my word!"

We all turned around to where the voice was coming from and saw the man who was talking. He was gesturing, drawing imaginary lines with his arms going back and forth. At the end we all laughed, and the man, whose name was Macky Tall, and I embraced each other. I realized then that I had been speaking English all along with my other friend and his companion from Sweden. We had completely excluded the two young women from our conversation, and had it not been for Macky Tall's interruption, we would have gone on like that for a long time. At that moment, I found it odd that we had chosen to speak English instead of French, the official language of Mali, or Bambara, which was most commonly spoken in Bamako. I could also sense some admiration for us on the part of the people sitting near our table, for they all seemed to be listening to our conversation in English. For them, we were a different kind of Malian because we had been in America and we no longer faced the obstacles that lay in front of them. English made us more powerful than even the French people who had colonized us.

But the evening was just beginning for me. Macky Tall, who had been speaking English with an accent and body language like those of a Brooklyn homeboy, took me away from my other friend and his companions. The place was now getting livelier, and people were dancing in front of the musicians, who were playing classic Cuban *sons* that had never gone out of style in Bamako since the 1960s. Macky drew me over to a table where another man was drinking beer and smoking a cigarette. As soon as we sat down, the man started an argument with Macky. He was talking about his sister, whom Macky had married just a couple of years ago and was now leaving behind to come to bars. Macky tried to introduce me to him in an attempt to change the conversation, but his brother-in-law was determined. He said that he had not been to America and did not speak English. "We are here," he continued, "and we don't need anybody from New York or Washington to tell us how to live our lives. This is Mali, and I don't care about America."

The man ordered another beer and lit another cigarette. He was looking me in the eye defiantly, as if the discussion were now between the two of us. I just stared back at him and said nothing. I knew he was drunk and wanted attention, so my best weapon was to deny him that.

"Don't mind him, man," Macky said. "He's fucked up."

"Don't worry about me," I answered in English. "I understand."

The brother-in-law fanned away from his face the smoke he had just released from his nose and mouth. He was now waving his index finger at us. For the first time, I noticed his face under the yellowish light bulb of the nightclub. He was good-looking in spite of the anger tightening his elongated jaws.

"Listen, Macky," he intoned, attempting to remain cool, "I've tried to be reasonable with you. I invited you to my home and drank beer with you. I don't have any problem with that," he said, turning his gaze on me.

"I bought beer for him and invited him to my home. Ask him, has he ever invited me to his home and bought me beer, even though he is married to my sister? Eh? Eh? That's what I am talking about." The brother-in-law inhaled a lungful of smoke from his cigarette, which glowed and crackled under the pressure of the drag.

"Let's get out of here, man, before I punch him in the face," Macky told me in English. We stood up to leave, but suddenly Macky pulled me back, saying, "Wait a minute, I'm 'a lay somethin' on dis muthafucka."

I got really nervous then because I thought Macky was going to start a fight. I restrained him, but he yanked himself away, went over to the table, and, assuming the posture of someone getting ready to fight, said in French, "*Est-ce que tu me connais?*" ("Do you know who I am?")

"I don't care about your sister," he declared. "You can come and pick her up if you want. Who are you to come here and insult me? And where's your wife? What are you doing here?"

"*Ça va, ça va,*" the brother-in-law said, gesturing disdainfully to show that he was finished with us. "*Ça va, ça va, tu m'as compris.*" ("OK, OK, you got my point.") He picked up his beer glass and took a large swig, leaving foam on his lips. He then resumed smoking, blotting us completely out of his existence.

I made another attempt to pull Macky away, and this time he did not resist. We went outside, where it took him a while to locate his car among the many cars parked in front of the club. We both had had a bit too much to drink. Macky said that we should go to the Tempo, another nightclub, where people were more fun. I was a bit worried about driving in the condition that we were in. But when Macky opened the door of his BMW for me, I got in anyway. When we were on the main road, Macky told me that it was a good thing I had stopped him, 'cause he was gonna bust that guy's lips, he was gonna punch his face, fuck him up, and to hell with his sister anyway.

Finally, he said, "So Manthia, how you been, man? Glad to see ya!"

"It's good to see you too, Macky. How are things here?" I asked.

"Baad! Business is bad; everything is at a standstill. People ain't got a dime in their pockets; it's all fucked up now."

"Yeah, that's what I heard too. But how are *you* doing?"

"Fine, Manthia, just fine. Dig it?"

"Yeah," I said, and we fell silent for a moment. Driving in Bamako at night like this was like going between several small towns. From the Akwaba to the Tempo, where we were going, we had to traverse the center of the city from east to west. The city center was completely asleep, except for the occasional dog that barked at our car when we came near the main marketplace. As we drove through a whole section of the city that was plunged in darkness, Macky explained to me that Bamako had changed a lot. There was a great deal of corruption, and only people involved in politics on the side of the ruling party were doing well. They had kept all the deals between themselves, leaving the market in the hands of people who knew nothing about business. All the people we used to know who had been powerful in Bamako in the old days had been pushed to the side today.

"But, Macky, how can you live here then, if there . . . "

"By kicking ass!" he proclaimed. "If anybody stands in my way, I put my foot up his ass. I was born and raised in this town, and ain't nobody here gonna stop me from getting what's mine. I kick ass every day, that's how. Dig it?"

We both laughed. Macky was still speaking English the way we had learned it in the 1970s from black Americans in Washington, D.C. We arrived at the Tempo, where several cars were parked all along the street. A young boy emerged from the darkness and appointed himself the guardian of our car. As Macky and I walked toward the door, I asked him whose ass he was going to kick this time. He said mine, if I did not behave. We laughed.

The Tempo was a club divided into three sections: an outdoor area with a live band playing Malian and Cuban jazz; a downstairs discotheque with Afro-pop music, Congolese *soukous*, and rap; and a bar upstairs with couches and living-room tables for people who just wanted to drink, smoke, and have a conversation. We stopped by the bar first, because Macky was hoping to meet some business associates there. He also told me that he did not like the discotheque very much because its clientele was mostly young girl prostitutes and tourists. The bar was better because it was air-conditioned and the atmosphere was nicer. I wondered how people were dealing with the AIDS epidemic in Bamako.

As soon as we entered the bar, I heard people greeting Macky in English from all sides: "Hey MacJohn, what's happening?" "How are you, McDonald?" "Gimme five, Mack!" I could not believe what I was hearing and seeing. There were mostly men in the bar, except for one of the bartenders, a woman in her thirties who was now exchanging jokes with Macky. Most of the customers were drinking hard liquor like whiskey and cognac. Two guys were whispering something to each other in a corner, pointing at Macky and me at the bar. A man by himself at a table was moving back and forth in his chair as if he were listening to imaginary music. He was surveying the room and us with a smile on his face. In fact, he gave me the chills. But the rest of the people seemed happy to see Macky and not to worry about him. They gathered around Macky, each one competing for his attention. They used expressions like "Hey, boy, where you been?" or "My main man, McDonald!" Macky answered all of them with even bigger words: "I ain't your goddamn man! And you! You better not call me 'boy' or I'll put my foot up your ass. Hey, you there! Leave my girlfriend alone before I fuck you up!" The barroom thundered with laughter. Even I laughed along with the people. A few admirers of Macky could not stop themselves from laughing until they had tears in their eyes and started coughing.

Then, suddenly, the man sitting by himself stood up and started walking toward me. When he got close, he pointed his finger at me, saying, "Irving Street, 65 Irving Street, Fourteenth and Irving, 1975!" He was now poking his index finger at my chest as he repeated each word. Everyone in the bar was looking at us. I was getting more nervous, and had Macky not intervened at that moment, I would not have known what to do. "Fuck you!" he said. "Leave us alone. Who gives a fuck about Irving Street? Been there, done that." Once again, people were delighted by Macky; they laughed until they were tired, and they waited for him to say some more smart things.

"Don't you remember him? They threw his ass out of D.C. in 1975," Macky said to me, but he was really not expecting me to answer, at least not right away.

"You know how Americans are. They don't mess with their laws," Macky continued.

"*Ah oui, ça c'est vrai, oh!*" ("That's the truth!") said a man. He was standing to my left, facing Macky and with his back to the bar. It was the first time I had heard someone speak in French there.

"Shut up! I wasn't talking to you. You don't know nothin' 'bout Americans! So hush your mouth!" Macky had everyone laughing again, like little children watching their favorite cartoon character at work.

"Don't say nothin' 'bout Americans in front of me and this man here." Macky was pointing at me. "He knows America like you know your whore. You know wha'm sayin'?" Mackey said, slapping his hand into mine. I was a bit embarrassed, because I did not want to give the impression that I was bragging about America.

"That guy over there is Johnny. You know, the same," Macky told me, pointing toward the man who had tagged me with Irving Street. He had gone back to his seat and again put the devilish smile on his face.

"Yeah, it's Ibrahim Diallo, aka Johnny. The same one who was in Washington, D.C., in 1975, when we were on Irving Street. He was caught working with a tourist visa, and they expelled him. Ever since then he's been obsessed with returning to America. But he's calmer now. He just be like that sometimes; he be in his own world and shuts everybody else out. It's just seeing you that's excited him so much, that's all," concluded Macky.

A woman's voice over the intercom announcing that Air Afrique has arrived pulls me out of what seemed like a nightmare, because it felt real. I'm glad in a way, for I am not sure I want to keep thinking about the story of that man when I am getting ready to board a plane for France. Some stories bring bad luck to the storyteller, and this one seems like one such tale. One day I would have to rid myself of the memory of that night in Washington, D.C., at the restaurant Chez Dominique, when they destroyed Johnny's American dream. Macky and I used to laugh with our friends in Washington about the way he was caught by the INS (Immigration and Naturalization Service), like a vampire surprised by sunlight, and sent home. We had thought then that we were so clever for passing for black Americans and for remaining undetected by the immigration officials. How innocent we were then! But in reality, I could never forget the way we had said good-bye, Johnny and I—he in handcuffs and I standing behind the pantry bar.

As I finally take my seat on the plane, I say to myself that the burden of memory is sometimes too painful to carry around. A white couple takes the seat in front of me, the man and the woman each holding a newborn baby. I tell myself that they must be working for some charitable or nongovernmental organization. Everybody wants to get out of Africa, even newborn babies. But I must take my mind off that, too. I am tired and determined to get my rest and be ready to do all my errands tomorrow in Paris. It is already past midnight on a plane that was supposed to take off two hours ago.

I pull one bag out from under the seat to open the compact discs I had bought this time in Bamako, the new ones from Salif Keïta, Oumou Sangare, and Habib Koité, which will keep me busy until I fall asleep. I look again under the seat for my black purse with the CD player and the old CDs. At first, I cannot find it, and I think that it must have been displaced when the plane was taking off. I undo my seat belt to look under the seat, but still cannot find it. As I comb with my hands the floor under the seats in front of and next to me, a horrible feeling begins to overtake me, from my head to my stomach. Did I lose it somewhere between the check-in counter and the lounge, or did someone steal it from me? If I had left it on the counter or in the lounge, perhaps there was a chance of recovering it. When I arrive in Paris, I will call my brother or one of my cousins to go check for me. Oh yes, my brother—I must have forgotten it in his car when he brought me to the airport.

I climb back into my seat and fasten my seat belt. Sweat is running down my face, and my body is hot enough to set my shirt on fire. Why am I so nervous because of a CD player and some albums that can easily be replaced? I comfort myself with the idea that I must have left the purse in my brother's car. That's my best chance of recovering it, for I know that my brother will keep it safe for me. I don't trust those people at the airport; they only have regard for bribes and for white people. Now I am wide awake, instead of sleeping like most people on the plane.

I pick out of my other bag one of the new books I had bought in Bamako, Ahmadou Kourouma's *Allah n'est pas obligé*. It's a great title that captures people's overreliance on God in this part of the world. Muslims in West Africa leave everything to God: The rich person is rich because God willed it, and the poor one is poor because God wanted it that way. It's Allah who gives some people good health and keeps others sick and handicapped. People's destinies are written before they come into the world, and they cannot do anything to change them. I remember that when I was young and in high school, I used to pray to Allah to let me get out of Mali, study in Europe, and live happily at least until age fifty. I said fifty, and not seventy or eighty, because I knew that I was asking too much of God; I was bargaining my place in heaven for happiness in this world. This dilemma used to keep me up late at night, or wake me up from a deep sleep soaked in sweat.

Allah n'est pas obligé (Allah is not responsible, or Allah does not have to hear your prayer if he chooses not to) is a title that reminds me of my own transgression against the will of God in our part of the world. By describing a God who is often blind to the cruelties we inflict on one another, and deaf to our cries of complaint, this title invites people to take their destinies into their own hands, to accept responsibility for their own actions or passivity. It is unfortunate that the literacy rate is so low in West Africa, or this title would have created a big controversy over its interpretation.

The book itself is about a young boy's search for his aunt in Sierra Leone and Liberia, and how he becomes a child soldier in the civil wars of both countries. The opening sections are brimful of amputations, gangrenes, and foul odors in a population caught between Islamic movements and animist witch doctors. The characters' complete surrender to these forces makes identification with them impossible and produces an exotic and Afro-pessimist effect that becomes the only pleasure of the text. I mean by this that as the novel relates its story of African-on-African crime through exotic scenes, one loses the sense that there is any hope for change in Africa, that good will triumph over evil, or that God loves Africa. My problem with people who make art out of Afro-pessimism is that they emphasize evil over good, and by doing so they naturalize poverty, violence, and incompetence as an African condition. Since Africans are blamed for their own miserable conditions, Europeans and Americans who still benefit from their exploitation of raw material bear no responsibility.

I put down *Allah n'est pas obligé* and try to find a comfortable position in my seat so that I can go to sleep. But one of the babies in front of me starts crying. If it is true that Mali is one of the poorest countries in the world, then these babies are lucky to be getting away to a country where they would have a chance to eat a proper meal every day, receive medical care, go to school, and prepare a better future for themselves. Surely I am not against that, and I cannot blame these white people for trying to save two Malian babies. I do not need anybody to remind me that Mali is a poor country and that children and women suffer the worst. I know the troubles I myself had endured running away from hunger and poverty in Mali—once in my village, where my parents had left me with my uncle, and later in Bamako, where I was staying with my father's other brother. I will never forget how, as a seven-year-old, I lived my last month in the village at the end of the rainy season. There was no grain left in my uncle's granary, and he had to go around the village to borrow a calabash full of corn or millet or beans from more fortunate heads of households. The women would cook it for our supper with a lot of salt and very little meat. Some nights we went without eating. And then I would wake up in the morning very hungry and unable to play with the other kids. Sometimes I would sit in the middle of the road, incapable of moving my legs. Coming from the well, women carrying their buckets of water on their heads would ask me to get out of the road, and I could not obey their orders. My mind would will my legs to respond to its command—but nothing happened; it was as if I were paralyzed. I remember how it used to embarrass me that I could not obey the women coming from the well.

Every time I could, I pleaded with my uncle to send me to my parents. At first he chided me for being spoiled by my parents in the city and not being able to endure life in the village like the other boys my age. But when he realized that I could not stop crying for my parents, he gave me a bundle of thirty sticks and told me to pull one out every morning. He would send me to my parents after I pulled out the last one. It was during that period that I began dreaming all kinds of food-related dreams. Sometimes I would dream that I had finished with the bundle and was with my mother eating from a bowl-ful of rice and plenty of meat. Sometimes, I would be with the boys in the village. We had caught birds in our traps—a sticky sap that we had extracted by cutting open the branches of certain trees—or lizards or crickets, and we were roasting them for a nice meal. But my favorite dream was when I was sitting in the middle of the street and could change myself into any of the boys in the village during mealtime and eat at their houses. I was able to fly into every compound I wanted to, or just make myself invisible and eat people's food. In those days, I was so afraid of the distinctive sound of the hyena—at night during mealtime—that I would lose my appetite upon hearing it.

In Bamako, too, I remember hard times. I went to school one time, the whole year, with one pair of khaki shorts and a short-sleeved shirt. I was in the eighth grade, and already by the middle of the year, the bottom of my shorts was worn out. The first hole appeared when a nail on my classroom bench caught me unawares. I went to my aunt's tailor to put a patch on it, but other parts in the back and between the legs began falling apart soon afterward, causing me embarrassment in front of the girls. Eighth grade was the most painful year for me because of the way my shorts made me feel self-conscious. Toward the end of the year, my shirt ripped open as well, leaving a big hole in my back like a window. Eighth grade was also the class where many of my friends dropped out of school, because neither they nor their parents saw any sense in continuing with an education that increasingly cost more effort and money. After school closed that year, I remember running away with my father's friend's cattle to Liberia. The trip took me twenty-one days, riding in trucks with cows or walking behind them with Fulani herds. I stayed with another of my father's brothers, who had been living in Monrovia for more than thirty years. I had never seen him before, but he was my only hope for finding some clothes for the next school year.

So I can see why people, including these two babies, run away from their miserable condition in Mali. During this trip, I have seen abject poverty from Bamako to Timbuktu, which leads me to believe that very little has changed since I was a little boy in my village. In a desert town called Goundam, on the way to Timbuktu, I saw a man working under the hot sun to earn a daily wage of less than one U.S. dollar. He cut grass with a machete and tied it in two big bundles, which he loaded onto the back of his donkey to deliver to people who owned horses in the town. I followed him to his nomadic settlement on the other side of the lake to see his family. The ride across the lake with him and five women returning from the market only cost about forty U.S. cents, which I paid. The owner of the canoe propelled it on the water with a long pole on which he leaned with all his strength before pulling it out and then pushing against it again.

When we got to the man's village, he showed me his three wives and more children than I could keep track of. They lived in tents built of millet stalks and thatched grass. There were no wells or toilets. None of the children in the village attended school in the town. They cautiously followed us at a distance as the man showed me around; as we approached them, the women covered their faces with the black wrap they used as dress. Even though I was from Mali and lived in the same times as they did, they looked afraid of me, as though we were from two different planets, and mine had been unnaturally pushed forward.

Yet there is something about those two babies on the plane that still bothers me. I know that I myself have contributed to the representation of Mali as the poorest country in the world. How can I therefore blame this white couple for their human-itarian gesture of adopting two Malian babies? I guess I have to admit to myself that I am embarrassed and angered by white people's coming to the rescue of poor Africans when they are responsible in the first place for causing poverty in Africa, maintaining African nations in a dependent situation, using racism to keep able and willing Africans from immigrating to Europe for better-paying jobs, and destroying African systems of values in order to replace them with their own. That's why African cities like Bamako are so dirty today: The government refuses to clean up after people because it has accepted the image of itself as poor and therefore cannot afford to clean the streets. After all, clean streets are a luxury of developed coun-tries, and Bamako is not Paris. The people, on the other hand, throw garbage everywhere because everybody else does, and no one can tell them not to. There is a danger that we have accepted an image of ourselves not only as poor, but also as worthless and undeserving of a clean environment. Waiting for white people to come to our rescue, we have all become infantilized in our own environment.

The pilot announces that he will be starting the plane's descent into Paris, apologizes again for the delay—which was not Air Afrique's fault—and wishes us a nice stay in Paris. The plane lands. I gather my stuff from the cabin above and from under my seat. The two babies are now sleeping in the arms of their new parents. I hope that they will be all right wherever they end up. It is past seven o'clock and it is still dark outside the windows. I can also feel the cold plastic window as I look outside the plane. I remember that it is November. I put on my coat and hat and follow the people in front of me outside the plane and hallway to the immigration police. The line stalls as we approach the exit door. When I reach there, I realize that the police have been stopping people to check their papers even before they get to the immigration line. They stop the couple with the Malian babies in front of me and tell them to stand aside with a group of Malian passengers who have also been told to wait. One of the policemen looks at my passport for a while, flipping the pages until he finds the visa stamps, and then orders me to move forward.

I wonder why the police are at the door of the plane to meet people coming from Mali. I have never seen them do that to planes coming from America. When I pass the second row of immigration police and while waiting for my luggage to arrive, I start thinking again about the couple with the babies. Maybe they were suspected of smuggling Malian babies into France. I once heard a story about a Malian woman who went into labor on a flight between Bamako and Paris. She was joining her husband, who worked in an automobile factory in France. The plane made an emergency landing in Algiers to leave her in the care of doctors before continuing on to Paris with the other passengers. After the woman had her baby in Algiers, she was told that she had to apply for a visa for the infant in order to continue with it to France. The French embassy in Algiers turned down her request on the grounds that deception was involved: She had wanted to have the baby in France so that she could have the right to stay there permanently. I pick up my suitcase and move toward the exit, concerned now only about finding a taxi and going through the rush-hour traffic. As I pull away from the line, I run into the couple with their new babies. They look as determined as ever. We exchange a smile for the first time.

Outside, there is a long line for taxis, and it is cold in Paris. When my turn comes, the cabdriver, who is African, tries to give me a hard time about where I should be putting my bag with my computer in it. I insist on taking it inside the cab with me, but he tells me that it counts as luggage and, according to the rules, has to go in the trunk. I am so tired that I do not want to argue with him. I let him take the passenger behind me rather than listen to him lecture me about the rules in France. I know how even Africans in Paris have internalized racism against other Africans in Paris and use all kinds of excuses to discriminate against them. It is obvious to me that this cabdriver prefers a white customer to an African, and I just don't feel like taking lessons or giving one this morning. The next cab arrives, and I get in front with my computer bag. The driver, who is white, tries to humor me with light conversation: where I am coming from, the Cameroonian soccer team, his French wife and Moroccan mistress. But the first cabdriver has already left a bad taste in my mouth, so I tune this one out.

By the time I get to my apartment, my son has left for school. I open the windows to let in air, and take my shower. Still too nervous to sleep, I go to la Rotonde to have coffee, read the *International Herald Tribune*, and catch up with the news of the world. I have plenty of time before my noon appointment with the prefecture in the fourteenth arrondissement. I am feeling good about myself again. La Rotonde is cozy. The glass walls protect me from the cold outside. I love watching people go by in the streets, looking for directions with a map in their hands, stopping at newspaper stands to look at headlines and magazine covers. Lovers looking back at each other as one of them disappears into the subway hole; motorists blowing their horns and cursing at others in the intersection; the 91 bus rolling into the Vavin stop like a giant green bottle tossed on the sand by ocean waves. I see an African opening a fire hydrant and placing towels to guide the water along the right-hand curve of the Boulevard Montparnasse. It brings me back to reality.

I finish reading the *Tribune*. It has two interesting stories on soccer: one on the multiracial makeup of the French national team, and the other on the Italian lawmakers' attempt to limit to four the number of non-European passport holders playing for the premier soccer clubs in Europe. The latter mentions some clubs that were fined for drafting Brazilian players with fake passports from Portugal. The Italians also believe that the presence of foreign players in their premier teams hurts the chances of homegrown players to dominate in international competitions.

I still have more time to kill before going to my rendezvous. So I take out the chapter I have written so far for my book on immigration. I am going to reread it to see if I still like it after my visit to Bamako.

II

We Won't Budge

I don't know why I care about Paris. Sometimes I feel that Paris does not care about me. But I keep telling people that Paris is my favorite city in the world. I love the cafés, the cuisine, and the big boulevards. They make me feel good, as if they were made for me and for people like me, who enjoy these vestiges of modernity.

Today, for example, sitting in la Rotonde, where I regularly have lunch, I was feeling good about myself and Paris. I was sitting facing the Boulevards Montparnasse and Raspail, with a panoramic view of the Hotel Raspail, cars and motorcycles going in every direction, the long buses that take you to Bastille, the metro station at Vavin, the taxi station, and the fish restaurant le Dome across the street. The pedestrians are the most fascinating. They emerge from the metro hole or the number 91 bus and rush to cross the street in front of speeding cars. Everybody is well dressed, and you can see at every traffic crossing somebody with a bouquet of flowers or a baguette. People also stand in front of the metro and kiss for a long time before saying good-bye.

I like it inside la Rotonde. The silver noise at the bar is not too loud to interrupt conversation, the waiters are cordial, and the customers are regular enough that I can already pick out some recognizable faces in the crowd of tourists who also come here because of the name of the place. Most of all, the lovers at la Rotonde are reassuring. There are those who come here after twenty-five years of marriage. If they are Americans, after they have finished their coffee they go outside to take pictures of themselves in front of the door. There are also lovers who are probably cheating on other people in their lives. I suspect this from the way they touch each other under the cover of the tiny café tables. Sometimes I also hear them talk about their children, their husbands, their wives, or other people at work. La Rotonde is a very discreet place. Everybody minds his or her own business, as if each couple or group is its own world at its own table.

What amazes me in general about Paris cafés is the tremendous power a café table has in giving people a sense of privacy. Once people settle comfortably at a café table, they tune out the rest of the world around them and behave as if they are in their own private spaces. At la Rotonde, there are tables that I find more comfortable than others because, once at them, it is easy to slip into my own world. I consider them charismatic tables, and they are coveted by all who are indolent like myself.

And today I was feeling particularly good because I had just had a great lunch: *maquerau breton au vin blanc,* or sardine-like fish cooked with shallots and served with potatoes and green salad dressed in a vinaigrette sauce. I had a *pichet* of house red wine to go with it. I was playing with my espresso cup and caressing in my mind some ideas that I had been mulling over for the last year in preparation for my sabbatical leave.

I had decided to move to Paris for one year to write a book on an African decolonization movement called Rassemblement Démocratique Africains (RDA). Using Paris as a base, I would go to the pertinent African countries for fieldwork and check books and newspapers at the Bibliothèque Nationale. I would also gauge the French intellectual scene and go to the Collège de France to attend the seminars of Pierre Bourdieu.

I still had a few minutes left before I had to step outside and go to my rendezvous at Oberkampf in the eleventh arrondissement. I could tell that the red wine had gone to my head because I had begun to fantasize about myself in Paris. I was changing from one identity to another. Sometimes I was a Francophone intellectual at la Rotonde with friends from Martinique, Guadeloupe, and different African countries. I could see Léopold Sédar Senghor, Léon G. Damas, and Aimé Césaire meeting at la Rotonde and talking about negritude and modernity. La Closerie des Lilas, another famous café, where their fellow symbolists met, was right up the street on the Boulevard Montparnasse. I heard James Brown's music in the background. Yes, la Rotonde, like most cafés, had a sound system; the music blended in with the clicking metal sound of the silverware, the conversations, and the cigarette smoke. Just at the point when my reveries turned to black America, I could see my African American friends turning up here and rocking this place with the hippest conversation, the best looks, and the coolest pauses. The 91 bus came sliding in smoothly right close to the curb. I stood up to go to my rendezvous.

When I went outside, Paris was still looking good to me from left to right. I did not want to go down the subway hole and deprive myself of this sight. I crossed to the middle of the street and got in the line for a taxi. I gave the driver the address, and he went straight on Montparnasse until we were on Port

Royal. When we reached les Gobelins, he took Saint-Marcel to cross the river. I sat back then and relaxed. I was dressed in a brown jacket over a brown vest, and I had on my brown felt hat. I put on my sunglasses and felt on top of the world. I saw the cab driver looking at me in the rearview mirror. Finally, he said to me, "Excuse me for being indiscreet. May I ask you where you come from?"

"New York!" I said without interrupting my reveries.

"I mean you do not speak French like Americans. Your accent is rather Parisian," he said. "Where are you originally from?"

"Me! I was born in Paris," I lied to him. The cabdriver had walked right into my fantasies, and I felt no shame in presenting to him the new identity I had fabricated for myself. Anyway, I was used to playing such identity games with racist cabdrivers in New York and Paris, who behave like detectives and think that they could tell from a person's accent where he or she was from. They like to show black people that they know us better than we think they do; they cannot be fooled by appearances; they know who is an American in New York or a Parisian in Paris, and who is an impostor. I easily play the cabdrivers' game by misleading them or by challenging their expectations. In New York, when they try to place me as a Nigerian or a Ghanaian, I tell them that I was born in Jamaica and raised in Brooklyn. In Paris, I try to pass for a black American.

The questions that came after "Where are you originally from?" contained all the traps that the cabdrivers lay in front of me to try to find some inconsistencies in my story. I enjoyed the game, because I knew that victory was mine if I kept my story straight and fascinating until the end of the ride.

We passed over the bridge, la Gare d'Austerlitz to our right, and turned left following an arrow pointing in the direction of

République. "I went to school in America, and now I live between New York and Paris as a writer. I love Paris," I told him.

"What kinds of books do you write?" he asked me. "Nonfiction stories," I said, a bit relieved that I was telling the truth this time. I told myself that the reason I lied in the first place was that I did not want to tell the cabdriver that I was from Mali, West Africa. I did not want him to know my Malian identity, which would have caused him to lose his admiration for me. I knew that he was fascinated with me because I was from America, because I was a black American, because I was powerful and free. The image of the West African in Paris, on the other hand, was that of an unwanted illegal immigrant, called here *les sans-papiers*.

"Are you American?" he asked me.

"An American? Me? I guess you can say that! America is my primary home," I said deliberately, tentatively sensing the trap he was laying in front of me. The game was not going to be easy with this cabdriver. "I live there, work there, maintain a family there, and make my money there in order to come here and afford to live here conveniently. So, I guess that I am an American," I added, hoping that he would not ask me another specific question about my citizenship and what passports I was holding.

"But how can you live in America, with all the violence and racism there?" he asked me, looking sincerely concerned this time.

I was relieved by his question because it was one French people typically asked black Americans to show empathy with their situation in the United States. The question also revealed the French people's belief that they are superior to Americans. The system of the République Française was unique in the world. It started by destroying the French monarchy and maintained the universal freedom and equality for every individual. French people did not judge people according to their birthright, religion, or race. The cabdriver added to these clichés by saying that he did not care if people were yellow, white, or black. For him, all men were equal.

We drove quickly by the Place de la Bastille, and we reached the eleventh arrondissement on the Avenue de la République. This side of Paris is as busy as the Montparnasse area, but it is more mixed with Asians, black Africans, and Arabs. The time was about three P.M. in late September, but the sun was still as strong as it is in August. The cab made many turns before taking the Boulevard Richard Lenoir. The driver said that he was trying to avoid the heavy traffic on the Boulevard du Menilmontant. So we took the Rue de Oberkampf north toward Père Lachaise, the cemetery where famous people like Yves Montand and Edith Piaff are buried.

"The way I see it," he said, "in fact, there are a lot of things I admire about Americans. They practice what they preach. When they say we're going to bombard Iraq, they go ahead and do it. Their market dominates the whole world today. We, in Europe, on the other hand, we must talk. We cannot agree on anything. But what I cannot tolerate about America is the violence and racism. Children carry guns to school, and the slightest provocation can lead to a shoot-out in the school cafeteria. That's why I never had the desire, personally, to visit America."

"Well, I think that you're right about America being a violent and racist country," I conceded. "But, it is more than that. It is a country that is permanently changing and creating opportunities for newly arrived immigrants. That's what fascinates me about America. In Europe, it's difficult to change tradition. There is therefore less opportunity for poor people and immigrants to change their lives."

"You're an intelligent man. I can see that you are different from the others," he said, looking at me in the mirror. "But let me tell you one thing. I've been driving a cab in Paris for four years, and I've picked up all kinds of passengers. Right where you're sitting now, I had Lionel Jospin before he became prime minister. I talked to him like I am talking to you now. For me, all men are equal. I believe that racism comes out of fear and ignorance. But let me tell you one thing. All politicians are liars. They'll do anything to get elected to high office. Look at Jospin; he promised to solve the problem of illegal immigrants, *les sans-papiers*, once he was elected. How many years has he been in power now, and we still have the same problem. We vote for nothing; all the politicians are the same."

By now we seemed to be going around and around. It was so easy to get lost in Paris. We passed several streets that I could not recognize. I was therefore relieved when we arrived at a big intersection with cars coming from more than five different directions. To the right, I could see the Père Lachaise Cemetery. I glanced at the meter to see how much I would have to pay. It had passed the eighty-francs mark. I was also listening to the cabdriver, who was jumping from one subject to another. I wondered how to respond to him. Should I get back at him for the racist way he was patronizing me, or should I address instead the issues of politics and immigration that he had raised?

We were reaching the Boulevard du Menilmontant at the other side of the crossroad when we saw two policemen, dressed in the traditional blue uniforms with caps, standing in front of the tall walls of the cemetery. At first I did not pay attention to them, except to notice how small they seemed in front of the great walls of Père Lachaise. One of them made a gesture with his arm going from the left shoulder to the right side of the waist. The taxi driver explained that he wanted me to put on my seat belt. "It is the law," he said. I reacted automatically by pulling down the belt and looking for the buckle to lock it. Meanwhile, I smiled nervously to acknowledge the presence of the policemen. I was ready to consider the whole thing a minor incident when I noticed that the driver was pulling to the right, near the building, and stopping the car.

"*Qu'est-ce qui se passe encore?*" I asked, wondering if the car did not have a problem this time.

"It's the *flics,*" he responded looking nervous. *Flics* is the French slang for cops. "They want me to stop. Pretend you do not understand French. Speak only English!" he instructed me.

The two policemen approached us, and one of them opened the back door where I was sitting. "Why didn't you have on your seat belt?" he asked me in French.

I noticed that he was addressing me as *tu,* instead of the more formal *vous,* which one uses to show respect for people with whom one is not familiar. But I had decided to play the cabdriver's game and had to pretend not to understand French. I stared at the policeman and said, "What do you want? I don't understand French!"

He said, pointing to the seat belt, "*Ta ceinture de sécurité! Pourquoi tu l'as pas mise?*"

"I didn't realize that . . . "

"*Ou sont tes papiers? Passeport!*" he said interrupting me.

I reached for my wallet in my back pocket and showed him my driver's license from the state of Pennsylvania.

"*J'ai dit: Passeport!*" he shouted. Then he lowered his voice but repeated the same question with an even more unpleasant tone. "Where is your passport?"

His tone reminded me of soldiers who guard national frontiers to keep illegal aliens from smuggling themselves in. I felt like telling him to speak to me in a more respectful French. After all, we had not raised cows together. But how could I? I had decided with the cabdriver that I was an American who did not understand French.

"I thought this whole thing was about seat belts!" I said. "Now you're telling me that I can't move freely in Paris?"

"Montres-moi ton passeport," he said, leaning over the taxi door.

I put my hand in and out of my vest pocket to show that I had nothing else on me. "I must have left my passport in my apartment," I told him.

"What's in the bag? Open it!" he ordered, pointing his finger at my bag.

Instinctively, I picked up the bag, which I opened and pushed toward him. "You want to see what's in my bag? There it is. Look!" I was actually relieved that the focus had shifted from my passport to the bag. I did not want to show my passport, because it would have put a lie to the game I was playing; it was easy to prove that I was not a criminal carrying drugs or concealed weapons in my bag.

The policeman looked inside every pocket in the bag except for the zippered one in the back, where I kept my checkbook and other important documents. It occurred to me at that moment that my passport was hiding there. I had put it there, with other relevant documents such as my employment letter, my lease, and my proof of insurance, that I was supposed to take to the prefecture to receive a *carte de séjour,* or a resident's permit in Paris. I thought to myself that I would be as good as dead if the policeman were to open that pocket and find the passport. Just then, he looked at me, directly in the eyes, before unzipping the pocket and coming out with its contents. He took the passport out of the pile of documents and searched inside for the visa. "He's Malian, not American! Humph!" he said triumphantly to his colleague.

He gave me my other papers to put back into the bag and held on to the passport for a while longer. When he was satisfied, he handed it back to me saying, "I thought you had said that you did not have your passport on you. I found a Malian passport with your picture and name on it. So you don't speak French, humph!"

I was full of rage. I looked him straight in the eye but I had nothing to say to him. I blamed myself partly for allowing myself to be caught in the cabdriver's game and denying myself the use of the French language. I could have at least demanded that he address me in a more polite and less condescending manner. Moreover, for the rest of the ride, I would have to face the cabdriver, who now knew that I was not an American. I had lost twice, to the policeman and to him.

Just then, the policeman turned to the cabdriver and asked, "Where did you pick him up?"

"Montparnasse," he answered.

"And where are you going?"

"Fifty-six Rue Oberkampf."

"That's not the way to Oberkampf from Montparnasse. You should have taken the Boulevard Voltaire from République. You did not need to come this far," said the policeman.

"But, but, . . . " the cabdriver said in his own defense.

"*Oui, oui,*" said the policeman, waving his hand to the driver to move along. "*Allez-y, allez-y,*" which meant "Go on, go on."

I noticed that the policeman addressed the driver in the proper manner, even though he had accused him of cheating on the fare. I noticed at that time, too, that the cabdriver had not turned off the meter during the entire time that we were stopped. He too had regrets, though. He kept apologizing for the incident with the policeman, whose behavior he considered a disgrace to all Frenchmen. He also tried to justify why he chose the way we came. He was attempting to avoid the heavy traffic. He said that it was easier for the *flic* to take the way he proposed, but he knew nothing about traffic in Paris. I told him to forget about it.

We passed alongside the Père Lachaise Cemetery in complete silence and humiliation in the taxi. This is the city where Jim Morrison is buried. The black American author Richard Wright is also interred here. If you had listened carefully to the silence surrounding us at that moment, you could have heard them crying for the Paris they too had loved for its cosmopolitanism and tolerance of difference. I was not angry with the cabdriver and the policeman alone. I was angry at France just as Wright had been angry at America for its racism.

Let us face it, this was not an isolated incident that I experienced while using public spaces or riding taxis in Paris. Less than two months later, I was stopped by three plainclothes policemen as I was getting out of a taxi on the Rue d'Avron in the twentieth arrondissement. They were tall and muscular, looking like bouncers for a private club. At first, I thought that they wanted to get in the taxi I was exiting and could not wait for me to get out of it. The most aggressive of the three leaned over me and felt my coat pockets before identifying himself as a policeman.

"Police," he said. "You did not have your seat belt on. Can you show us some identification?"

"But how can I have my seat belt on and get out of the cab at the same time?" I responded, feeling ready for their aggression this time.

He ignored my response and started patting my pockets from my shoulders to my feet, asking me, each time he felt a lump, "What do you have in there?"

I was so upset with him that I began shouting: "Why don't you put your hand there and find out for yourself?"

"Monsieur," said the second policeman, "calm down. We're just doing our job. Nobody put a hand in your pockets. We're just asking you to cooperate while we do our job."

"But why is it always me?" I asked. "This is the second time that I have been stopped like this. And I thought that people could move freely in Paris, the most cosmopolitan city in the world."

"You were stopped before by the police? And where and when did that take place?" asked the third policeman. They were all looking curious now.

"Less than two months ago, in the same city, near Père Lachaise. Is it because I am black that you are always asking for my papers?"

"*Allez, ça suffit,*" said the first cop, meaning that he had heard enough. "Show us what is in your breast pocket."

"I said that you had to get it yourself if you want to know what is in my pocket. Why don't we go to the police station, and I can explain myself there to the commissaire. Go ahead, arrest me," I said, putting up my hands.

"Would you stop playing the clown and talking so loud?" the first policeman shouted at me.

"*Non, Monsieur,* I am very upset by the way I have been treated here in Paris. I know that you are doing this to me simply because I am black."

A crowd of passersby now surrounded us. I kept my hands up and raised my voice. I talked about how racist French people had become and how the treatment I was suffering was contrary to the image of Paris.

"*Bon, Monsieur,*" said the second policeman, "show us your passport and we can put an end to all this."

I gave him my passport. He looked at it and handed it back to me.

"Have you heard of the CRS [Compagnie Républicaine de Sécurité], Monsieur?" he asked.

"No," I said. "But what does that have to do with my being stopped in Paris more than two times in less than two months? I am really getting tired of this."

"Monsieur, we are simply doing our job."

I was going to tell him that they singled out black people, when I saw the first policeman reach for my bag on the floor. He opened it and looked inside between the pockets. I screamed at him, ordering him to show me his identification card. I was going to hire a lawyer and report him to the justice system. He refused to show me an identification card. He just turned away from me and got into the car in which his two partners were waiting. I only had time to write down the license/registration number of the car, the date, and the time. While I was doing that, the first cop shouted at me, "If I were in Bamako and the police asked me to show my identification card, I would do it without playing the clown."

I just stared at him as the car moved away. I understood what he meant by that statement. In fact, it was not the first time that someone had thrown that in my face. But, if only they had known the messy history that tied our fates together, they would not have been so quick to remind me of where I came from and to subject me to abuse for it. Did my police-man know that France had a longer history of immigration in Africa than the other way around? And what kind of French immigrants we had in Africa! The French merchants had taken more out of Africa than the African immigrant workers would ever have gotten out of France. The Catholic missionaries had violated more sacred customs in Africa and imposed their god on us in a more shocking defiance to our cultures and civiliza-tions than the African immigrants would ever have attempted in France. Finally, the French soldiers had destroyed African empires and would continue to fight any African government today to maintain and protect French political and economic interests in Africa, which would always be bigger than African interests in France.

Meanwhile Paris in particular had been held as a mirror, as the symbol of opportunity, progress, and civilization for Africans who wanted to enter modernity. Whereas France exploited Africa and reduced the opportunities of Africans to succeed in their own countries, Paris lured them to come to work in the factories and study in the universities. Thus, French immigration in Africa and African immigration in France have always been politically and economically linked and more to the benefit of France than Africa.

I wondered whether my policeman had thought about the consequences of ending immigration between France and Africa. It not only would cost the Parisians the cheap labor that the Africans provide by cleaning the offices and sweeping the streets, but would also affect France's foreign trade and political prestige in the world. In Francophone Africa, French businesspeople and corporations own most of the important industries, including oil, cocoa, cotton, and technological and manufactured products imported from Europe. Compared to this economic interest and France's political hegemony in Africa, the African immigration in France, no matter how politicized it had become of late, would just be a drop in the bucket. The situation was more complex than my policeman and anti-immigration peers understood.

As for me, I wondered what my next move would be. What was I going to do about these humiliating incidents? Ignore them and keep on emphasizing only the beautiful things about Paris? I often advise my black American friends to move around the obstacle of racism to find the positive in themselves and to define their own actions. "Move on," I keep telling them as if racism could be indefinitely ignored. For the first time, I was beginning to question the philosophy of "move on," which had served me so well in America.

But what to do about it? There were no civil-rights lawyers, per se, in France, to whom I could go with my demand for justice. The very republican constitution of France, *Liberté, Egalité, Fraternité*, did not leave room for the recognition of differentiated communities. Unlike in the States, one could not belong to the French Republic and have minority status at the same time. In the absence of the recognition of different communities in the French Republic—groups such as blacks, homosexuals, Jews—it was therefore difficult to generalize one's mistreatment as racism, homophobia, or anti-Semitism in France. Characteristically, France contrasted sharply with the States in that France experienced no resistance movements built around identity politics.

When I spoke to different friends in Paris about my being stopped twice by the police in less than two months, I soon found out that none was surprised or shocked as I had expected them to be. Diafode Sacko, a childhood friend of mine living in Paris since 1979, best characterized the African community's reaction to such incidents. Referring to the first incident at Père Lachaise, he thought that I could have inadvertently done something wrong to cause the spirits and my angel guardians to stop protecting me from the police for a while. Right away, he said some prayers for me and entreated Allah to protect us all from evil and the French police. He told me that God was nonetheless with me because I got out of it right away without blame. Diafode added that I should not venture outside too much until Friday, when he could take me to the mosque, where a sacrifice of one liter of milk and fifty francs (about $7.50) was due to a needy person.

Another Malian, Mamadou Baraji, who has been living in Paris since 1962, where he now runs a travel agency, responded to the second incident on the Rue d'Avron in similar terms. He said that the *Baraka* was with me, meaning that I was protected by the prayers and benediction of the elders and the saints. That was the reason why the three policemen could not do anything against me. He told me to keep doing good so that the *Baraka* would stay with me. "Mighty Allah, protect us all." "Amen!" I replied automatically.

For Baraji, another reason they let me go so easily was that I was educated and could speak French well. Had I been like one of those uneducated Malians who do not know their rights, the police would have taken me in. They have the right to arrest you on suspicion and keep you locked up for forty-eight hours without trial. And you had to be careful not to get into trouble with them, because during those forty-eight hours, they could be very violent with you. They could even kill you and claim that you had an accident or were beaten to death by gang members.

I asked Baraji why he thought I had been stopped so many times. I had been in Paris for only two months. I bought all my clothes here and I tried to be clean. I was not a drug dealer or a bank robber, and all my papers were in order. Baraji said that maybe, because I was dressed in expensive clothes compared with other Africans, they found me suspicious. He told me that, from seeing me, the police knew right away that I was not a black Parisian. They said to themselves that maybe I was a black American or somebody dangerous.

I asked Baraji if he knew of a lawyer whom I could hire to sue the police for violating my civil rights. I was spending a lot of money to live in Paris for my sabbatical year, and I was not about to let the French police spoil it for me. How could black people live in such a blatant violation of their right to move freely in Paris and not pose a challenge to the police?

Baraji said that I was clearly operating with a different reality from the one that prevailed in France for African immigrants. He could see from the way I talked and my behavior that I would never be able to adjust to the life of the black people in France. When a person had lived in America, he or she could never live in France again. The people are not the same. The Americans are too advanced in comparison with the rest of the world. They have too many rights.

But it would be a waste of time to sue the police. Nobody would be my witness. The French people always stuck together. How could I win a case against the government?! Besides, Baraji added, a lawsuit could turn things against me, for no matter how successful you have become in life, as a foreigner you should never challenge the laws of your hosts. You should always be grateful that they let you into their country and gave you the opportunity to succeed and prosper. If ever you were to forget that and believe that you were more powerful and smarter than your hosts, then you would end in failure. Even if in the first place you should win your case against them, someone would get you down the line one day and you would be ruined. Baraji, the successful businessman who had been in Paris for more than thirty-five years, advised me, in his turn, to "move on." The key to success for an immigrant was to keep a low profile.

I spoke with other Africans with different backgrounds and origins. I also told my French colleagues at different universities and journalists at *Le Monde* and Radio France Internationale (RFI) about my ordeal with the police. They all expressed sympathy for me. They agreed that the police in Paris were out of control and that I was surely a victim of racism. Some said that the twentieth arrondissement, where I was, around the Rue d'Avron, was a hot spot and always under the surveillance of the police on the lookout for drug dealers and the *sans-papiers*. Others recounted to me how many times they too had been stopped by the police, and how mad they were about it. They also explained to me that the seat belt law was real and that the fine was three hundred francs. They found it curious, however, that I was not fined for not having on my seat belt, which led them to believe that I was stopped for other reasons. But none of them could tell me what steps I could take to obtain justice. My French friends seemed embarrassed by the crude behavior of the French police, but had no clue as to how to fight it. I had the impression that they were all wishing that I had not brought up the subject, or that it would quickly go away. Even the black Parisians were uncomfortable with the subject.

As I listened to them, it became clear to me what my task was going to be for my sabbatical year in Paris. I was going to write to protest against racism in Paris. I was going to expose the CRS and the silence of the Parisians about the brutality against African immigrants. I was going to challenge the French intelligentsia on its lack of advocacy for Africans' rights to move about freely in Paris. For example, why weren't there today in Paris men and women like André Gide, Marcel Griaule, Michel Leiris, Jean-Paul Sartre, Simone de Beauvior, and André Malraux, who fought next to Africans against colonialism and racism? Where was the French intelligentsia when the CRS broke into the Saint-Bernard Church in 1997 and yanked out in handcuffs all of the *sans-papiers* to expel them to Bamako in Mali? Finally, I was going to write about Africans themselves, not simply as victims, but as people who had participated in creating a multicultural society in France. It was time to write a modern-day slave narrative set in Paris.

I was going to add my voice to the song of protest by Salif Keïta, "Nous Pas Bouger" ("We Won't Budge"). This song, the second cut of the CD *Koyan*, relates the suffering of black people in the lands of whites from slavery to colonialism. Then came independence and freedom, and white people from everywhere came in solidarity to help build Africa. The Africans called them brothers and sisters, whether they were French Co-operation workers, U.S. Aid (USAID) workers, or Canadian and Japanese workers sent to Africa by their governments. Nongovernmental organizations from Europe and elsewhere also came to work in Africa and were treated by Africans as their brothers and sisters.

When Africans, on the other hand, traveled to France to find work, they would find only shame and humiliation at the hands of the French police. Every day, they ran into arrests; every day, there were planeloads of Africans being sent back home:

> *My sister, look after my things.*
> *The C.R.S. are everywhere.*
> *They only know violence and nothing else.*
> *To push us around!*
> *We won't budge; we won't budge.*
> *No way to make us budge.*
> *We won't budge.*

When this song came out in 1992, I remembered dancing to the tune in various nightclubs—S.O.B.'s in New York, Keur Samba in Dakar, or Black and White in Bamako. The beat was something between "Rock Steady" and *soukous,* with drum sounds at the rhythm section in the foreground. I also remembered Keïta in a concert at the Beacon Theater in New York. When he sang "Nous Pas Bouger," the African immigrant community stood on its feet on the metallic chairs.

For African immigrants, "Nous Pas Bouger" was like a national anthem, a song that told their history and validated them in this world. It was a defiant song, an in-your-face denunciation of racism and the people who had rejected human solidarity and fraternity. At the Beacon Theater that night, the immigrants demanded an encore performance of "Nous Pas Bouger."

But I had to confess that, even though I had let myself go with the ambiance in the auditorium during the performance of "Nous Pas Bouger," it was not among my favorite Salif Keïta songs. On the *Ko-yan* album, I preferred the song "Primpin," which was about the abuse of alcohol and drugs. Beside the superiority of the melody and the beat of "Primpin," I also found that "Primpin" was more artistic because of the complexity of meaning and the sense of humor embedded in it: "If alcohol does not kill you, it's you who is going to kill alcohol." This ambivalence of the artist toward alcohol and drugs reminded me of my favorite blues singers. "Nous Pas Bouger" had seemed to me, on the contrary, to be too populist and literal. Perhaps, because of a certain Western fatigue with protest art in the 1980s and 1990s, I thought that *Ko-yan* had not risen to the level of Keïta's other albums, like *Mandjou, Soro,* and *Folon.*

"Nous Pas Bouger," on the contrary, revealed the complicity of those who were silent about the actions of the CRS. The song stated that Africans had learned to speak French, to speak English, and to speak Japanese—all because they had wanted to live in peace and harmony with other people. But it had not been enough, for the CRS and the silent majority still discriminated against them, still excluded them from the human race.

By the beginning of the twenty-first century, "Nous Pas Bouger" embodied a prophetic significance to me and to other Africans in Paris. I put on my earphones and listen to it at la Rotonde to prepare myself to write. Sometimes I listen to it while riding in a taxi or on the subway in Paris to give myself a sense of belonging. I listen to it on the plane during my back-and-forth flights between New York and Paris, or Dakar and Paris, to get myself ready for the CRS at the passport check point.

I listened to "Nous Pas Bouger" on several occasions while standing in line or waiting for my name to be called at the *préfecture de la Cité* in Paris. I had to keep going there because I had applied for a one-year residency permit, the *carte de séjour,* for my sabbatical year in Paris. This would enable me to avoid the long and complicated process of applying for an entry visa each time I left Paris. After being stopped by the police, I also realized that the prefecture, where all the foreigners came to apply for the permits, provided me with an excellent opportunity to observe the French police and their treatment of African immigrants.

With "Nous Pas Bouger" in mind, I began to realize my role in Paris. I was going to do a reverse anthropology of the CRS and the Africans in Paris, the French intelligentsia, and its attitude toward multiculturalism. By *reverse anthropology,* I meant that I was going to look at Paris as a field for anthropological research, and at Parisians as natives. I was going to observe them in their everyday way of life. I believed that it was the French intellectuals' lack of tolerance for a multicultural Paris that was keeping them silent about the CRS's treatment of

Africans. Their preoccupation with a united Europe was also a factor in the creation of a new social order in Paris that tended to exclude all those perceived as non-Europeans. For example, I was surprised to see a near total absence of Africans in the Latin Quarter, from Saint-Michel to Odeon, on the Boulevard Saint-Germain, or from Saint-Michel to Chatelet across the river, or even from Luxembourg to Montparnasse.

I used to live on the Boulevard Saint-Germain in the early 1970s, before I left for America. In those days, the Place Saint-Michel in front of the metro was a choice meeting place for young people of all origins, including the newly independent African nations. I used to meet my friends there either to go to the American bookstore, Shakespeare and Co., or to our favorite café, le Relais d'Odeon, which faced the movie theater on the Boulevard Saint-Germain. African students would meet at the café to impress each other with the extent of their assimilation to Parisian life—an assimilation that was usually measured by the ease with which one acquired the Parisian accent, the way one dressed, or the Parisian woman or man in whose company the student was. Café Odeon was also a place to find new friends or just to meet old friends and reminisce about home.

Shakespeare and Co. was different. It attracted American students and aspiring writers, who constituted its largest audience for the evening poetry and fiction readings. The rest of the audience was made up of Anglophiles like myself who had first discovered American culture through film and the popular music of the 1960s and 1970s, before coming to language and literature. I remember buying my first English/French dictionary at Shakespeare and Co. It was also there that I met the black American poet Ted Joans and discovered the works of literature by LeRoi Jones (known later as Amiri Baraka), Edgar

Allan Poe, Jean Toomer, Aleksandr Solzhenitsyn, and especially Ernest Hemingway and F. Scott Fitzgerald. The bookstore had these authors' pictures on the wall, signed and dated.

On the Boulevard Montparnasse today, the only Africans who pass by are the street sweepers with their green uniforms, green boots, and green plastic brooms. People speak predominantly American English. I have noticed in fact that most waiters in this neighborhood speak fluent English, which they employ to communicate with anybody—Japanese, German, Italian, Scandinavian, Russian, or Korean—who does not understand French. The absence of black people in this area makes it threatening to me at times. Since I was stopped twice by the police, their presence always make me self-conscious.

Some of the friends with whom I have discussed my neighborhood have told me that the Latin Quarter and Montparnasse were now overrated and passé, anyway. Only 1960s nostalgics and tourists who rely on old Paris guides still come here. Besides, the neighborhood is so expensive that only Americans can afford to live here. The "branches" spots or the hip neighborhoods today are Bastille and Oberkampf. It is there that you will find the new face of Paris: the designers, the artists, the filmmakers, the musicians, and all the underground culture that you need to see. The other places where I could find Africans in Paris today, I was told, were the eighteenth and twentieth arrondissements. They were like little Bamakos, Doualas, or Dakars inside Paris. You would only see black people: Senegalese restaurants, African grocery stores, cosmetics and hair salons, and Malian women selling roasted corn at street corners. "So who needs Montparnasse or the Latin Quarter?" they told me.

Their mocking tone made me wonder whether I was making a big deal out of the absence of Africans in my neighborhood. I was also wondering if it was not I who was out of step, after they had explained the makeup of the neighborhoods of Paris in terms of class and social movements. But how could these theories account for my being stopped twice in the so-called branches and predominantly African enclaves? If the high cost of living had driven most Africans out of the Latin Quarter and the Montparnasse area, then the arrests and human-rights violations by the CRS had played a role in pushing Africans to the outskirts of Paris, out of sight of the well-to-do white people.

III

Les Sans-Papiers: Menace to Society

I HAVE TO GO TO the police station in the fourteenth arrondissement to get an appointment at Cité, the main office in Paris for all residency permits. I had already gone to Cité before my visit to Mali, where they sent me to one place to get my letters of employment in America, insurance, income, and proof of residence translated into French. I went to another place for a health test for tuberculosis and HIV. I will go back to Cité for one last time after this visit to the prefecture of my neighborhood to prove that I entered France legally, that I have a certificate of lodging signed by my landlord, that I can pay for my expenses in Paris, that I have insurance, and that I will not seek employment in France.

I wonder why they make me go through all this bureaucracy for the right to stay in Paris during my sabbatical leave. I have already provided the French consulate in New York with all the information they are now asking me for. I have to do the whole thing all over again, and sometimes I wonder whether it is worth it. But I say to myself that it is my right to be in Paris and have an apartment near Boulevard Montparnasse without people treating me like a Malian street cleaner or a *sans-papiers*. Perhaps if I document my experience and ordeals with the French police, cabdrivers, and waiters, it will help the French people to change their attitude toward Africans in the public sphere, to make them less prejudiced and more hospitable.

The prefecture in the fourteenth arrondissement is near the Montparnasse Tower, not far from la Rotonde. I walk along the Montparnasse Cemetery, where Jean-Paul Sartre is buried. The street air is filled with the smell of fresh fruit from the market at the Edgar Quinet station. The vendors draw attention to their stands by yelling the names of the fruits—strawberries, cherries, apples, apricots, oranges, tangerines, figs—and the prices, both by the basket and by the kilo. The aroma of fresh-baked bread replaces that of the fruits and vegetables as I advance, and the peddlers of collectibles and rugs obstruct the entrance to the metro. If I were not in a hurry, I would have stopped to buy some fruit and look for a rug for my living room.

At the police station, they direct me to a big room with a receptionist who checks people's papers at the entrance and hands them a red, yellow, or green card, telling them to have a seat until their number is called. In the back, there are windows with other bureaucrats who call the numbers. I take my seat and go through my papers to make sure I have everything. The receptionist gave me a green card; I wonder what that means. Around me, there are black Africans, Arabs, Vietnamese, and Chinese people. The three young men sitting in front of me have red cards. The number of one of them is called out from the window facing us. They turn to me to ask if it was their number. I say, "Seventy-five," pointing to the man holding that number.

"*Ils ne savent même pas lire, ces gens,*" says the woman at the window ("These people don't even know how to read").

While the young man walks toward the window, I hear his friends say in Soninké—my native tongue—that Mamadou is unlucky today to encounter this woman. She is a mean person who does not like black people. She gets irritated once she sees a black person at her window. The man adds that he hopes the sacrifice Mamadou offered this morning before coming here will assist him. He also hopes that Mamadou's parents' prayers are with him. But before he is even finished, the woman has dismissed Mamadou, sending him to go get his birth certificate to prove that his passport is really his. Mamadou is beside himself; every time he comes, it's the same story—they ask him for additional paperwork.

When my turn comes, the same woman calls me. I hope that I can control my temper if she becomes rude to me. I do not have my birth certificate with me, but I am not going to let her cast doubt on the authenticity of my identity. With a lit cigarette dangling from the corner of her mouth, the woman looks at my file. She appears to be in her thirties, a brunette with short hair, about five foot three. Her round bifocals and pointed nose give her the look of a laboratory mouse. Again, she looks over the pages of my passport. I wait for her to find something wrong with my file so that I can blow up and tell her who I am. I don't need a job in France; I am doing very well in America; and in that case, who needs France? I will be here for one year, on a sabbatical leave, during which time I will spend a lot of my own money on rent, food, clothes, and my son's private school. I guess a person like her cannot understand that. Most French people, in fact, cannot see Africans as anything other than their inferiors, as people who are desperately trying to move to France. The woman who looks like a mouse takes my passport over to the next window and shows it to another woman, whom she calls Sylvie.

"*Regarde, Sylvie,*" she says, with excitement in her voice, "*une perle rare. Un Malien avec tous ses papiers en ordre.*" ("Look, Sylvie, a rare gem. A Malian with all his papers in order.")

The bureaucrats at the other windows join them as they look at my passport, as if I and the other people waiting do not exist. When she comes back to her window, the mouse-woman asks me if I had done my medical visit. I calmly respond yes and note that it is in the file. She opens the file again and goes over it while her cigarette continues to burn from a corner of her mouth. Then she hands my passport back to me with a stamped piece of paper. "*Vous avez rendez-vous à Cité le quinze décembre à onze heures. Merci, et bonne journée,*" she tells me, and calls out the next number even before I have time to remove my stuff from her window.

I go back home the way I had come on Rue de Maine, lost in thought. I had already gone through this procedure at the French consulate in New York, where they gave me three months to go to Cité once I got to Paris. At Cité, they sent me to the prefecture of the fourteenth arrondissement. Now I am being sent back to Cité on December 15. In January, I have another appointment in New York with the immigration services for my citizenship application. I have decided to become an American to avoid being harassed at the airports of the world, suspected as everybody's illegal immigrant from London, Lisbon, Hong Kong, Stockholm, and Johannesburg. I am tired of people questioning my identity, chasing me down, and looking at me with contempt. I say to myself that I am lucky that my country of origin, Mali, allows dual citizenship; otherwise, I would be faced with the dilemma of choosing between the United States and Mali. But as it is, if I become an American, it will be mostly for practical reasons, and I will not have to break any commitment to my native country. That's what all my friends who have become Americans tell me. They too are tired of being discriminated against at airports. They say that the green card is only good when you are inside America. Once you leave the States, you are known by your passport. With a passport from an African country, you are mistreated everywhere, especially at African airports when traveling to Europe or America. Once, in Dakar, Senegal, the police held my passport and green card for more than four hours, trying to ascertain their authenticity. My colleagues with American passports breezed through security checks and waited for me in the reception lounge.

I know that getting my residency permit in France and my American citizenship within one month of each other will be like amassing wealth of another kind. I can travel to any country I want without the hassle of long lines for visas at foreign embassies. To apply for a visa to go to America, people spend the whole night in front of the embassies. Fights break out, bribes are taken, and applicants are treated as less than human. The doors close at eleven o'clock in the morning, and those who cannot get through by that time have to come back again and again. If one's contact with countries like France and the United States were limited to their embassies and consulates, one would consider their people the rudest and most insensitive in the world. Once, with my green card, letter of employment, several credit cards, insurance, plane ticket, and hotel reservation, the French consulate in New York would not grant me a visa, because I had not supplied the balance of my checking account. They were closing their doors for lunch break, and I had to come back the next day. Luckily for me, it was a Thursday and my flight was on Saturday.

With the residency permit in France and my American citizenship, I will be exempt from these frustrations and mistreatments. It's funny, I will still be the same person with the same income and worldview, but I will be treated differently. I will play games, alternately using my American passport and my Malian one with the visa stamp to enter Paris. I bet that each entry will be different, depending on the passport I will present to the police. If that is not a human-rights violation, I don't know what is. If that is not discrimination, I don't know what is. When I am holding a Mali passport, I get hassled first by the security officers of the airline on which I am traveling. Before I reach the check-in counter, they take my passport to their supervisor in the back—for what, I don't know. Maybe they think I am a terrorist. After all, Mali has such a history of terrorism. Maybe they think my green card is fake. But how could mere airline security officers tell a fake green card from an authentic one? I hate the way they give themselves the air of real Scotland Yard agents. They ask me stupid questions like What is my favorite movie? That's because I have told them that I was a professor of film and literature, and they want to seem friendly and sophisticated. But I let them know that I do not like their game, because they have just let the guy behind me pass with his American passport.

After checking in and passing the police, the same airline security officers wait for me for another passport control before boarding the plane. I once lost my temper with them right before boarding a USAir plane from Roissy Charles de Gaulle to New York. The same young woman who had looked at my papers at the check-in counter was flipping through my passport again. When she told me to be patient while she discussed something with her superior, I told her to give me my passport first. I was tired of her holding onto my passport as if I were a common criminal. She was visibly shaken by my sudden outburst, and another man, brown-skinned, dressed in a dark blue suit, and looking like a Moroccan, had to come to her rescue. But by then I was talking loud enough for everyone to hear me. I was tired of USAir's singling me out in the crowd. My passport and ticket were as legitimate as those of anyone else. What was the problem then? Was it because I was black and from Africa? The guy who looked Moroccan interrupted me at that point and said, "Look, Monsieur, I am black like you, and I am from Africa like you. So don't tell me about racism."

"You are stupid," I retorted, "if you haven't heard about institutional and structural racism. You are stupid if you think that a black person cannot be racist against another black person."

At that moment, their supervisor arrived and took my papers from them, saying, "That's enough, that's enough. Follow me, sir." He had a British accent and looked like Klaus Kinski. People were looking at us out of the corner of their eyes. I was sweating under my shirt and did not know whether I should feel embarrassed for losing my cool in public. The chief handed my passport and ticket to the flight attendant and said, "Bon voyage!"

Now I need only go to the prefecture at Cité to receive my papers. I know I will not be needing them by the end of next summer, in nine months' time. But I will have had the experience of an African immigrant in Paris: his struggles to legalize himself and his status as a permanent-resident cardholder.

For a France that is against segregation on the basis of race and origin, the police station at Cité is an embarrassment. It is compartmentalized into different wings, sometimes according to the cases the station handles—like the status of foreign students in France—and other times according to race and origin—like a wing reserved only for African immigrants. The last time I visited la Cité, I was surprised by that. There were only black Africans in the room, as another was only for Eastern Europeans, and another for Asians. I guess it is not surprising to find a police station that discriminates between criminals: murderers here, petty thieves there, and juvenile delinquents over there. What is shocking is that immigrants are compartmentalized in the same way here, with the worst treatment reserved for Africans and Asians. After examining my papers, a woman ordered me to take a seat and wait for my name to be called. I sat in the same row with an immigrant worker from Mali who was accompanied by a white woman. She was instructing him how to organize his papers in a folder. He was missing his last pay stub, and when she asked him where it was, he answered that he did not know. She searched through his papers and was irritated by the way they were crumpled and torn up.

"You have to keep your papers neatly together," she said, looking at him severely. "Look at this, Samba, it's your electric bill, and this is your rent. They are all torn up. I can't help you if you're not organized. You understand?"

"*Oui, Madame*," answered Samba, looking like a schoolboy who had been scolded.

I was observing the scene between Samba and the maternal white woman, when another unusual event in the room attracted my attention. I became aware that since my arrival, all the names they had called began with D-i-a. Each time, I had jumped, thinking that my name was being called. They had gone through the Dias, the Diaos, the Diabys, the Diabiras, the Diagnes, the Diagouragas, and the Diallos before I had become conscious of the pattern of the roll call. Then came Diameh, Diarisso, Diarra, and Diawara. I had wondered how many names there were in Mali, Senegal, and Guinea that began with D-i-a and that were not present in the room that day.

The first Diawara they had called that day was a young man of about twenty. When he had deposited his papers at the window and come back to his seat, I went over to him and tried to find out who his parents were. But he was not in a mood for talking. He spoke French like the young kids born in the suburbs of Paris, and I knew from his attitude that he did not want to have anything to do with me merely because we had the same last name. I felt stupid; I could see that the young man wanted to be an individual, too, and that by invoking my kinship with him, I was denying his right to live as such. It was hard enough for him, as a young man probably born in France, to have to appear in a place for immigrants to justify his right to be in France. The last thing he would have wanted was an immigrant like myself clinging to him as a relative.

When I reach la Rotonde, after my visit to the prefecture, it is four o'clock. I decide to have a coffee before going up to my apartment to wait for my son. His school ends at three, but he is home by five after hanging out with his buddies from the International School of Paris. They are all American kids, or British, Scandinavian, or Irish. I wonder whether he'll learn some French before the end of the year. I am surprised by the way my son loves Paris. I was worried that he would miss his friends from New York and that he might not like French people. But for him, it is like love at first sight. He loves the long boulevards with wide sidewalks for pedestrians, the crowds in the streets, the food vendors, the cafés, and the metro. Most of all, he tells me that he feels free in Paris, that people do not look on him as a young black man who is a menace to society.

In New York, living near Washington Square Park, he has always felt under the surveillance of the police. He also resented the old ladies and men who held onto their purses and bags when they saw him and his friends coming. Here, in Paris, no one looks at him; there is no peer pressure at his school; and he is even beginning to like French food.

I wonder how my account of Paris can be so different from my son's. I love Paris, but I am always struggling to belong here. I feel constantly watched by the police. The waiters in restaurants ignore me until I can't stand it anymore. The neighbors in my building look at me as if I am an intruder, and the French intellectuals with whom I interact berate my position in America as a result of quotas and political correctness. It means that they are smarter, harder-working, and more deserving of their jobs. I wonder when they will wake up. I suppose that some of the difference between my son's attitude to Parisians and my own can also be explained by the difference in our ages. As a young man—he just turned fifteen—he is immune to some forms of racism. He does not constitute a threat to anybody, and the fact that he only speaks English makes him exotic in Paris. He's a black American, not an African. French kids want to befriend him so that they can be as trendy as kids in New York and learn about rap music and the latest movies and fashions. Some even want to visit him when he's back in New York. It is just wonderful how kids at this age do not see color, but only friendship.

With me, however, it is another matter altogether. I speak French, and despite my living and working in America, I am considered an African immigrant. My colonial tie to France gives French people a privileged impression that they know me better. No matter how long I stay in America, they feel I will want to return to France. How could I be happy in America after knowing French culture, freedom, and universalism? Paradoxically, this is also why my presence in France constitutes a threat. People like me want what French people have, and if immigration is not kept under control, we will invade France and destroy its precious culture. Therefore, instead of reserving for us the generosity of French hospitality, they watch over us as if we were criminals. I am glad that my son is not exposed to this side of Paris.

As a general rule, kids move around freely in France until their eighteenth birthday, when they have to apply for a residency permit and prove that they have entered France legally and do not constitute a threat to public order. In other words, if during their sixteenth and seventeenth years they have run into trouble, they could later be considered a threat to society and denied the residency permit. I read this information in a notorious *circulaire*, an open letter to the prefects of France written by Charles Pasqua, the minister of the interior, in 1994. Pasqua is to French immigration what the most conservative Republicans are to the immigration of Mexicans into the United States. During election time, politicians use the immigrants to get votes, and border crossings become political football games for the decline in the quality of life, the corruption of culture, increased unemployment, drug trafficking, and the rise in crime.

The 1994 Pasqua *circulaire*—he had written another one in 1986—constitutes a direct assault on immigration and those people who have already migrated to France. Under cover of euphemisms like family reunification, integration, and the protection of law and order, the *circulaire*, an articulation of the 1993 revision of the 1945 immigration codes, constructs a stereotypical image of immigrants as criminals and mobilizes the police against them. In 1974, the year I left France for the

United States, the immigration laws had already been changed, making it more difficult for new arrivals to get entrance visas and favoring the integration of Africans already in France into French society and culture. I did not know why, but many of my friends with me in Paris returned to Mali between those crucial years of 1974 and 1977. Among my close friends, only Diafode Sacko is still in France today. I left France to go to America because I had always dreamed of going to the land of Wilson Pickett, Aretha Franklin, Bob Dylan, Muhammad Ali, and Woodstock. But like my friends who had returned home, perhaps I was running away from the increased policing of immigrants and the lack of opportunities.

The immigration laws became even tighter in the 1980s, when François Mitterand's Socialist Party lost the election and had to share power with the conservatives. This was the first time Pasqua was named minister of the interior. In 1990, the Schengen Treaty united all of Western Europe under one immigration law and protected individual countries against the illegal entry of people from neighboring countries. The 1994 Pasqua *circulaire* tops all these anti-immigration laws by demonizing the immigrant. Some say in France that the right-wing politicians seized upon immigration to wrest votes away from the National Front Party, which is known for its racism against Africans and which by 2000 was continuing to gather momentum in France. That may be so. But how can the immigrant tell the difference between Pasqua and Jean-Marie Le Pen—leader of the National Front—if they both prevent him or her from moving about freely in France?

A person might wonder what my problem is with French law and order. After all, I have nothing to worry about if my papers are in order. All I have to do is comply with the law during the police checks, and go about my business afterward. So

I may seem to be whining about nothing. Sometimes, there are police campaigns called Opération Vigi-Pirate. When the police have probable cause that there are terrorists or drug dealers in a Paris neighborhood, they invoke that law and proceed to check people's identity cards in that district. We all know that recent activities in Algeria and the terrorist bombing of the subway at Saint-Michel have made such police interventions necessary. It is clear that most of the drug dealers in the suburbs and the eighteenth and twentieth arrondissements are *les sans-papiers* who give law-abiding citizens and immigrants a bad name. Aren't the police just doing their job?

I would argue, on the contrary, that the Pasqua *circulaire* constitutes a serious threat to individual freedom in France. The Pasqua law dramatizes the crime of illegal immigration and creates an atmosphere of fear and suspicion of the immigrant as a threat to the fabric of French society. The crime of the illegal immigrant is thus made to fit all the contemporary problems that France is facing: social security, politics of births, overcrowding of schools, housing, medical care, unemployment, and the defense of family values, as well as serious crimes like murder, terrorism, kidnapping, burglary, money laundering, and drug trafficking. By linking *les sans-papiers* to all these issues and crimes, the Pasqua law has constructed an image of the illegal immigrant as Public Enemy Number One. Thus, it is against this enemy that the police must fight as they go to war against murderers and drug dealers. The frontier police must hunt the illegal immigrant like a foreign enemy trying to invade the country. The politician must denounce this enemy in the reforms promised his or her constituency. Finally, the citizens themselves begin to consider the country to be at war against the illegal immigrant and suspend their judgment against the violation of his or her human rights.

The Pasqua law easily transfers these prejudices against illegal immigrants to legal residents and some citizens whose rights are constantly suspended in the zeal of the police's search for the enemy. One can argue that the Pasqua law targets the legal resident as well when it encourages the prefects to reduce the number of residency permits delivered and to reinstate the old law of "acceptable behavior" as a condition of eligibility for the residency permit. This old law—which was in effect during World Wars I and II to deter the immigration of spies into France, and subsequently dropped during periods of détente—has been resurrected by Pasqua to discriminate against Arabs and black Africans in France. The concept of "acceptable behavior" can now be used to an unlimited degree to expose not only immigrants who practice polygamy in France, but also those who engage in minor public deviations, such as dressing or behaving differently. Anything can be considered unlawful conduct and lead to the examination of one's right to reside and move about freely in Paris.

The reinstatement of the law of "acceptable behavior" in peacetime is truly racist because it encourages racial stereotyping of blacks and people from Muslim cultures as illegal immigrants and criminals. Consider the example of my cousin Bintou's son, Komakan, born and raised in Paris and twenty-five years old in 2000. A philosophy student at the Sorbonne, he stays at the apartment with my son whenever I am traveling. During our brief encounters to exchange keys, we often discuss philosophy and why there are no black philosophers like Martin Heidegger or Hegel. When I ask him if he knows the negritude movement, Frantz Fanon, Cheikh Anta Diop, and Amadou Hampâté Ba, he answers that he is talking about real philosophers and that it has often bothered him that African civilizations had not produced great thinkers like Hegel.

I know that my nephew is trying his best to become a serious philosopher, but I also feel that he is placing too much of a burden on his own shoulders by faulting Africa for not having a philosopher like Hegel. Consequently, I enter into a discussion of Hegel's racist dismissal of Africa and Heidegger's complicity with Nazism. I do this to undermine what I consider to be his uncritical acceptance of these philosophers. At first, it bothers my conscience that I might be bursting his bubble and destroying his love for philosophy. But from the way he looks at me, I gather that he does not believe me. Komakan has always seemed reserved, even distant. The only time I apparently have had his undivided attention is when I have spoken of my preference for Nietzsche's work. But I have since realized that he wanted to make sure I really knew Nietzsche.

So one day, when I asked Komakan what he thought about the police's stopping a black man in the streets to check his identification, he shrugged his shoulders and said, "I do not let it bother me, I just let it go."

"But why do you let it go without protesting?" I asked. "You were born here, and you are French like everyone else. Why do you let them treat you like that? It's racist."

"Oh, as I said, I do not let it bother me. My parents raised me with a strong moral character, and that's what helps me survive. I've known discrimination since I was young and growing up in the suburbs. The teachers put you with other kids who are Arabs or black, because they don't think you're smart enough. All of us end up in technical schools, where we learn manual labor or drop out. After high school, I went to a school to learn how to be a cashier in supermarkets. I didn't like it. So I worked twice as hard to pass the entrance exam for the university. I am the only black in my philosophy class. All the black students I see on campus are foreign students. We do not get along, because they believe that the blacks born here in France think they're French, and that we're all lazy. Me and my Arab friends, we always get stopped by the police. One day, we were coming from a party. My girlfriend was driving. Two policemen pulled us over to the side of the highway. They asked for our papers, checked our pockets, and looked in the trunk of the car for drugs. One of them just looked in my eyes and said, 'If you don't like it, go home.' I didn't say anything, because I know myself. I knew I had a stronger moral character than he did. It's not that I don't understand my rights, or that I don't think it's wrong for the police to single out Arabs and blacks. It's just that I don't want any trouble with them, so I rise above them. I exercise, in Kant's words, a critique of pure reason."

"But," I remonstrated, "if you do not protest, nothing will change for you or your children."

"Uncle," he replied, looking me in the eye, "I believe that black people have to work twice as hard to get what they want. That's the only thing that is going to change our image here. That's how it is, and no one is going to change things for us. We are newcomers here, and we have to pay the price. I am going to do everything to get my diploma in philosophy and do my doctorate. That's how it is. I have to do it by myself. In America, they give black people degrees and jobs for which they are not qualified. I don't believe in that, because I think that quotas are a form of racism. I'd rather work twice as hard as white people to earn my degree. Here, you do not get anything because you're black; you have to prove that you're a man and deserve your place in society."

I pay for my coffee, still wondering about my nephew's answer to my question about policing in France. On my way to the apartment, I stop by the *boulangerie* to buy bread, and the *boucherie* to buy a roast chicken. Now that I remember our conversation in its entirety, I feel my nephew's resentment toward me for insisting on the topic. It was as if my criticism of racism in France was also directed at him, as if I had hurt his pride by attacking France. I also believe that my nephew might have been challenging my characterization of policing in France as racist. Why else would he have reminded me of quotas in America, if not to tell me that, on the contrary, it is America that is racist? Many people here believe that Americans are quick to bring race into everything. My nephew, like most French people, has accepted the notion that Africans and Arabs—as the last wave of immigrants in France—must work twice as hard and comply with the police when they are doing their work, as the price of their integration into French society. After all, since Opération Vigi-Pirate was put in place to protect everybody, everybody must accept some sacrifice. That was why my nephew had spoken of strong moral character and hard work.

But how about the social profiling embedded in the Pasqua law? Clearly, when "Frenchness" is defined against the immigrant's culture, behavior, and appearance, one has to label the policy of integration and assimilation as racist. I remember once riding in a cab in New York between Penn Station and my apartment on Bleecker Street. I was wearing a suit and tie and had a nice conversation with the driver on the way. He was an old, Irish cabdriver. When we arrived at my destination, he said, "Have a nice day, buddy. If everybody dressed and behaved like you, they'd have no trouble finding cabs." How was I supposed to take that, as a compliment or as a racist remark?

I walk all the way down the Rue Bréa to turn right on Rue des Champs, where I will turn right on my street, Jules Chaplain. The sun is not even down, yet already there are lights in the shop windows and in the streets, and *café* and *tabac* signs are flashing. This is also what's attractive about Paris. Nightfall, like sunrise, is another invitation to life: to sit in cafés, to dine, to go to the movies, or just to walk down the boulevards. As I turn onto Rue des Champs, I see a woman wearing high heels and trotting behind her dog, which looks more like a reptile with a long, furry tail dragging behind it. The dog stops and starts sniffing the concrete sidewalk as if there is a cat hiding underneath. As I pass them, I hear the woman having a very serious conversation with the dog about running too fast. She looks beautiful. I wonder if she is going to clean up the sidewalk after the dog.

Suddenly, I am not feeling well. My head aches and I feel as if I am coming down with a cold. Maybe I need my sleep, or perhaps I caught something on the plane. I also need to eat properly, take an aspirin, and go to bed. I try to think back to my conversation with my nephew about the Pasqua law to take my mind off dogs in Paris and my allergies. Komakan thinks he is misunderstood by everyone. The French treat him as a foreigner, and his own family considers him too French, meaning a spoiled son. Komakan once told me that he wished African parents communicated more with their children. When you go to my cousin Bintou's house, what's lacking—in spite of all the noise, laughter, griots, food, and drink—is openness between parents and their grown children. Komakan told me he had no privacy in his mother's house. Visitors come and go out of the apartment. They have no appreciation for his studies or for philosophy; on the contrary, they believe that philosophy alienates the youth from religion. Komakan does not really understand why his mother and the other African women give so much of their money to the griots. Sometimes, he just wants quiet in the house, not only to read a book, but also to be close to his mother. They never have time to talk seriously about anything. Most of their exchanges are limited to Bintou's telling him, "Don't do this, don't do that," or "You are too French; this is not African."

I guess my nephew is a bit like my own son, and I am like my cousin Bintou. We were raised in Africa, where children are showered with love and affection until they reach puberty, when they are left on their own. Mothers create a distance between themselves and their grown sons, and fathers begin to see less of their grown daughters. We never discuss sexuality with our parents. They communicate everything to us in orders, and we obey without asking why. Our children, on the other hand, are American and French. That means they are individuals, with an identity—acquired since childhood—that cannot be violated without putting the whole system around them into question. If you tell them not to do something, you must explain to them why. The state defends their right to be against you, your values, and your religion. In fact, many people from Africa feel that the state has corroded their influence on their children and has left them to themselves. That's why many immigrant kids grow up selfish and distant from their parents. I wonder who is right: the parents or the children. The most frightening thing, however, is that our children are growing so far apart from us.

I push the button to unlatch the door in my building, check my mailbox, and begin climbing the stairs. My headache is still there, and I am feeling enormously tired. What of the future for my nephew and the other children of my cousin Bintou in France? And all the children of African immigrants living in France? In France, the criminal police and the immigration police are one and the same. And they see every immigrant first as a potential lawbreaker, a drug dealer in disguise, or an enemy of France. Who can emigrate from Africa to France nowadays?

These stairs are really tough. They go around in circles, and they are hard not only on my legs, but also on my head, which is giving me a sharp pain through my eyes every time I look up to see how far I have to go. I feel like stopping to rest for a while, but I do not want to obstruct the staircase or stand in front of someone's door. People will be startled by me, afraid that I am going to attack them. My apartment is on the fifth floor. In America, that is equivalent to four flights, but here it is five. I did not feel the difficulty of these steps this morning, when I arrived. Now I am sweating after having climbed only one and a half flights. There are twenty-three steps in each staircase, which now seems like the peak of a mountain. I must be really sick.

Under the Pasqua law, the cultural differences of Africans are not exotic, but criminal. In the suburb of Saint-Denis, I once visited a cousin who lives in one apartment with two wives and seven children, from age five to twenty-five. He lives in a building inhabited only by other Africans from Mali and Senegal. In Mitterrand's time, it was said that such *foyers* were specifically built for West Africans to accommodate their cultural environment and habitus. Today, Saint-Denis is considered one of the most dangerous of Paris suburbs, and the police are constantly there on the lookout for illegal immigrants, drug dealers, and even American-style gangs.

My cousin had welcomed me in his living room, which had a canopy against the wall on one side, and a mat on the floor on the other, exactly the way living rooms used to look when I was young. My cousin told one of his sons to bring two chairs for me and my companion, and he sat on the canopy himself next to his griot, who was playing a stringed instrument called a *ngoni*. The griot welcomed me on behalf of my cousin, as custom dictated in West Africa. He said that I should consider myself at home, that, France notwithstanding, my cousin's children were my children and his wives, my wives. Then there was a long line of children and wives who came out of the hallway to greet me and my friend. The women sat on the mat, and the boys brought in more chairs to sit behind each other. We ate together, with our hands in the same dish, and started drinking tea as the griot resumed playing his instrument and praising our lineage.

Then they asked me what I was doing in France. I answered that I had come to do research on immigration to contribute to the understanding of the plight of Africans in France and to facilitate their integration into French society. At that point, my cousin said to me that what I should tell French authorities was to stop meddling in their affairs, that polygamy and female circumcision were long-standing customs they had inherited from their parents and their parents' parents, that they should just leave them alone to do their work. My cousin said that it was better during Mitterrand's time and the times before that, when the government did not pry into grown people's private lives and tell them what to do. My cousin said that French people had their value system, and Africans had theirs. "C'est comme ça, quoi. Chacun a son choix," he concluded ("That's how it is, to each his own"). The griot played harder on his *ngoni* and said that my cousin had told the truth as his ancestors once told it to their adversaries. He said that our people would not abandon polygamy and our daughters would always be circumcised. Then, turning to me, the griot summarized what my cousin had said, and added that everybody was proud of the work I was doing by coming all the way to France to defend our values. I thought of reacting, and then said nothing. What was I supposed to tell them? That the point of my research was not to defend polygamy and circumcision? The place was not right for such a discussion in front of wives and children.

My head is really hurting now, my legs are weak, and my hands are beginning to shake when I hold onto the banister. I am reaching the last stairs of the third floor, where my friend Moune de Rivel lives. I am tempted to knock on her door and pay her a visit to rest a bit. But she's not expecting me. How could I barge in just like that? It's just not done. Even someone like Moune would be surprised by such a visit. I had met her on the stairs one day when she was carrying two heavy grocery bags, and I had offered to help her. She had politely declined my help, saying that she was used to it, and that at her age it was important for her to know that she could still do it. She had complained about her knees, which were hurting her, but she had promptly added that climbing the stairs was good exercise for them. "*Ça fait du bien,*" she had concluded.

That was how Moune and I became friends. She had told me that she had seen my son on the stairs, and he too had offered to help her with her bags. She had said that my son was a very nice and handsome young man. I had told her that I too had heard about her from my friends at the publishing house Présence Africaine. Moune had responded that she was very fond of Madame Diop, the owner, and that any friend of Diop's was her friend, too. She had invited me to stop by her apartment one day and have a glass of wine with her, and maybe I could also come to listen to her play her guitar and sing at l'Auberge Antillais.

I discovered later that Moune is not only a great musician and living legend of Antillean culture, but also a monument of the culture of black Paris. She knows everybody in the negritude movement, the surrealists, the Communist Party, and the existentialists. She can talk all night about the trip she took in the 1940s—during the war—to New York City with Henri Matisse. She remembers, with much emotion and nostalgia, visiting Harlem, the Cotton Club, and other jazz clubs. She then tells you that the best part of her visit to New York was when a black woman in Harlem invited her to move in with her. Moune adds that the woman was named Mrs. Morgan, and asks if I knew her. She also says that during her brief stay in New York, she married and divorced a jazz musician. Another measure of the important place Moune occupies in the culture of black Paris derives from her acting roles in many classics of the French cinema of the 1940s, such as Jean Renoir's *French Can-Can*. One day, Moune confided in me that she had been told by the administrators of the sixth arrondissement that they would rename our street—Rue Jules Chaplin—after her. Maybe during my next visit to Paris, the street would be called Rue Moune de Rivel.

Thinking about Moune gives me more energy to keep climbing the stairs. Maybe someone will make a film about her for French TV someday. I like Moune, and I like what her Paris stands for: *Liberté, Egalité, Fraternité*. She is warm and hospitable. Yes indeed, it would be nice to walk down a street rebaptized Moune de Rivel. My Paris, now, is trapped between two extremes of cultural exception: the desire for cultural purism implicit in the Pasqua law, and my cousin and his griot's attachment to polygamy, circumcision, and inalienable cultural rights. I wonder about the extent to which these two extreme forms of cultural specificity need each other. The application of the Pasqua law depends on a reductive view of all African immigrants as supporters of polygamy and excision. That the majority of Africans who come to work in France view polygamy and excision negatively has little bearing on how the police see them as a group. Oh, how permanently alienated by these two positions I feel!

I open the door to my apartment and find my son watching TV and my nephew packing his bag. I place the bread and roast chicken on the kitchen counter and proceed to the bathroom to take two aspirins before making a salad to eat with the chicken. My son says that school was fine, except for two of his friends who got in trouble because they were busted near the school for smoking marijuana. Surprised, I ask, "Do kids do that at your school?" My son laughs and says that kids do worse than that at school. "How about you, Komakan, how was school?" I ask my nephew. "Fine," he answers. They have finished with Hegel and are now reading Kant. My nephew says that the reading is hard, but what hurts most is the professor's total indifference to his views. He has been trying his best to write papers, but the harder he tries, the less impressed his teacher is. I ask him if he needs my help. He laughs and answers that he prefers to keep on trying by himself. He wants to prove to himself that he can do it.

I spread the salad on a flat tray, cut the chicken into pieces on it, and place the tray on the table so that we can eat. We usually eat with our hands, sitting around the table. This is the only kind of French food my son likes. My cousin Bintou has offered to bring us African food, but my son does not like that, either. He takes carry-out sandwiches from Greek restaurants and fast-food places like McDonald's and Hippopotamus restaurants. I found out, to my surprise, that he liked the food made by my nephew while I was away. They ate frozen pizza, canned corned beef, and spaghetti and meatballs. The two of them get along well and communicate better with each other than the three of us together.

I have no appetite for the chicken. I do not know what is wrong with me today. The aspirin helps my headache, but I don't feel like eating or even drinking a glass of red wine. After the meal, my nephew washes the dishes and picks up his bag to go home. I renew my offer to help him with his homework, and finally, he promises to show me his next assignment before turning it in. He bids us good-bye, and I lock the door behind him, before throwing myself on the couch in front of the TV. "Do you have homework to do?" I ask my son, as I try to find a comfortable position in the couch, with my head resting on one arm of the couch and my feet on the other.

"Don't worry, it's under control," he answers automatically.

I feel like asking him to show me his homework, but I am cold and tired. So I tell him instead to bring me a blanket from my bedroom.

"Are you OK, Dad?" he asks. "Because this room is very warm. That's the way Komakan likes it."

"I don't, but suddenly I feel very cold," I answer.

He brings the blanket and covers me with it. But I must have fallen asleep right away, because the last thing I remember before waking up three hours later, soaked in my sweat and about to vomit up everything I had eaten, is the silhouette of a young man standing over me. I get up and run to the bathroom, put my head in the toilet bowl, and throw up. After I finish, I sit on the floor between the bathtub and the toilet seat, not feeling like getting up and cleaning up after myself. I manage to take my clothes off, and suddenly I lie down on the cold floor, which for some strange reason feels very comforting. I would have gone back to sleep there if my stomach had not started turning over in a violent attack of diarrhea. There is no doubt about it: I have malaria. After calming my stomach down, I take a shower, and the water has both a cleansing and soothing effect. I clean up the place as best I can and go to bed.

After my son had put the blanket on me, I looked at him for a while, admiring how tall he had grown. But soon I had fallen asleep, and the man standing over me, taking care of me with a blanket, had turned into Ibrahim Diallo ("Johnny"), who was trying to hurt me. His eyes were red, and he had a short rusty knife with which he was going to cut me. I had tried in vain to run away from him, because I did not want to catch tetanus from his knife. Macky Tall and other people were there, watching and laughing. I kept screaming that it was not my fault that the immigration police had expelled Johnny; I could not say a word in his defense, because I was afraid for myself; there was nothing anybody could do. But he kept touching my arms with the knife, and I was dying of tetanus. Everybody else was laughing, except Johnny. It was then that I discovered the most horrible thing about him: He had no mouth or ears. There were scars like burns in their places. His nose and red eyes looked implacable, and even though I was feeling a burning pain each time he touched me with the knife, I noticed that he was touching me gently. I had woken up sweating because I could no longer bear the pain, and I had to go to the bathroom. I had gone to sleep with the television on, and when I had woken up, it was as if the people had come out of the tube to be in the room with those who were laughing at me.

Johnny Be Good

Now I can face Johnny's story, because I am feeling better after the shower, and I am not sleeping, anyway. It's every immigrant's story. That's why seeing him that night in Bamako, in the state he was in, was so unsettling to me. Every immigrant, no matter how successful and well integrated, has, deep inside, a doubt. Has the immigrant really made it? Has he or she overcome the roots of the past? Is the person's new, self-made reputation unassailable? Or can it all be taken away by an immigration officer with a single stroke of the pen?

Handcuffs, officers dressed in somber uniforms and tall boots, pushing you—Johnny—in the back and shoving you into a blue van; and the ride to the immigration jail with your ears full of the sound of the sirens. Fingerprints and computer searches that reveal the different names you have used to sneak into the country; the public defender who gives you a glimmer of hope but is unable to help you because you cannot afford his price. The two or three nights you spend in jail awaiting expulsion are the hardest. You go over your whole life in seconds. What went wrong? Why did your luck run out? You had always been careful not to get into trouble with the police; you avoided bold women and places where the crowd hung out; you dressed like an ordinary black American so as to blend in; and you said little at work and on the bus for fear of revealing your African accent.

If only you had not run away that night, giving the immigration officers reason to believe that you had something to hide. Which god had you offended to keep your mother and father's blessings from protecting you? Just last month, you had sent your savings to your old mother, asking her for more prayers and good wishes. If only you had saved some of that money now, you could have used it toward the lawyer's fees. You had called the Malian embassy in Washington, D.C., for help. The staff answered through your lawyer that it was not part of their responsibilities, that they could not interfere with the immigration laws of a sovereign state. You thought about that for a while, and it made you angry. All the money that Malian expatriates sent home from abroad to build houses, subsidize poor farming, keep the marriages and naming ceremonies going, observe the religious holidays, and pay the medical bills—surely all these should have convinced the embassies to set aside funds to help those in trouble with immigration.

You had asked your friends—James, Americain, Blanc, and Manthia—to lend you some money until you got out. But it was the end of the month, they had paid the rent like you, they too had sent the rest of their money home, and those who had not done so had said that they were paying their school fees to maintain their F-1 immigration visa status. You still had hope that one of them would come through with the down payment

for the bail. They did not even call you back to say whether
they had been in touch with Tidjani Diarra. For only he could
help you now. He was the most successful Malian in D.C., with
a restaurant on Eighteenth Street and a truck that delivered
fresh groceries to other restaurants in the city and all the way
to Silver Spring, Maryland. Tidjani was known for his tightfist-
edness and mistrust of other people, particularly Malians. But
this was an emergency; you had never asked him for a favor
before. Surely he ought to understand.

Macky Tall had come one day to bring you your suitcase
with some clothes, your French/English dictionary you bought
in Paris before leaving for Washington, and some platform
shoes you had just purchased from a store on Connecticut
Avenue and K Street. You bought them one day at four o'clock,
on your way to work at Chez Dominique on Pennsylvania
Avenue and Nineteenth Street, because you had been looking
at them in the shop window for a month and you could no
longer resist the temptation. After work that very evening, you
changed your clothes and put them on to go dancing at Bixby's
nightclub. What could have brought you this misfortune and
made you lose all your protection? You had never liked
Dominique, the boss, anyway. When French people came to
America, they became more racist than Americans. He used to
shout in racist terms at you and the other Africans in the
restaurant. He would tell you to work faster, or he would call
Idi Amin Dada and Mobutu down on you. That used to make
everyone laugh, and you laughed too, going along with what
everybody knew was not funny. Maybe your defenses had been
broken by such public humiliation. Maybe you were also being
punished for buying such expensive shoes. Sixty dollars was a
fortune in Mali, and you had spent that on a pair of shoes to go
dancing in.

Macky Tall had said that all your friends—James, Americain, Blanc, and Manthia—had gone into hiding until things
cooled off. They did not want the immigration services to link
them to you and start looking for them. Macky Tall was laughing. He had said that your friends were cowards, that you
should not count on seeing or hearing from them until this
thing was over. He had said that Tidjani was a selfish bastard
who would be happy to see you expelled. He had said that the
best thing for you was to leave the country and come back with
a different passport. You could get a passport from Zaire or
Kenya easily. But if you challenged the immigration and lost,
you would leave behind a paper trail with your fingerprints,
photographs, and blood samples that would make it impossible
for you to get back.

Macky Tall was a lucky guy, because he had the green card.
He obtained it through marriage with a black American
woman. Some even said that Macky Tall was an American citizen now. You understood why your friends and roommates
were hiding away; you might have done the same thing if you
had been in their place. You were angry with Macky Tall for not
taking things seriously. How could he have failed to see the
gravity of the situation now? You so wished that some miracle
would happen and free you. This was not your fate. This place
was for criminals who did not deserve to be in America, those
who were dealing in drugs, counterfeit banknotes, prostitution,
communism, and other anti-American activities. Yes, you liked
your work, you went to school, and you loved rock and roll.
You wrote letters home to your friends praising America for all
the opportunities it had given you. You told them about the
steady progress you were making in your studies and at work.
You were going to take your degree in business administration
at a university called Federal City College. You had explained

to them that in America, a college was the same as a university. In those letters, you slightly exaggerated your success in America. You were only learning English, not taking college classes yet. But you were sure of going to college and finishing your degree.

Most of all, you loved the way your life was changing in America. Every day you noticed improvements about yourself. You earned a regular paycheck, bought your own food, paid your rent, and sent money to your family in Mali. There were no such opportunities in Bamako. You and your friends were nineteen and twenty years old in Mali, high-school dropouts, without ever having held employment. There was nothing for a person to do but sit around and wait for the opportunity to leave the country. Everything you had was a handout from a relative or a friend. Some of your friends had even begun picking people's pockets in the market and at the train station. A few had been in and out of prison. No, this was not your fate; as Bob Dylan used to sing on the album you had left behind in Bamako, "there must be some way out of here."

One night, you stole your mother's sewing machine and sold it to pay a truck driver carrying cattle to Abidjan, in the Ivory Coast. That was how you got out of Bamako, like a thief in the night, looking straight ahead, and determined to leave the past behind. Sitting around and drinking tea all day was not for you. You were also too young to be a regular at the mosque, where everything was only about those who would go to hell or heaven. You had chosen to live in this world; you had decided to take your destiny into your own hands. Unlike your friends in Bamako, you had refused to believe that it was Allah's will that some people were poor and others rich. You had wanted to be part of your other friends, who had left Bamako and changed their lives for the better.

In Abidjan, you had realized for the first time the true meaning of exile and suffering. You were hungry, and no one gave you food. You had no place to sleep, and you wandered around town looking for a job or someone from Mali who could help you. You were picked up by the police with other young men from Upper Volta and Guinea and thrown in jail for not having proper identification papers. They called you a foreigner, a savage, and a thief. It was in Abidjan that you had lost your innocence about African Unity and Pan-Africanism, which had been taught to you since elementary school and which you were still hearing on the radio.

You finally found work with a Lebanese businessman who owned several stores in the city. He first employed you as a watch boy in front of one of his stores. When he realized that you were educated and intelligent, he took you in as his helper. You ran errands for him: retrieving containers full of merchandise from the port of Abidjan, depositing his money in the bank, and even managing the stores while he was involved in diamond trading. He had taught you how to drive with his own car, a Peugeot 404. You had met his wife, Marie, whom you began to accompany around town for her shopping sprees and visits to her friends. You even went with her to the swimming pool, to the tennis court, and to the movies when her husband was away on business. She had opened up to you, telling you how bored she was in Africa. She missed her friends and family. Her husband was too involved in his work to pay her enough attention. He was only interested in showing her off at big ceremonies with African ministers and businessmen. He believed that money could buy happiness, and so he gave her all the money she needed. But that was not enough. She was missing her friends, some of whom had gone to France and the United States to study or work. The man she really loved had gone to France. But her parents did not want her to marry him, because he was from a poor family.

Your boss's wife was not much older than you. She began to share things with you; she introduced you to Italian photo-novellas, which were about romance, betrayal, and true love. When she found out that you liked music, she bought you Johnny Hallyday and Rolling Stones records. Whenever she took money from her husband, she gave you some. Then people started noticing that you were getting too close to her. The Lebanese community in Abidjan had begun to talk about you. They said that you had suddenly grown too arrogant and that it was time to remind you that without them, you were nobody. Your boss at first told you to stay in the store and keep out of Madame's way. Then he accused you of stealing from him and had you arrested by the police chief, who was his friend. You spent a whole week in jail without food until Marie threatened your boss that either he would free you or she would leave him.

At that moment, you decided it was time to leave Abidjan, too. You had written your friends in Paris, asking them to send you an invitation so that you could apply for a visa. It was so easy in those days to get a visa from France that all your friends who could afford it were already there. You had taken your savings to buy an airline ticket for about two hundred dollars and had sent the rest of your money to your mother in Bamako. She had forgiven you by then, because soon after you had found a job, you had sent her money to buy a new sewing machine. You were still feeling guilty, though, for what you had done to your mother. The machine was her sole means of earning an income for the family. People said that after she found out that you had left with the machine, she cursed you every morning and every night. You still wondered whether those curses had been stronger than the blessings she was now bestowing on your behalf.

In Paris, you found the same friends you had grown up with in Bamako. Life was easy enough, because they had found you employment in the glassware factory where many Malians worked. The pay, they had said, was good, if you could do the job. You knew that you were not afraid of work, because you had already been used to that in Abidjan. But you did not find in Paris the same opportunities for self-improvement and financial gain that you did in Abidjan. In Paris, no one paid attention to how intelligent you were, no one asked for your opinion, and the supervisor did not like it if you talked too much. You were expected to be alert, to make sure that you had removed all the glasses, no matter how hot they were, from the table while the machine was running. Your wrists and the palms of your hands were always sore from the heat. You were exhausted in the evenings and barely had the strength to eat your dinner before falling asleep.

Most of your friends had worked in this factory during the first months after their arrival in Paris. They then left to find other employment or to join the ranks of the unemployed. You had stuck to it because you had made up your mind not to stay in France. You were going to go to America; you were already dreaming of being in America with your friends—James, Americain, Blanc, and Manthia. Every weekend, you wrote them letters and they wrote you back. The exchange of letters between Paris and Washington, D.C., was what had kept you going, making you daydream and taking the pain out of your job. You had kept these letters with you until today. Even after being in Washington for almost a year, you still were able to enjoy them.

The thought of the letters reminded you of the shoes and the suitcase Macky Tall had brought to you. You had opened it to see if the letters were there, and when you had found them, you opened one to read:

Washington, 30 April 1975
Manthia Diawara
2130 R St., N.W.
Washington, D.C. 20008

My dear Johnny,

I am so busy with every day that passes that if I had taken more than a month to reply to your letter, it would not have surprised me. You see, dear friend, I have too many commitments this month. I wake up every day at 7 A.M. to go out, and I don't come back until 1:30 A.M. The University where I take my classes is all the way in Virginia, a state bordering on the District of Columbia. I leave school at 2 P.M. and take the bus back to Washington, D.C., to go to work, and I don't get off until 1 A.M. But in spite of all of this, something inside me was telling me to respond to your letter right away. I hope very soon to save enough money to quit this job so that I can have enough time to write to everybody in the group. Maybe I have bored you enough with my problems. So let's get to the point.

I wrote to the guys in Bamako and told them about a Led Zeppelin concert I attended at RFK Stadium here in Washington, D.C. They are the biggest group in the world now. I sent their latest album to the guys in Bamako. By the time you receive this letter, your I.20 should also arrive from my university. With that, all you have to do is go to the U.S.

Embassy in Paris, and they'll give you a student visa. Tell them during the interview that your parents will pay for all your expenses while you are studying in America. Remember, do not tell them that you will be working to pay for your studies.

You will see, my dear friend, that America is very different from France. There are more opportunities here to study, and you can work and earn good pay. There are many Gambians and Nigerians here, and very few Francophone Africans. France lures us without giving us the opportunities. Here, there are Black Americans who fight for you and help you to go to school. I am telling you all this, my friend, so you don't get discouraged. When you get here, we will have lots of fun together.

Amitiés,
Manthia "formerly Jimi Hendrix"

P.S. I heard that our friends in Bamako are all ready for marriage. Alas, for me, nothing doing. I would not think about even getting a fiancée before four years are up. That is, after I earn my diploma. If I were to get married now, I am sure that I would be divorced in less than two months. Love does not exist here. Every category of man corresponds to a category of woman. Since I believe that I am superior to my present class of women, I have no choice but to limit my relations with women to flirting, pedantic conversation, and casual sex. The day society sees me as important as I see myself, only then would I think about marriage. I have thought about this mathematically; there is no room for errors.

Good luck to the lovers.

La folie des grandeurs, Manthia

You had placed the letter back, slowly, in its place. For a while, you had debated within yourself whether to read another letter. But the realization of the situation you were in had made you angry. Suddenly, the letters had made you feel the full weight of your despair. You had held onto them in Paris because they represented your dreams; they had kept you going; and they were the light at the end of the tunnel. They had taught you to have courage, patience, and resilience at your job in Paris. You had held onto them in Washington because they were a witness to how far you had come from, and they were fellow travelers. They were also like a magic charm, a talisman that knew your secret and was protecting you from your enemies.

Now, like the shining shoes, the letters seemed to have betrayed you, to be laughing at you. It seemed as if Macky Tall had appeared in their place, sitting in a dark corner of your cell, grinning at you. He was telling you that this was the end of your road and that there was no way out of this; that you had been dreaming all this time; that you were going back to Bamako in chains, like a thief caught with a sewing machine. You will be back there as you had started, with all the others, stuck, without an exit. You will have it worse than in Paris and Abidjan, with no job, and your head bowed like a criminal. You will resign yourself to being poor, and like a hypocrite you will find God again. They will laugh at you everywhere you go, a failure worse than your friends who had never left Bamako. You were seeing Dominique too, in another corner of your cell, calling you a monkey and threatening to send you back to Africa. You had fire in your eyes this time; you took the suitcase and flung it against the wall. The letters fell out and you started tearing them to pieces. Then you grabbed the shoes between your teeth and hands, trying desperately to tear them apart.

At that time, the guard came in, ordering you to stop it and be quiet. You went after him that very instant, wresting the club away from him and ripping off his shirt. You climbed the cell bars, attempting to get out. Several guards came in to control you and give you an injection to put you to sleep. You woke up the next day in a hospital bed, surrounded by guards and doctors who were drawing blood and urine samples from you and giving you all kinds of painful treatments. They asked you if you were still being chased by armed soldiers, if there was war in your country, if you slept in trees there, and if you were still taking yourself for a monkey. You answered no to all of this, but they did not believe you, which led them to perform more tests on you.

The results came in. They diagnosed you as a paranoid schizophrenic and dangerous to yourself and to others. They had said that the treatment was long and expensive, and you had had no insurance.

Any one of us living in D.C. at that time could have been in the same jam that Johnny had fallen into. His story reminds me of our beginnings in America and how a wrong turn with the immigration officers could have taken away everything that my friends and I had worked hard to realize. We had all been law-breakers in those days, for how could anybody have believed that we were being supported by our parents while we lived in America? We were coming from one of the poorest countries in the world, and America was the richest country in the world. Of course, there were a handful of African students whose parents worked at the World Bank or the United Nations. There were also the sons and daughters of military dictators and corrupt politicians and diamond smugglers. But those privileged African students had nothing to do with us. We were also set apart from political refugees from Ethiopia, Sudan, and apartheid South Africa. These refugees were immediately granted work permits and given scholarships from different churches.

Poor and powerless, we had left our homes to come to America, to return rich and with an abundance of knowledge to change our wretched condition. Another challenge facing us at the time was that we were coming from countries with French and Muslim backgrounds, compared with our counterparts from Nigeria, Kenya, and Ghana, who had come from English and Christian backgrounds. We had turned to America because France had stopped being hospitable to us. In America, everybody spoke English, and Protestant culture permeated every aspect of life. Americans prized hard work, moral rectitude, and cleanliness. At first, what surprised us in America was how conservative the people were. We had this image of Yankees as individuals and nonconformists who were casual in their appearance. Coming from Paris, one was particularly surprised by how religious Americans were and how much they loved their country and their politicians. Those of us who had come to America expecting only freedom were surprised to find rules everywhere. Those of us accustomed to ridiculing politicians and God in public had found out that in America, such conversations were no joking matters.

We had to learn quickly to fit into American culture. Whether one was dirty or not, one showered every day, changed one's underwear and shirt, and neatly combed one's hair. Unlike our Anglophone counterparts, we had to learn English and pass the TOEFL (Test of English as a Foreign Language) before going to the university, where we also had to write all our papers in English. We had to conform to American civilities such as saying "Hi!" instead of shaking hands, and to black American vernacular forms like "What's up, man?" and "Gimme five!" We also had to find out soon that the Islam we were brought up on in Africa was different from the Islam of Black Muslims, who were clean-shaven, always dressed in black suits and ties, and opposed to white people. We finally had to get used to people asking us—once we had opened our mouths to say something—things like, "Where are you from?" Our only satisfaction in our failure to pass completely for black Americans in those days was the realization that even the so-called Anglophone Africans—from Liberia, Ghana, and so forth—could not speak English like natives. Some of us had even believed that we could pass more easily for black Americans than those Anglophone Africans because we were learning our English in America. We were so determined to be American-ized in those days that we copied all the street slang and the hip expressions in the movies, on television, and in music. But who could have thought that they would send Johnny back home like that?

But as I have said, we were all lawbreakers back then. Everyone must have known it, and the immigration officers were closing their eyes, reserving their serious investigations for real criminals who ran international prostitution rings, engaged in money laundering or spying, or trafficked in false identity cards. We had gone to America primarily to get educated and to work to support ourselves. Some of us would eventually abandon school for work, because the money was more tempt-ing, but we were all aware that we were breaking the law by working. So we made sure to hide our night-time jobs from the school administrators and the immigration officers. As long as we were keeping a good record of school attendance and were not involved in any visible violation of laws governing our stu-dent visas, they did not bother us. We were living in fear of them, which motivated most of us to stay in school until we had finished or received a green card. And they pretended not to see us.

Our school environment and our jobs were in separate worlds. At school, we were succeeding the same dreams with young people who knew nothing about our past, where we came from, or our existence outside the classroom. All the student body seemed homogeneous in our eyes; even the black Americans looked privileged to us. They all had cars, and they did not seem to have problems paying their tuition at the end of every semester. We too had to let on that we had no other worries than majoring in math or English. We had to make our situation look romantic enough to the students and professors, by emphasizing our Frenchness over our African identities and by painting a rosier picture of our stays in Paris before coming to America. Even the girlfriends we met in that world had wanted us to satisfy their dreams for romantic French lovers, knights in shining armor, and Prince Charmings.

We were so caught up in our roles as black Frenchmen that it almost cost the life of one of our friends, whom we called "Bo" for Charles Baudelaire. Bo was more like Lamartine in his affair with Madame de Staël than Baudelaire. His strange, melancholic manners also recalled those of someone trapped in the love poems of Alfred de Musset that we had learned by heart in high school. Bo was from Timbuktu, in the desert north of Mali. He had met Francine, a white American girl, while she was working in the Peace Corps there. They had fallen in love in Timbuktu, because Francine, like Bo, loved poetry, even though she had majored in economics and development. Bo used to tell us how he would take her to the banks of the Niger River and recite to her poems full of nightingales, doves, and flowers. They would sit together, facing the water, and cry silently. Then he would kiss her passionately until they had both run out of breath. Bo's stories used to make us feel homesick, but they were also capable of making us dream erotically.

We were envious of Bo for being able to live completely in the world of nineteenth-century poems and for having some-one like Francine to take care of him. Since arriving in Wash-ington, Bo had not worked once. Francine had a job at the World Bank on Pennsylvania Avenue, and she was taking care of both their expenses with her World Bank salary. Bo had told us that her parents, who lived in Alexandria, Virginia, were also very rich. Fran and Bo, as Francine's friends called them, had a beautiful apartment at the beginning of Columbia Road, near Connecticut Avenue and the Hilton Hotel.

Bo used to ask himself, in front of us, how we could work in restaurants as dishwashers and cooks, as if we were peasants. He would say that, because he was from a noble family in Tim-buktu, and an intellectual, he would never lower himself to such menial jobs. That was why he had remained unemployed all the time he had been in Washington. He had to keep his pride and not cross certain lines. At first, we had all thought that Bo would come down to earth sooner or later, and better sooner than later. This was not Africa, and everybody here was working. Even people from wealthy backgrounds were working to support themselves. As a result, we were used to talking a lot about Bo behind his back, wishing him ill, because many of us did not like him. But Bo was so sure of himself, so full of con-tempt for the restaurant jobs we had, that he had passed a whole year in Washington, in Francine's beautiful apartment, without having changed his mind about work.

Then, one morning, it happened. Macky Tall came to wake us up with the news. Bo had poured kerosene on himself and set himself afire on Pennsylvania Avenue while reciting poetry, right below Francine's World Bank window. At first, we thought that Macky Tall was pulling one of his usual pranks. He said that the whole of Pennsylvania Avenue was full of fire engines and police cars, all the way up to the White House. Some people were even afraid for President Ford's life. "Poor Francine, she had never been so humiliated in her life," Macky Tall concluded.

"Come on, McDonald, tell us you're joking," we all entreated him.

But he had sworn on his mother's grave that he was being serious, that he was telling the truth. Bo had taken himself for Alfred de Musset, or Romeo, or some crazy stuff like that. He was shouting his eternal love for Francine, that it was better to die than to live without her, that the flames with which he was going to cover his body were the symbols of his undying passion for her. People at the World Bank and in other office buildings were all standing at their windows and watching. Francine had begged him to go away because it was all over between them. At that moment, Bo had laughed, saying that the whole world would sing about their love. And then he ignited the lighter.

Macky Tall said that Bo had been rushed to Saint Elizabeth Hospital. He had disappeared from the scene ever since. Some of us were glad, though, because we were getting tired of his continual put-down of our working in restaurants. Our world in the restaurants was mostly composed of immigrants from France, Bolivia, El Salvador, and Guatemala. In this world, no one had had more than a high-school education, except for us, the Africans. Our fellow dishwashers from El Salvador and Guatemala had barely finished elementary school, and somebody always had to read them their letters from home. They only spoke in Spanish, and so we had no choice but to learn their language in order to communicate with them. Like us, they were fun-loving people, and they taught us the foul words first: *carajo, callate la boca, culero, montañero, hijo de perra*, and *jabon pa'la paja*. Unlike us, though, they were not interested in moving up from dishwasher to assistant cook or to the position of pantry chef. They were afraid of making mistakes and getting fired. The language difficulty was also a major obstacle.

The French were always coming in as cooks, waiters, and chefs. We were always surprised to find out in Washington that some of our French co-workers had less than a high-school-level education. They too had poor English skills, and we often had to translate letters and bills for them. They were always proud to speak in French to their American customers, who in turn were flattered into mispronouncing French words on the menu. It used to amuse us to hear these French co-workers making grammatical errors. They were a bunch of chosen migrant workers, though, because all the good promotions went to them in front of our very eyes. A French guy could land in Washington from Normandy, with less than a sixth-grade education and no English, and climb to the position of head cook or restaurant manager in six months to a year. Some of them might not even have set foot in a cooking school. But once they came to Washington, they had it made. If they were not happy at Chez Dominique, they could move to Sans Souci or la Bagatelle or Chez Robert or Café de Paris. They could even get married to an American woman and, with their green card, get a loan from a bank to open their own restaurant. In those days, French restaurants were burgeoning everywhere in D.C., from Pennsylvania Avenue to K Street to M Street and Georgetown.

We, the Francophone Africans, obviously had some advantages. We were second to the French and ahead of the Latin Americans. Even though the people from El Salvador and Guatemala were considered harder working and more docile than we, we were moved up the ladder ahead of them because of our linguistic versatility. We were serving as intermediaries and translated between the French and the Spanish, and the French and the Americans. But instead of giving us credit for being better educated than our French and Spanish co-workers, those among us who got promoted were simply considered smart or intelligent—as one would say of monkeys.

In the restaurant world, education was apparently the enemy. Our boss, Dominique, was against hiring students, whom he considered lazy and dishonest employees who stole food from his restaurant. Although many of us students took home forks, knives, and food from the refrigerator, we were not alone in doing that, and we were only helping ourselves to old silverware, leftover food, and steaks that were more than a week old. But Dominique was so evil that he sometimes checked our bags on our way out, at the end of the workday. And if he were to discover something that belonged to him, he would start screaming racist epithets and drag the culprit back into the kitchen to empty the contents of the bag into the trash. He was more vicious with those of us who exhibited our education at work, either by speaking proper French and English or by carrying a book to work in front of him. We had to be careful, therefore, not to reveal any connection between our school life and our existence at work. It was as if one became a different person between school and work.

It was only at home that we were free to feel like ourselves. But even there, we did not have stable selves, because our lives were rapidly changing as a result of the education we were getting and our jobs. At the beginning, we were used to spending our free time drinking tea and talking about friends we had left behind in Bamako and Paris. But soon, many of us had bought our own cars and were taking girlfriends out. Some of us became busier and busier doing homework, and some had stopped school to take on a second job. At that time, the four of us—Americain, Blanc, Johnny, and I—were staying at Irving Street. We had left behind two of our friends—James and Ousman—in the Columbia Road apartment, which had become too crowded, and moved into this one-bedroom place. It was located near Fourteenth Street, where there was a Shabazz restaurant run by Black Muslims.

While we were on Columbia Road, James was the first of us to have a girlfriend. Every time he had her over, we were forced to stay outside until they were done with the bedroom. Sometimes we would come back from work at 1 A.M. and find them there, making love until two or three o'clock. We then had to hang out in a crabmeat joint across the street, with drunkards listening to the blues all night. It was there that Macky Tall learned the black American slang that he used to impress us with. The crabmeat joint was also a dangerous place where men pulled knives on each other just because of one look at their girlfriends. One guy who lived around the corner from us and whom we thought we knew well had surprised us there one night, while we were waiting for James and his girlfriend to finish with the apartment. The man was talking to Macky Tall about some woman, when suddenly they got into a big argument. Macky was only joking, not realizing that the man was not appreciating his mocking tone. Macky was winning the argument, hurling such epithets at the man as "punk-ass, jive turkey, faggot." The whole joint was laughing at the man, and when he stepped outside, we felt for a while that he had run away because he could no longer take the tongue-whipping by our own Macky Tall. But the man soon returned with a pistol, pointing it at Macky Tall and screaming, "Who you callin' a faggot, you fuckin' African? Who you callin' a faggot, you fuckin' African? Huh? Huh?" If Jimmy the owner had not stopped him at that moment, he would have killed Macky.

We were so shaken by that incident that we never set foot in that crabmeat joint again. Some people had told us that black Americans were different from us, and that we should not mix with them. Macky had put his own life and ours at risk by playing a game without knowing all the rules. The man Macky had provoked was full of a kind of rage unknown to us Africans, but familiar among black Americans. It was also said that black Americans had nothing but hatred for Africans for being black and for being the cause of their own blackness. Not for nothing were some white people afraid of black Americans; some whites believed that blacks could kill a man without thinking twice.

It was because we did not want to go in the crabmeat bar or sit outside to wait until James was done with his girlfriend that we moved to Irving Street. The move also marked a moment of transition in our lives as immigrants in Washington. Some of us had decided from then on never to have anything to do with black Americans again. For others, James was also to blame for putting his girlfriend ahead of friendship and immigrant solidarity. In fact, it was the beginning of the end of such friendships. First, James was not alone in preferring the company of a girlfriend to that of the group; second, we had to scatter after Johnny's arrest, lest we get in trouble by standing out as a group of foreigners.

Johnny's arrest marked the beginning of our integration as individuals into American society. Because we had wanted to erase all traces of our foreignness, the better to hide from the immigration officers, we had to disperse into different parts of the city. Some of us even had to move out of Washington, down south to Atlanta or up north to Baltimore, Philadelphia, and New York. It was as if we had used the incident of Johnny's arrest as an excuse to break the community that we had formed until then. We no longer wanted to be each other's caretakers just because we were from the same country. In fact, we had begun to enter into a competition with one another, each of us struggling to become the first Malian to succeed in America.

James married his girlfriend for the green card. Before him, only Tidjani and Macky Tall had their green cards. Macky had also received his permanent resident permit through marriage with an American woman who was a professor at Georgetown University. Tidjani had only gotten his after he was sponsored by the owner of a restaurant where he used to work as *chef cuisinier*. He would later open his own restaurant and jazz club on Eighteenth Street and start a vegetable delivery service, before disappearing one day amid speculations about what had happened to him.

As I said, what happened to Johnny could have happened to any of us. In a sense, one could say that Johnny was a scapegoat. He was used by the immigration authorities to remind us that if we were not careful, we could lose everything. His bad luck was not unlike the random manner in which the Internal Revenue Service audits a few people to remind every taxpayer that Uncle Sam is watching. Johnny's expulsion reminded us of how close we were to the abyss and how agile we always had to be in order not to fall into it. We therefore had to treat every arrest of one of our colleagues—even if we did not know the person—as an occasion to evaluate ourselves, to restrain ourselves from excessive greed and arrogance, which could lead us into trouble with the immigration officers. We had to carry out a soul-searching, change our attitudes, and renew ourselves.

I remember sending that letter to Johnny and other letters to my Uncle Mody Diawara and my friend Seydou Ly ("Sly") in Bamako. I had written them at four A.M. on Saturday, April 20, 1975. Coming back from a Led Zeppelin concert at RFK Stadium, I was so excited that I could not sleep. So I had written to Johnny in Paris and to Sly and my uncle in Bamako to share my happiness with them, but also to keep my friends informed about the latest news in rock and roll.

After I finished that letter to Johnny, I felt good about myself. The morning light was beginning to reveal the shapes of things outside my window and to enter and disperse the artificial light of the Columbia Road apartment. I turned off the light at the head of my bed and lay down, looking at the ceiling. Instead of being tired, I was feeling rejuvenated with the new morning. I looked at Yassoun Camara ("Blanc") sleeping on a mattress on the floor at the other corner of the room. He had his head covered with the sheet to prevent the light from bothering him. We had all attended the Led Zeppelin concert together—James, Americain, Ousman, Blanc, and myself. James and Ousman were in the other bedroom, and Americain, who had joined us from Paris, was sleeping on the couch in the living room. They were all tired from the concert and wanted to sleep throughout Sunday morning, until one P.M., when some of them had to prepare to go to work in restaurants. Typically, on weekends, we used to sleep all morning and get together at noon to cook a big dish from home—a *maffé*, a *yassa*, or a *tiebudien*. We tried to exchange the latest news of our friends at home and in Paris. We would also reminisce about the past and make fun of each other. We were competitive among ourselves and with our friends in Paris and Bamako.

I don't know why I was not tired that morning, like all my roommates. I looked at my life so far. I was happy with everything that was happening to me, up to the concert the previous night. At my university, I was learning new things that were also exciting me. My history teacher, Dr. Swann, was a black American woman who was among the first to integrate the University of Arkansas at Little Rock. She had taken me into her office to show me a picture of herself as she was being escorted by the national guard, surrounded by white people holding signboards that read "Nigger Go Home." She had explained many things to me that day in her office—things, she said, that would not go into the classroom textbooks. Before I left her office, she had given me a book on West African history in which she had written: "To Manthia Diawara, my student. Keep your history alive. Dr. Swann."

I don't know if it was because of what I had read in Dr. Swann's book, or the Led Zeppelin concert, but I decided then to write a letter to my uncle, too, before attempting to go to sleep. By then, it was six o'clock in the morning. My Uncle Mody was the one who had adopted me after my mother passed away. Because he was a manager of a Shell gas station and gave away free gas to politicians, he was considered an important person in Bamako. The government even used him during electoral campaigns to go to our region of the country and spread a good word about the president's party. He was also a good Muslim whose reputation for being generous to the poor was unequaled in Bamako. I had wanted to write to him to tell him what I had discovered in Dr. Swann's book. I called him "father," as did his own children, because in our culture,

you refer to your father's brother as "father" instead of "uncle."
So the letter went as follows:

Washington, D.C., 30 April 1975
Manthia Diawara
2130 R St., N.W.
Washington, D.C. 20008

Dear Father,

I am doing fine here in Washington and I hope that everybody is doing well in the family in Bamako. Please give my
greeting to everybody: my mothers Sokhona and Nana; my
brothers Bandiougou, Madou Diawara, Gagny, Bouba, and
Vieux; and my sisters Bintou Diawara, Lalia, Safia, Rokia,
Kadiabu, Assatou, Zeinabou and Penda. All my friends are
doing well here; they send their greetings. Dear father, I hope
that you received the $200 that I gave to Bokar Diop when
he was here to attend a conference at the World Bank. I know
that it is nothing and that the important thing for you is that
I study hard. I am doing just that, and, with your continued
blessing, I hope to earn my diploma soon. My school is doing
well and my work too.

Dear father, I am discovering many things in the books
about us. I learned that we had our own empire before the
Moslems' jihad in the 19th Century. The books say the
Diawara kingdom extended all the way to Kaarta with the
Bambara and Manden with the Mandingo. I learned all about
our ancestor, Daman Guilé Diawara, who descended from
Assouan and founded the empire. He was said to be a great
warrior and hunter. I heard that his sword is in a museum in
France. The books blame the Jihad warriors and the Euro-
pean colonizers for destroying the Diawara civilization. Dear

father, I want to study for my doctorate and restore our history and civilization. I want the whole world to know that we had our own kings and queens before the Moslem and French arrived in our country. My father, what can you tell me about our past? I feel proud of Daman Guilé and all of his descendants.

Dear father, I hope that this letter will find you in peace, and that you'll continue to bless me.

Your son in America,
Manthia Diawara

By the time I had finished writing these letters to my friends in Paris and Bamako and my uncle, it was seven o'clock. My friends in the apartment were all busy sleeping. The blanket that was covering Blanc rose and fell as he snored, and from the way he had tucked himself under the sheets—from head to toe—he clearly did not want to be disturbed. I was still not sleepy; in fact, I was too excited to feel tired. I was feeling the way I felt every time I finished writing my friends. It was as if they were in the room with me; I could hear them as I was now hearing Blanc snore. I could look at them sitting down or standing up and appreciate the subtle details of their behavior.

V

Let the Good Times Roll

It is four o'clock in the morning in Paris. The fresh air coming through my window feels good. But it is becoming difficult for me to go on enjoying the air and the tranquillity of the sleeping city, because of the noise of the first garbage trucks in the streets. I get up from my bed to go drink water in the kitchen. I feel cold, and yet my shirt is wet from perspiration. I definitely have malaria. I go over to close the window, thinking that I have to call the doctor first thing in the morning. Back in bed, I cover myself with sheets and the blanket. As soon as I close my eyes, I see myself in Washington, D.C., again. The year was 1975, and the reality was so overwhelming that I could not awaken from it, no matter what I did. It was the morning after the Led Zeppelin concert, and I was still writing letters to my friends.

Manthia Diawara
2130 R Street, N.W.
Washington, D.C. 20008

Hello, Rockers [my group of like-minded friends in Bamako]! This is your leader; I want to speak with the acting President of the band in Medina-Coura, Bamako, Mali.

Sly! Is that you on the line? Good! Well, this is the former Jimi, now known by his real name, Manthia.

First of all, my thoughts go to Ali of the Desert, the Emperor of Bamako; I have named Watt from Sogodogo, the lover of all women and tall joints. He must be as free now as bird. So much the better for him. He loves Led Zeppelin the most, and now all his wishes have come true, because Led Zeppelin is the biggest band in the world. Too bad for the fans of Mike Farmer and the Grand Funk Railroad (Joe Cuba and myself included). Led Zeppelin is touring the U.S.A. for three months, in spite of the fact that Jimmy Page had just broken the third finger of his left hand, while coming out of their private jet. And they are stronger than ever for it. The tickets vanish ten to twenty days before each concert. In some places, they are gone a month before the show. This goes to show you how mad Americans are about them. It's a real state alert here. According to the press, Madison Square Garden has never seen anything like it. So much bestiality! Here, in the District of Columbia, women were giving themselves up for a ticket.

Like you know me, I, Manthia—me and myself—I was there on D-day, in the stadium, looking as cool as someone at a funeral, and waiting for Led Zeppelin to appear on the scene. I was not disappointed. They opened here with a combination of "Black Dog" and "Whole Lotta Love." But the crowd responded even better to "Ramble On," a piece which, I believe, is in the second album. They then played new songs that I am not familiar with: "Kashmir," "Sick Again," "The Song Remains the Same," and an interpretation of "In My Time of Dying" by Bob Dylan. After that, they played "Where the Levee Breaks," "Rock and Roll" and that piece in *House of the Holy:* "Over the Hill and Far Away." They closed with what you, of course, know I know, Watt knows, Vignon knows, Joe Cuba knows, Diafode knows, Mack knows, Abou Boly knows, Blanc knows, Subor knows, Douss knows, Debro knows, Ly Check knows. Did I leave out anybody? It is true that even the part-time Rockers like Franky, Horse, Harley, and Sylla know. Even Laurent and a few other members of the Beatles of Medina-Coura know. So do our younger brothers like Jeff and Brian. So guess what it is in your reply letter. I must confess that nothing compares to it.

The album was released on March 10, in the U.S.A., and I bought you one right away. I am sure that you will receive it before most people, except for a few diehard fans of Jimmy Page and Robert Plant. It is not yet out in England or Sweden, nor in the other European countries. Happy? I have to congratulate the Rockers because I see that we were ahead of everybody in music. We had discovered Led Zeppelin in 1969, not in 1975. In addition to your Led Zeppelin album, I have also sent to the group a record of Bob Dylan—of course it is the latest release—one by Stevie Wonder—three months old—and one by the Ohio Players—which came out in January. I like a lot the last two albums. The Stevie Wonder, especially, with songs like "You Ain't Doing Nothing" and "Boogy on Reggae Woman." In the Ohio Players, I dig "Jive Turkey," and "Fire." You know, "Reggae" is the music they play in Jamaica. Before Stevie Wonder, others had copied it: Paul

Simon, "Mother and Child Reunion"; Neil Young, "Harvest"; Paul McCartney (Beatles), "Love Is Strange"; and Johnny Nash, "I Can See Clearly Now." It is in style here, and all the musicians are copying it. Do you remember "Rock Steady" by Aretha Franklin? It belongs to the genre. Reggae music consists, basically, of playing the guitar in a sharp manner, with a staccato drum accompaniment.

I really love soul music now. You know, it's really two worlds here: Rock and Soul music. If you want to enjoy yourself with artists who are full of talent, and who reflect on politics and society—not too deeply—then you must necessarily go to black American music. On the other hand, if you want to see the style of Little Richard enriched by the likes of Jimi Hendrix, then go to white people's music. You will get David Bowie, Rod Stewart, Mick Jagger, Jimmy Page, Lou Reed, Bad Company, Yes, Velvet Underground and Pete Townsend. These guys are taking all the money. They are loved by the youth from 16 to 25, and even older. Their style is a little gay (too transvestite even). They dress in satin and expensive paraphernalia. (I forgot to put in this category Sly Stone, Mark Farner and Don Brewer). The third clan includes Crosby, Stills, Nash & Young, Dylan, Richie Havens, Steve Winwood, Judy Collins, Paul Simon, Carole King and Arlo Guthrie. This is what I like now. There are many more, but I can't remember all of them. These guys think deeply and sincerely. Their music is understandable. But, I'll repeat, the richest are Jimmy Page, Alice Cooper and the like. That's why you only see their pictures in the magazines. The whole world follows them.

I hope, one day, to talk to you about the real greats: the jazz singers, the Blues men and black rock musicians: B. B. King, Aretha, Nina Simone, etc., etc. . . . I hope that you are happy in your new quarters in Bamako, the original home without too much hustle. Please do not envy those renegades in France. I also hope that you'll like my letter. Let me know when you get the records. I put them in two different parcels, and they are registered. They'll get there then.

As you can see, I still remember everything. So I'm still a Rocker. As they say, a good friend is better than a corrupt brother.

P.S. I wrote to some of the guys at your address, back in November. Did you receive my letters?

Manthia "High Way Child"

It used to please me that, through my writing, I could discover things about my friends that I did not know before. I could be more indulgent of their eccentricities and find beauty in each of them. Take Watt, for example, who was crazy about Led Zeppelin. To put it another way, he was crazy about a girl named Maï and when Maï died suddenly, he stopped caring about anything except the music of Led Zeppelin and Steppenwolf. Watt's real name was Amadou Ouatara. His father was a policeman who was very strict both outside and inside the home. He was a devout Muslim who locked his compound door after six P.M. and forbade his wives and children to go outside. One day, when Watt got caught picking somebody's pocket in the market, his father repudiated his mother and threw her out with Watt and his brothers. When we used to play music in Bamako, and Watt was intoxicated by smoke and certain guitar chords, he would start crying like a baby, asking for his father, begging him to take his mother, his brothers, and himself back home. In the beginning, this scene was always too dramatic to watch, until Vignon, Watt's best friend in the group, told us one day that Watt was lying. He didn't have a father in Bamako, Vignon said; Watt and his mother and brothers were staying with his uncle—his mother's brother—who was a policeman. Watt's mother had left his father in their village to join her brother in the city. Vignon then added that Watt was a pathological liar who would do anything to be the center of attention. A handsome boy with a shiny, dark complexion, Watt liked wearing tight, white jeans and a big black belt around his waist to emphasize his good looks from top to middle to bottom. When he was in a good mood, he would stand there with a Craven A cigarette between his white teeth and look like James Dean in *East of Eden*.

Maï was what we used to call in Bamako *une fille de bonne famille*, that is, a girl from a respectable family. Her parents were Catholics, and her many brothers and sisters had gone to France to study. Maï was among the first liberated girls I knew in Bamako. She used to wear pants and skirts in the daytime and smoke cigarettes in public. She was more comfortable with us boys than were any of the other girls in the group. She would smoke with us and enjoy the same music that we did, not hesitating to tell us what certain songs made her feel like doing, and in what state they put her. Maï's attitude used to embarrass some of the girls, and some of the boys didn't like her. But she didn't care. She had the same dream that we boys had: She wanted to leave Bamako one day and achieve her full potential in France, Italy, or the United States.

Maï was not particularly pretty; that is, she had big bones and a large nose, which excluded her from what we used to consider then as a beautiful and feminine woman. But she was attractive because she was the only girl who was an intellectual like us. She could be as passionate about the rock stars as any of us, and she knew all about movies and politics. I also

respected Maï because she was the only person in the group
who knew and had read all my favorite writers: Dostoyevsky,
Balzac, and Richard Wright. Finally, people in the group
admired Maï because of her love for freedom, the way she
dressed like French girls, and how she spoke French by rolling
her r's as if she were from Paris. Maï was the personification of
our dream: the idea that we would one day go to France, get
our diplomas, and come back to Bamako speaking French like
Parisians and being as free as them.

Watt and Maï had met at a going-away party for one of our
friends who was in the same high school as Maï's. The friend
had passed his baccalaureate exam and received a scholarship
to study at the Sorbonne in Paris. He was the best student in
his class, and his send-off was attended by Maï, as well as many
other girls from respected families and all the members of the
Rockers, which included Watt.

According to legend, it was Maï who had first asked Watt
to dance. As usual, Watt was standing in a corner, wearing his
white jeans and smoking a Craven A cigarette. Maï had walked
up to him and asked him for a dance when they were playing
"Midnight Hour" by Wilson Pickett. The legend concluded that
there was a slow song after that, "Pain in My Heart" by Otis
Redding, and Maï had waited until the moment when Redding
sings the refrain "Come back, come back, come back, Baby,"
and she had kissed Watt, or as Watt used to put it in Bambara,
she had taken his tongue. There were many girls from
respected families at the party that night, but they were all
with boys of their class. Only Maï stepped outside her rank and
chose Watt. She was a Christian and he was Muslim; she was
about to finish high school and, like her brothers and sisters,
continue her studies in France; he had already dropped out of
school and was hustling in the streets.

When Watt and Maï started going out, he became a full-time pickpocket. Our group, the Rockers, was always divided into two camps: those of us still in school and those who had dropped out. While the first camp was in school during the daytime, the second spent its time wandering in the market-place, in front of banks, the train station, and the movie the-aters. When we got together after school, the second group brought us the news of what new films were playing in town. They also had their pockets full of the money they had stolen from innocent travelers at the train station or from business-men in the marketplace. Our dropout friends were so success-ful at picking people's pockets that those of us still in school began to question the value of education and honesty. They always had money to buy the nicest clothes, the latest record albums, and magazines, not to mention that they were dating the most beautiful girls from our school. They moved around in taxis, ate at expensive restaurants, and could afford to pay for everybody's drinks in nightclubs.

At first, Watt only ran with the gang (of pickpockets) when he was broke. Even then, he told us that he was only holding the money and the wallets for those doing the real job. But once he started going with Maï, he decided that it was time to make his own money. She was from a respected family and deserved to be taken to the best places, so he had to become a *nussi*, or cat, himself, as they used to refer to professional pick-pockets then, and "kill" some *gawa*, or victims. "To kill" in their language was to rob. But Watt lacked the courage of a thief. He therefore had to take drugs in the form of pills to accumulate enough audacity to stand behind people and put his hand in their pockets. Whenever he was successful, he would buy new white dungarees, rent an overpriced Kawasaki double-engine motorbike from his neighbor, and pick up Maï in front of her school. They would ride the Kawasaki, glued together like Johnny Hallyday and Sylvie Vartan, from one end of the newly paved street of Medina-Coura to the other. People watched them go by, identifying them as Watt and Maï. Some young people admired Watt because he looked good in his white jeans—which had become trendy in Bamako because of him and Elvis Presley. Others resented him and called him a thief whenever they saw him pass with Maï on the Kawasaki. In those days, when Watt and Maï descended upon the group at our headquarters in Medina-Coura, we could not help but see how their styles matched each other and resembled the rock stars we were seeing in the latest pop magazines like *Salut les copains*.

Soon, Maï's parents heard that she was going out with one of the boys from the Rockers group. We had earned in those days a reputation for being a bunch of juvenile delinquents who were always high on drugs and picked people's pockets. As I described, we had in the group a camp, which included Watt, that was guilty of all those accusations. They were school dropouts with nowhere to go during the day. In the 1960s in Bamako, as it is some forty years later, it was easy to drop out of school. The literacy rate was less than 15 percent, and people saw no benefit to staying in school. The government could not afford to keep everybody in school, and Muslim parents thought that school was bad for the religious and social education (development) of their children. When boys dropped out and began to steal or when young girls got pregnant and had to leave school, their parents blamed it on the bad influence of Western education. Consequently, there was never any program or other mechanism to pick up kids from the streets and send them back to school. Indeed, some schoolteachers were glad to get rid of the slow learners or disruptive students.

But we could not get rid of our friends just like that, because they had dropped out of school and had become pick-pockets. We had grown up together and had deeper ties that could not be easily broken. Some among us were even related to the so-called bad apples. In such instances, how could one tell his brother or his homeboy to stay away from the group because he had dropped out of school? Instead of taking that kind of action, we had let the group naturally divide itself into two camps, according to people's affinities. We had internal conflicts as in all groups. But the division in the group could have been attributed to the corrupting effect of the money that was flowing between the hands of Watt's camp.

So, when Maï's parents found out that she was going out with Watt, they had to lock her up in the house after school to prevent her from going outside. But as soon as their vigilance diminished, Maï was out again, running with Watt. It was during that period that she got pregnant. She was only sixteen and Watt was eighteen. She had no one to talk to, because she was afraid of what her parents might do. In Bamako, in those days, men were known to have repudiated their wives because their daughters had an illegitimate child. In some cases, the daughter was banned from the family house or sent to a village where she and the child were hidden. When we were growing up, one of the worst insults was *nyamoxo den*, or "bastard."

Maï had heard somebody say that aspirins could cause a miscarriage. She started taking them in excess; when she ran out of them, she would ask the other girls in the group for some. I remember that she had lots of bumps on her face in those days, she was becoming more nervous by the day, and she was always in the toilet. Suddenly, one day we heard that Maï was dead.

I still remember the day Maï died as if it were yesterday. It was one o'clock in the afternoon, and I was coming back from school. My friend Sly met me in front of our house and said, "*Ce, Maï ban'a!*" ("Man, Maï is finished!") To be finished in Bambara means to be dead. I asked him what had happened to her. Was he being serious? Was he sure that it was Maï, Watt's Maï whom he was talking about, and not someone else? Oh, how I wished that day that I was back in school, so that I could take another route home, by which I would not have run into Sly and which would have brought everything back to order again. But the more Sly talked, the harder it was to reverse the reality. He said that people did not know what she had died from. They said that she had just complained about a headache. She had died suddenly, as Allah alone could cause a person's death. The elders say that Allah has a date marked in the calendar for each of us. One never dies before or after that date.

But how could Maï have died just like that? I had seen her the day before, after school. She was with Watt at the group's headquarters in Medina-Coura. They were rehearsing a dance step—launched by James Brown's new hit "I Feel Alright"—which they were going to show the world this weekend at the Black and White discotheque. I could never remove from my mind the image of Maï, dressed in blue jeans, taking one step here and one step there, two steps here and two steps there, and turning around with Watt with carefree laughter. Maï was dead. She was the first sacrifice of our turbulent, but very fragile, youth in Bamako.

We called ourselves the Rockers, and we considered ourselves to be the vanguard of youth in Bamako. We wore Afro hair to show our affinity with black Americans; we listened to rock and roll to rebel against our parents and our socialist government; and we smoked pot to open our imaginations and, as we used to say, enter totally in the music. Some of our friends even became lawbreakers, going in and out of jail. Maï's death

made all of that clear to me then and pushed me to begin taking my distance from some of the bad elements of the Rockers.
Her death made me realize how trapped we were in Bamako:
The girls fell pregnant, and the boys dropped out of school to
become unemployed and petty criminals. We were young and
powerless, and our parents were poor for the most part and
with no investment in modernity. With Maï's death, all these
things had become clear to me. I made a decision, therefore,
not to make any girl pregnant and to stay in school until I was
able to leave Bamako.

As I said, Watt was crazy about Led Zeppelin's music. In
retrospect, I can now see his many qualities. In addition to
being handsome and stylish, he was generous and sensitive. He
too was a victim of the youths' lack of resources in Bamako and
the parents' neglect of their children's education. If Watt had
been born in France or America, he would have discovered his
talent as an actor or a model sooner and become successful.
Alas, in Mali there were no such opportunities; we had to go
outside to look for them.

Thinking about those turbulent years in Bamako with Maï
and Watt, I appreciate better my friendship today with my
childhood buddies from Bamako. The closeness that I enjoy
with Diafode Sacko, my only Bamako friend left in Paris, dates
from those years. No visit in Paris for me is complete unless I
spend some time with him, during which we reminisce about
our childhood. One day, he and I were coming from my cousin
Bintou's house at Créteil. The tape player in his car was blast-
ing "Every Picture Tells a Story," by Rod Stewart, one of our
favorite rock stars in the late 1960s and 1970s, when we were
teenagers in Bamako. Diafode said in his characteristic manner,
"Tu sais, Manthia, c'est le bon vieux temps, ça." ("You know,
Manthia, those were the good old days.")

We were entering the Paris beltway from the Créteil road, and in front of us we could see highway signs that said "Porte de Charenton" and "Paris Centre." The tape was now playing "Stay with Me." I used to love the way Rod Stewart sang, "Red lips, hair, and fingernails / But you ain't no Jezebel" in that song. I tried to sing along with him on the refrain: "Stay with me / Stay with me / For tonight you'd better stay with me." Knowing one line here and there in the songs used to make me feel good among my friends who could not speak a word of English.

With a wide smile on his big face, Diafode teased me with a translation question: "Manthia! Now that we know that you really speak English, tell me what Rod Stewart is saying in this song." I knew that he was reminding me that more than twenty-five years ago, I had pretended to understand—with only my high-school English and the experience of a brief visit to Liberia—the lyrics of James Brown, Hendrix, the Who, Otis Redding, and Rod Stewart. He continued mercilessly, "Now that you are a professor of English in America, tell me, just between us, what the song really means. I promise I won't tell anybody that you were lying."

"Come on, Diafode, what do you mean by that?" I pretended to be offended. "So that's how you repay me for all my hard work in translating the songs for you all in Bamako?"

We exited the beltway by the Place d'Italie entrance. The traffic slowed down to a virtual stop as cars converged from many directions to cross the bridge. It was a Sunday evening in late June, and people were coming back to the city. Even though it was past seven o'clock, the sun was still shining. I noticed people looking at us from their cars. The music coming from the tape player made the whole car vibrate. We had let ourselves slide into the sweet world of nostalgia and forgotten the real world around us. We had been caught in the middle of a song called "Cut Across Shorty." Stomping our feet and banging on the dashboard, we joyfully sang along with Rod Stewart: "Cut across Shorty, Shorty cut across / That's what Miss Lucy said / Cut across Shorty, Shorty cut across / You know it's you that I wanna wed."

Diafode turned down the music, and I stopped my foot-stomping and singing. The white people on either side of us on the bridge also stopped looking at us, as if recoiling.

"You know," Diafode said, "they are surprised that we even know this kind of music. They have no idea that we grew up listening to the same rock and roll as them. At my work, people are always surprised that I know about Traffic, Steppenwolf, the Grateful Dead, Jimi Hendrix, et cetera. They ask, 'How'd you know about that?' And I say to them, 'You know, we used to listen to them in Bamako when we were teenagers.' I swear, Manthia, they can't believe their ears when they hear me say that. You see, for them, we aren't in the same class as they are. In spite of all the evolution in the world, the media, the new communication systems, and the historical ties that link our countries to France, they still think we live in the trees, that we have no electricity and no music."

Diafode did not seem embarrassed by our being caught acting like children and listening to Rod Stewart. In fact, he kept his big smile as he explained to me the mentality of French people, their manner of behaving as if they knew more than others and were therefore the best in the world. Diafode loved showing French people that he was in the same class with them, that he knew the same things they did, and that he was even ahead of some of them when certain matters like rock and roll were taken into consideration. From the Place d'Italie, we went in the direction of Montparnasse to go to my apartment.

Diafode was driving his Renault with all the confidence of a man who had triumphed. He was not at all embarrassed.

I, on the other hand, had issues with myself and the incident on the bridge. By letting myself go down memory lane with Rod Stewart, I was no doubt betraying my natural class standing. Unlike Diafode, I had wished that the French people had caught me in the middle of enjoying the music of Miles Davis, Yusef Lateef, or Salif Keïta, instead of some kitschy white boys like Rod Stewart and the Faces. In America, a person of my class and race must not be seen in public abandoning himself to the pleasure of white rock and roll music. Not only is this music considered racist because it derives its popularity from the suppression of talented black musicians, but it is also regarded as inauthentic, not to say bad, music. From this perspective, being caught with Rod Stewart's music on the bridge constituted a betrayal of my class and race position. So although the scene put Diafode in the same class with French people, it put me out of my class by revealing my bad taste in music and my lack of solidarity with my race.

I have always wondered why the history of rock and roll raised so many emotions and controversies. In Bamako, we loved Rod Stewart, Joe Cocker, John Fogerty, and John Mayall as much as we loved Aretha Franklin, B. B. King, Otis Redding, and Wilson Pickett. Some of us even loved the white stars more. For the most part, we were ignorant of the context of music production in the West. For us, the meaning of the labels—Atlantic, Motown, Columbia, and Stax—lay in the quality of the graphic design on the record more than anything else. They were like sugar and milk companies: The more beautiful the brand name, the sweeter the product. We associated record companies with the names of musicians, who we thought owned them. That is to say, we were unaware of the behind-the-scenes history of rock and roll, at the level of promotion and distribution. We had no idea of how artists were packaged for promotional purposes; of the discrimination against black artists; of the exploitation of all the artists by the agents and music companies; or of the monopoly of distribution outlets, like radio stations and giant retailers, by a few big companies. We had not even questioned the racism of American and European fans who chose their favorite rock groups along racial lines. We had taken for granted that Elvis Presley and the Beatles were famous only because they were great musicians. We had never asked why equally talented black artists were not as famous.

Let's say that by the time it reached Bamako, rock and roll had been depoliticized at the level of production and distribution. In this respect, music is not unlike other consumer objects produced under capitalistic conditions and detached from these conditions to be consumed as objects that symbolize revolution, liberation, or the social status of the consumer. To us, rock and roll was like blue jeans, platform shoes, or Afro hairdos: We had to have them. They were as necessary to us as Colombian coffee or South African diamonds were to the elite in the West. Even before globalization as we know it today, the success of the market depended on the invisibility of the real conditions of production in the objects we consume. Rock and roll is no exception.

By the time it hit us in Bamako, rock and roll was reduced to the history of its reception and cut off from the history of the conditions of its production in the United States and United Kingdom. All we saw in it was its revolutionary content and its universal message of love and peace. We saw black and white musicians as contributing equally to this theme and to our liberation in our own societies. By the time rock and roll hit us, it was all rebellious lyrics, prolonged guitar riffs, and foot-stomping drum rhythms. We had no idea that the music producers and promoters had selected mostly white male youth to convey the revolutionary message of rock and roll. As Joseph Conrad wrote in *Heart of Darkness*, if only the housewives in England knew that the coffee and tea they were drinking every morning were produced through human suffering and exploitation elsewhere.

What we liked most about rock and roll at this end of its reception was its capacity to inform us about world politics, to give us pleasure and excitement of a kind totally new to our culture, and to connect us to the youth of the world. Through rock and roll, we discovered and adopted for ourselves the V sign, which we used to make to each other by spreading our two middle fingers, to symbolize the primordiality of love, peace, and happiness. It was a measure of the V sign's importance that it contributed to shaping our behavior in those days: the sign was a central part of our bodily gestures, our language style, and the way we dressed. Rock and roll strengthened our sense of inner spirituality against organized religions and pushed us to rebel against tradition. Our rock and roll habitus also made us allergic to everything old and yearn for what was new and different.

We were always rediscovering new musicians with different attitudes: Jim Morrison, Hendrix, Janis Joplin, David Bowie, Elton John, Frank Zappa, and Prince. As I said, at this end of reception in Bamako, it did not matter to us what color the rock star was. It was the music and the attitude that grabbed our attention. Such was our innocence at that time in our total embrace of rock and roll that we shocked everybody in Bamako but ourselves. Even the white expatriates lagged behind our knowledge of rock and roll. Perhaps it was that sense of class superiority in music that still animated my friend Diafode in Paris.

This brings me back to Rod Stewart, whose music I was caught digging when we were stuck in the traffic on the bridge. Our first introduction to the music of the Faces, whose lead singer was Stewart, must have been in 1970 or 1971 in Bamako. I can still remember the first Faces album we had. It had a gray cover with a square frame in the middle containing an impressionist photograph of a puppet band in performance. One could recognize Stewart as the lead singer with the microphone at the center of the foreground. The puppet had long, blond hair, strands of which were falling over his face; pink jacket and pants; a red, black, and white striped scarf; and very high, white platform shoes. Ron Wood was beside him, playing his wicked guitar, which brought wit and excitement to the Faces' music. The rest of the band was playing in the middle ground, and in the background, a giant horse puppet was dressed in the same colors as Stewart's scarf, with a tail that matched his strawlike hair.

At the top of the album cover was written "Faces," and below were these words: "A nod is as good as a wink . . . to a blind horse." I remember pondering the meaning of this statement for a long time, as I played over and over such songs on the album as "Stay with Me," "Memphis, Tennessee," and "Love Lives Here." My friends in Bamako also used to ask me what the Faces meant by the statement. Surely, they insisted, it was not intended to be interpreted literally. Surely there was a secret code behind the statement, and we had to know it to fully enjoy the album like other Faces fans.

In our group that gathered then in Bagadadji—a neighborhood of Bamako—to listen to rock music and drink green-leaf tea, there were some people like me who liked Stewart, and others who preferred Wood or Ronnie Lane among the Faces. Clearly, "Stay with Me" was for us the album's hit song. We spent a lot of time arguing either for the drum section, the guitar, or Stewart's voice in the cut. Some said that what made the song great was the drum reprise, which came in a crescendo immediately after the refrain "Stay with me" and exploded like a bomb. But, countered others, what tantalized you in the song was the way Wood challenged Stewart's voice with his guitar. The Wood supporters would then turn to the seventh cut on the album, "Memphis, Tennessee," and say that we should listen to it if we did not believe them. They would add that Wood was even better than Chuck Berry, who had originally sung that song.

This statement would provoke another argument. The rest of us knew that they were just saying this as an excuse to play their favorite song once again. But that never stopped the debate from getting heated or everybody from getting excited. We would start screaming and shouting at each other under the mango tree, with each person trying to take center stage and demonstrate his knowledge of rock and roll.

On our side, we argued that Stewart was the best because his voice had soul like a blues musician from the Mississippi Delta. There was something broken, not sweet or perfect at every level, about Stewart's voice, but it was also sexy, unconventional, and perfect for rock and roll. His sleepy, guttural voice reminded us of the great soul singers like Clarence Carter, Pickett, and Percy Sledge. Stewart's sexy rendition of a soul classic, "I'd Rather Go Blind," was one of the all-time hits in Bamako. He was also sufficiently playful with his voice and performance that he reminded you of Sly Stone or Tina Turner.

One might even say that Stewart had succeeded where many rock and roll singers had failed, because he had accumulated the habitus of black soul singers in his body and his voice, while at the same time preserving unchanged the kitsch of rock and roll. I remember that this duality was one of the reasons I had so much esteem for him. I imagined him to be comparable to a black soul singer on stage, communicating the feeling of the blues. In those days, I believed that Stewart, Mick Jagger, and Joe Cocker, because of their voices and bodily dispositions, were good intermediaries between us and black soul music. Their imitation of black music and rock and roll was doubly empowering for us: Where it was perfect, they increased our appreciation of the black musicians who were at the origin of the songs; and where it was kitsch, we took it for the real thing, and it opened the door for us to improvisation, creativity, and magic. To me, that was what the statement, "A nod is as good as a wink . . . to a blind horse" was all about.

We too began to imitate rock and roll and, by the same token, acquired the resources of the black soul music habitus. It was rock and roll that brought us to the Afro hairdos of Angela Davis and the Jackson Five. Clearly, therefore, as we imitated Stewart imitating black soul musicians, we were also participating in and helping to shape the rebellious, worldwide movement of rock and roll. Furthermore, the lyrics of the Faces and other rock and roll bands—with their themes of outsider status, nostalgia, love, and peace—corresponded to our own desires in those days for freedom, as well as our feeling of melancholia, self-importance, and heroism. We were always in extreme need of something and always desiring, without making any distinction between the objects of our desires. We were kitsch, political, and apolitical all at the same time.

To return now to this incident on the bridge to the Place d'Italie, where Diafode and I were caught with Stewart's music, let's say that we were rebuilding some continuity between our childhood and the present, consolidating our ties of friendship with music. But how was that still possible after all these years and with our different experiences in France (for him) and America (for me)? My taste in music had changed to become more consistent with my ideology in black America. That is, I had begun to take more seriously the sociology of music production, to consider the so-called British invasion as simply usurpation of black music, and to espouse the idea that black music was an integral part of black culture that rock and roll producers stole from black people and diluted.

My class position had therefore required me to break with rock and roll as we had known it in Bamako. I sought truly authentic music that was recognizable in the tradition of black survival from slavery onward, with African roots, and that had made its own contribution to that tradition. My class of people had raised black popular music to the esteemed level of high culture with its own genesis and formal autonomy.

For example, Jazz at Lincoln Center in New York City provides black and white audiences with firsthand knowledge of the genesis of jazz, as well as its formal autonomy. That is, under the authority of the esteemed jazz critic Stanley Crouch and the brilliant musical genius Wynton Marsalis, the audience is taught to appreciate the music of Louis Armstrong and Duke Ellington, all the way to the present.

Although Jazz at Lincoln Center is the most explicit example of linking jazz to black cultural nationalism, rhythm and blues and rap also have their own modes of inclusion and exclusion, legitimation and devaluation. Historically, black music, musicians, and audiences—to survive in racist America and Europe—have had to protect themselves with the label of authenticity and formal continuity against the imitation and kitsch of white musicians. When I was caught on the bridge with Rod Stewart, I had broken this aesthetic contract with black America. Surely I was also breaking the aesthetic contract with the white people who had recoiled in their cars on the bridge, because they had caught me with Rod Stewart. The history of the rock and roll that Diafode and I had was made in Bamako.

VI

La Bagatelle:
The Four Hundred Blows

It might have been ten o'clock in the morning. I was still lying in bed, looking at the ceiling, and thinking about Bamako. It might have been ten o'clock, because the light was forming a mirror-size frame on the wall behind Blanc's side of the room. Yes, a look at my watch revealed that it was ten past ten. Soon the sunlight would take over the entire room and begin to heat it.

During those years in America, I maintained my relationship with home and my friends through my letter writing. It was also the one activity, besides reading, that enabled me to conquer the loneliness of exile. Writing also gave me a sense of power over our existence as alien immigrants. Through writing, I could define reality in my own terms and make myself the agent of my own destiny. In other words, as I described my activities to my friends in my letters, they become reality for me in Washington. Writing also provided me with a sense of individualism and autonomy: a belief that I had a unique point of view and that, one day, the world would discover me as an intellectual—that my name would go beyond the circle of my friends and family.

Because of my love for writing and reading, I had also discovered a place to be happy by myself. I was writing to my friends in Bamako and Paris, but I saw my destiny as distinct from theirs. Nor did I take for granted the view of my friends in Washington that home was the only place where one could be really happy, that exile was nothing but hard life and suffering at the hands of people who did not know you. All I had to do to be happy was to read a book or write a letter in which I described my existence as I saw it. To me, the idea of home was also becoming universal. I identified every place I was able to find happiness as home. I mimicked people's idea of home in other places, and if I liked it, I adopted it. In the end, Bamako became the place that had marked me the most, but not the place that would satisfy me totally as home, because it would leave me missing Paris and Washington. In all those letters to my friends, a consistent theme that kept me going was the sense of independence that I had found in exile. I said in one letter after another that I liked Washington: I was on my own, responsible for my daily bread, and not afraid of hard work, because it guaranteed me a measure of stability in life. I was tired of the situation in Bamako, where life was full of uncertainty and one never knew where one's next meal was coming from. Here I more or less knew my future.

I have always been happy because I have always been dreaming. I have never let the present situation bring me down—hard work, racism or contempt toward foreigners. All I had to do to transcend adverse situations was to raise myself above them and plunge myself into a world in which I had put such things behind me. To pass the time, I would start humming a song in my head or thinking about a character in one of the novels I was reading. People at work, looking at my blank face, often teased me to try to get a smile out of me. But, whereas they thought I was unhappy and lonely, I was singing a song in my head. When there were a lot of customers in the restaurants and we had to work faster, I would find myself humming songs like "Chain of Fools," "Venus," "I Can't Get No Satisfaction," "Memphis Train," and "Papa's Got a Brand New Bag." And when business was slow or when we had to get the restaurant ready before service began, I would sing slower songs in my head: "When a Man Loves a Woman," "The Times They Are A-Changin'," "Like a Rolling Stone," "A Whiter Shade of Pale," "Angie," "On a Night Like This," "Hey, Jude," "A Stairway to Heaven," and "Another Girl." Sometimes, it was the lyrics that I hummed, and sometimes, I imitated the guitar or the drums in the songs.

In those days, I was working as a pantry man at Chez Dominique. When Johnny joined us later, from Paris, I found him a job there as a dishwasher. Before that, I myself had started as a dishwasher at the Bagatelle, where James used to work as assistant to the cook. The chef owner of the Bagatelle, at Twentieth and K Streets in northwest Washington, was Monsieur Robert. He was a nice guy. He addressed his employees by their last names and treated them like important people. When he called "Monsieur Diawara," I would forget that I was just a dishwasher who was less important than the dishes that had to be quickly cleaned for the most important person in the restaurant: the chef. A dishwasher was the one to blame whenever there were not enough clean dishes for the cooks to place the food on. The pots had to be cleaned right away, once the cooks had thrown them on the sink—no matter how hot they were. The dishwashers must also get the glasses and silverware ready for the waiters. On top of that, the kitchen floor must be constantly mopped and dried to keep people from slipping and falling. In many restaurants, therefore, the dishwasher got shouted at the most, when the customers waited too long for their food. But when everything worked smoothly, he got no credit, whereas the owner, the cooks, and the waiters congratulated each other.

Monsieur Robert's approach was different from the other owners of French restaurants in D.C. He would say, for example, "Monsieur Diawara, please do the pots first because that's what we will be needing before the plates," or "Senor Manuel, would you bring the mop here? Let's clean this spot before somebody falls down." His tone used to make us feel human and therefore care about our jobs. Whenever he came into the kitchen, we made sure that we were doing the right thing. We knew that his visit signified that some customers were getting impatient for their food. We gave each other a hand to expedite the service and save him the trouble of giving orders.

The Bagatelle was famous for its fish dishes—*bar au four*, a fish stuffed with special herbs and cinnamon sticks; *sandre au gros sel*; *dos de turbot roti*; and *dorade á la Sainte Louisienne*, a sea-bass-like fish in a bed of an exotic-looking béarnaise sauce; and the varieties of lobsters, called *langoustine* in French. There were also steak dishes, from the chateaubriand to the tournedos and *steak frites*; and all kinds of casseroles, bouillabaises, and soups; *coq au vin*; and *boeuf bourguignonne*. Employees were never hungry at the Bagatelle; Monsieur Robert did not mind if they ate the food left over by the customers. When large portions of a *bar* were returned from the restaurant to the kitchen, cooks and dishwashers alike gathered around the plate and peeled the fish off the bones. The leftovers at the Bagatelle were so good that I can still taste the food in my mouth. Some customers bought bottles of wine costing more than two hundred dollars and drank only half the contents. When the waiters brought back the half-full bottles, we would all hold out our glasses for a taste.

Monsieur Robert was a great chef himself. He cooked the *bar*, because only he had the secret of cooking it the way he did, and he did not want other chefs to steal his recipe for rival restaurants. So, although the Bagatelle had an excellent chef named Jean-Pierre, when Monsieur Robert's customers ordered *bar*, he came to the kitchen, put on an apron, and did it himself. It was said that Monsieur Robert learned to cook the *bar* at a famous restaurant in Paris—le Dome—from one of the most famous chefs in the world. Jean-Pierre was no slouch himself; he had a cooking diploma from a school in Lyon, supposedly the best in France. He was from Marseille, and with his curly hair, he almost looked Algerian. He had lived in Abidjan, Côte d'Ivoire, before coming to America, and he got along well with Africans.

It was Jean-Pierre who taught me how to make baked Alaska, soufflés, and crème caramel while I was still a dishwasher at the Bagatelle. Whenever there was an order for one of these, he would ask me to bring him the ice cream, the eggs, the lady finger biscuits, or the Grand Marnier liqueur. He would say, "Break three eggs, separate the white from the yoke, and beat it. Add some sugar. . . . That's enough!" Jean-Pierre told me that cooking was easy and that anyone could learn it. It did not bother him that Monsieur Robert was keeping secret his recipe for cooking fish. He used to tell us that anybody could cook anything and add his own style to it. For Jean-Pierre, it was styles, not their recipes, that separated good cooks from great cooks. When Jean-Pierre himself used to cook a rack of lamb, his style was unmistakable. When the sweet smell of cooked garlic and parsley butter slowly came out of the oven, we knew that Jean-Pierre's dish was ready. He would take the rack out just then and place it on a wooden board to cut it. His knife went between the bones without any obstruction, the juice from the meat flowing onto the board. He then picked up the pieces, dipped the bony ends into a bowl of parsley I had chopped earlier for him, and arranged them successively, one leaning on the other on a rectangular wooden board before shouting "Pick up!" at the waiters. I used to say to myself that the day I became rich, I would come to the Bagatelle to order a rack of lamb cooked by Jean-Pierre.

I learned many things from Jean-Pierre before leaving the Bagatelle to go to work at Chez Dominique. I remember one day Jean-Pierre had given me twenty-five cents to buy him the *Washington Post* at the vending machine. I went to the machine full of papers and did as he had told me: I introduced the coin into the slot and pulled the door open. Then I took out the entire stack of papers that were placed there and took them back to the restaurant. When I arrived, Jean-Pierre was shocked. "What did you do?" he asked me in French.

"Well, when I put in the coin, instead of finding one news-paper, I found all of these. So I brought them," I told him, feel-ing proud of myself.

"Mais non!" Jean-Pierre said to me, laughing. "You should have just picked one for your quarter, and shut the door back." He proceeded to explain to me that what I had done was ille-gal, and if caught, I could go to jail. He took the stack from me and went out to place them back in the machine. There was a review of the Bagatelle restaurant that day, and everybody was excited about it. But throughout the busy night, Jean-Pierre

kept teasing me about what I had done. I remember being puzzled for some time about this American system: How could
people be trusted to just pick one newspaper every time they
put in a quarter? Were they doing it out of honesty or fear of
the law? As for me, I thought that I had reacted as would any
normal person. After putting in the quarter, I figured that I
would somehow only have access to one paper. So when the
door opened and I had in front of me a pile of papers, without
anyone blocking my way, I thought that I was just lucky that
day. It was like winning a lottery. After all, I did not believe that
in America, of all places, people could be that careless with
their property.

It was at the Bagatelle that I first learned the importance of
solidarity and the complicity between employees and em-
ployer. Monsieur Robert was more than kind to everyone in the
restaurant. He helped some people apply for their social security numbers so that they could be officially on the payroll.
Whereas most restaurants will not get involved with you unless
you show them a social security number, he would take you on
and pay you cash for the first few weeks, until your number
arrived. My boss had a heart, unlike other restaurant owners
who only cared about their own interest. He made his employees' problems his own and did not rest until they were solved.
I worked as a dishwasher with two other guys—James Brown
and Manuel Sanchez—who felt more indebted to Monsieur
Robert than did anyone else. Both these guys were exceedingly
loyal to our boss. Brown, whom we referred to as "J. B.," was
also called "Peroleros" because he was in charge of washing
pots. They referred to me as "Africanos," and I was stationed at
the other end of the dishwasher, where the hot plates and
glasses came out. Manuel was in charge of rinsing the plates
before arranging them on a rack, which he pushed inside the

machine. I took them hot off the rack and stacked them before arranging them for the cooks and waiters.

J. B. was an ex-convict who had spent five years in jail for robbing a liquor store with a gang. After doing his time, he looked for a job everywhere in Atlanta, his hometown, without success. Then he moved to Washington, where again he found it impossible to secure a job with his kind of record. That was until he met Monsieur Robert. J. B. was straight with him; he did not hide anything about his past and was hired. Monsieur Robert simply told him that he deserved a last chance to prove himself and that he (Robert) was giving it to him. Within a week of his employment, our boss had given J. B. the keys to the restaurant to lock up after cleaning and putting out the trash. Vacuuming the restaurant and mopping the kitchen floor on the weekends took until three or four o'clock in the morning; we would be left in the restaurant by ourselves—J. B., Manuel, and me—to clean up and lock up. Both Manuel and J. B. had keys, but I never understood to this day why I was not given a key to the Bagatelle. Monsieur Robert seemed to like me, I spoke French, and everybody knew that Africans never stole from people.

J. B. was the first black American friend I met at work. He used to come to the restaurant dressed in a vest with a peace sign drawn on the back. He liked this vest so much that he almost never parted with it. During the winter, he put it over long-sleeved shirts or sweaters, and in the summer, he wore it with nothing underneath. Only at work did he have to remove both the vest and the scarf that he always tied in a band around his head, to swap it for the white shirt and checkered pants that we all had to wear. J. B. also carried with him everywhere he went a boom box that played the latest tapes of the Isley Brothers, the O'Jays, Barry White, the Ohio Players, and Graham Central Station. He always used to play "Fight the Power," by the Isley Brothers. Being a chain smoker, whenever he had a five-minute break, he went outside to smoke.

I liked J. B. and admired how hard he worked. He was always concentrating on his station and was rarely caught distracted. I gathered that, like me, he too sang a lot of songs in his head to pass the time. He was muscular and strong, and from the way he handled the heavy pots and light skillets alike, it was clear that he was a tough guy, too. People did not talk with him much, either because they did not understand his English or because they were afraid of him. When I started befriending J. B., I first teased him for his taste in music. Then he would get back at me, calling me "Franchise." When I asked him later why he was calling me that word, he told me that I was getting along so well with everybody that you'd think that I had a share in the restaurant. He said that Jean-Pierre never tried to teach him how to make soufflés or crème caramel. Here I was, newly arrived, and I was speaking French to white people, speaking Spanish, and moving about the kitchen as if I owned it. He had been at the Bagatelle for more than three years, and Manuel for more than ten years. People here came and went, or got promoted. But no one else—except for Monsieur Robert—looked in his direction, let alone spoke with him. He said that it proved how racist white people were—it did not matter if they were Italians, Irish, or French. So J. B. would also make fun of me, saying that he wasn't sure whether to trust me, because I got along so well with white people.

If J. B. was loyal to Monsieur Robert beyond doubt, Manuel was even ready to put his life on the line for him. Supposedly he did just that one time when burglars came with guns to the restaurant, at three o'clock in the morning. They must have slipped in through the back door while Manuel was putting the trash outside. But when he surprised them breaking into the cash register, he locked himself inside the restaurant with them and set off the alarm. The story goes that he single-handedly fought the two thieves and subdued them before the police arrived.

Manuel was a taciturn guy, around his midthirties, not too tall, and very fit. He did not talk much, even to the Hispanic waiters who were known to tease him often. They would call him *cavron* to get a reaction out of him, but he always responded with a "Hum!" or *"Bueno"* or a short smile. Even though our shift started at four P.M., he liked coming in at three and peeling English potatoes for Jean-Pierre. In one hour, he could finish a whole sackful of those small, red and white potatoes. He washed them in a tall pot and put them in the refrigerator for Jean-Pierre. The cooks would then cook a big steak for him—his favorite meal—which he would place on top of the shelf near the dishwasher and eat slowly as he worked. He always accompanied it with a loaf of French bread, which was longer than my arm, and a Heineken on the side. Once Manuel had his meal and his drink next to him, he seemed satisfied. The dishes would pile up like a mountain, and he was only pleased because he preferred that to slow nights, when he often had to turn off the machine.

As I got to know Manuel well, I also realized that he liked it very busy because it enabled him to test me. He took a certain pleasure in pushing me to see how fast I could work. As the restaurant reached its peak hour on Saturday nights, he liked to line up the racks, fill them up with dishes, and shove them into the machine, one after the other. As the racks began coming out at my end of the machine, I could see him relentlessly rinsing other dishes and putting them on racks to push toward me. The idea was to overwhelm me with racks so that

I would beg him to give me time to remove the plates from them or so that he would run out of empty racks and have to wait for me to send some over. I knew that I had to meet the challenge if I wanted Manuel to respect me. This was our way of combating, of communicating through the machine, and the whole restaurant was aware of it, so that it was important for me to keep up with him, not to accept J. B.'s offer to give me a hand, or to ask Manuel for *"uno momenquito, por favor."* My biggest satisfaction, then, at the end of the rush was Manuel's calling me *Moreno,* or *compadre,* and winking at me.

Manuel was from El Salvador, where he used to fight in the guerrilla movement against the government. Some said that he had achieved the rank of officer with a Catholic antigovernment coalition that organized strikes, nonviolent demonstrations, and took over a government building. Manuel also purportedly led guerrilla incursions secretly against the right-wing militia in El Salvador. That was why he was marked for death and was listed as "Wanted" by such extreme right death squads as FALANGE and Union de Guerreros Blanco. The Catholic Church had had no choice, therefore, but to sneak Manuel out of the country, to Mexico, Texas, and then Washington, D.C. Our boss was supposed to have known all of Manuel's background before hiring him. In fact, some of the Hispanic waiters had said that Monsieur Robert had hired Manuel because of his support for the Salvadoran People's Liberation Movement. Monsieur Robert's reputation was that of someone whose family had fought in the Resistance in France and whose wife was a Jewish émigré from Poland.

As I have said, Manuel did not talk much; he did not seem to trust the other employees from Latin and Central America. So he always kept to his corner, unless he was busy peeling potatoes for Jean-Pierre or mopping the wet floor. At first, my many attempts to engage Manuel in casual conversation failed. Unlike the other Latinos, he did not respond to name calling and other forms of teasing. It was only after he realized that he could not break me at the dishwashing machine that he began to smile when I brought him a beer from the refrigerator or called him "Lieutenant," or "General Manuel." J. B. warned me not to trust him, because he was a spy for Monsieur Robert. But I figured that since I had nothing to hide, it did not matter.

Everybody in the restaurant was loyal to our boss, but the degrees of loyalty varied. J. B. was grateful to Monsieur Robert for giving him a second chance in life. For Manuel, Monsieur Robert was like a father. As for me, I had no intention of remaining a dishwasher for the rest of my life. So, while I appreciated working at the Bagatelle and liked my boss personally, I could never feel totally at home the way some of the staff felt in the restaurant. For me, it was a job I had to do to pay my way through school. And, perhaps, Monsieur Robert sensed this, because he never gave me the keys to lock up the restaurant.

One day, Jean-Pierre took me outside the kitchen to tell me that he had told his friend Jean-Michel about me. Jean-Michel, the chef at Chez Dominique, needed someone to work in the pantry and would like to meet me. Jean-Pierre told me that he knew I could do it because it was more or less the same as at the Bagatelle: making vichyssoise, hearts of palm, vinaigrette dressing, soufflés, crème caramel, baked Alaska, *île flottante*, and cold asparagus. He said that I already knew how to make these and that he would teach me the rest. He ended by telling me not to worry about Monsieur Robert, for he would find another dishwasher to help Manuel. At the same time, I knew that Jean-Pierre did not want the boss to know that he had recommended me for the job.

That was how I left the Bagatelle and moved to Chez Dominique. It was difficult for me to tell Monsieur Robert that I was leaving him for another restaurant. Because he was so nice to me and to everybody else, I felt as if I were betraying his trust in me. It was like abandoning one's old friends for new ones. When I went to the Bagatelle a week later to pick up my last check, I still had sentiments of guilt, embarrassment, and fear. Luckily for me, Monsieur Robert was not there and I had to get the check from Jean-Pierre, who encouraged me to come in the kitchen and say hello to the employees. I went in to talk briefly with my old colleagues. Everyone was nice to me except for Manuel, who virtually walked away from me by pretending to be looking for something in the refrigerator. J. B. told me later that there had been a big fight between Monsieur Robert and Jean-Pierre over my departure. Manuel had informed Monsieur Robert that it was all Jean-Pierre's fault that I had found my job at Chez Dominique. J. B. said that Monsieur Robert was shouting at Jean-Pierre in French and that my name and the name of Tidjani kept coming up. Tidjani was another African from Mali who had worked at the Bagatelle. Jean-Pierre had trained him to be the second cook in the restaurant, and Monsieur Robert had sponsored him to get his green card. After receiving his green card, Tidjani had left the Bagatelle for a better-paying job at Sans Souci Restaurant. Monsieur Robert was furious at Jean-Pierre for encouraging Tidjani to leave him. I said good-bye quickly to J. B. and left the Bagatelle before Monsieur Robert returned to find me there.

Dr. Feelgood

"ARE YOU ALL RIGHT, DAD? Dad, Dad, wake up! The doctor is here!" I hear the voice of a man leaning over me and shaking my shoulder to wake me up. It is my son. At fifteen, he is already grown into a man.

"Dad, you're soaking wet. Are you all right? The doctor is here," he says, looking concerned.

"What time is it? You didn't go to school today?" I ask in my turn.

"I was waiting till the doctor gets here. It's ten o'clock," my son replies. "When I woke up and you were still sleeping, I got worried. At first, I thought that you were tired from your trip. But you were having an argument with somebody in your sleep, and you were sweating like mad. You told me last night that you had malaria. So I got really scared because I thought that you were dying. I ran downstairs to tell the landlady. It was she who called the doctor."

I get out of bed to meet the doctor, a Monsieur Eric Le-jeune, in the living room. He is a medium-sized Frenchman, five foot six, wearing a light blue shirt with no tie and a blue blazer. Mild mannered, with the demeanor of a cultivated man, he is at first interested in knowing more about me, instead of giving me a shot against my malaria.

"Where do you come from in Mali, Monsieur Diawara?" he asks me.

"Bamako," I say, wishing to put an end to the conversation.

"But where is your village? I mean, the Diawaras, aren't they from Kingui, in the province of Nioro?"

"Yes, but I am from Bamako. As a matter of fact, I grew up in Guinea before returning to Bamako for high school, " I reply in the hope of changing the subject while trying my best not to show my dislike for people who think that they know more about me than I know about myself.

"*Justement*, Monsieur Diawara," he rejoins, "I know that your people, the Soninké, like to travel. But they always remain very attached to their origins. I know, because I spent two years in Mali, for my military service, and I am still very close to the Malian immigrants here, in Paris. I have many patients among them. I love Malian culture: the music and the food in the *foyers*. It's delicious."

"That's their downfall," I say, unable to control myself.

"What's that?" he asks.

"I said that their culture is their downfall."

"What do you mean by that? I don't understand," he says, looking at me with kind, but surprised eyes.

"I mean that Africans should take on less of their cultures here, and assimilate more of the French culture that will help them to get ahead."

"I do not agree with you, Monsieur Diawara," he says. "On the contrary, I think that people should hold on to their cultures. Take the French culture, for example. I wouldn't want to lose it for some opportunistic reasons. I think that everybody needs his culture, and Africans too need their cultures. That's what makes the world beautiful."

My head is pounding. I am cold and my body is shaking. I am really making an effort to give coherent answers to the doctor's questions without having my teeth chatter against each other. I look around me to make sure that the doctor is real and not part of my hallucinations and that I am really sitting in the living room with my son standing over by his door and watching me and the doctor sitting on a chair in front of me with his black bag resting near him. I wonder when he is going to open the bag and give me something for my malaria.

"Daman, you can go to school now. I'll be OK," I say to my son. But really I had wanted to hear my own voice, to make sure that my mind was not playing a trick on me.

"Are you sure, Dad?" my son says, reluctantly going to his room to pick up his bag.

"Yeah, I don't want you to miss school."

The doctor is observing us, as if we had come from Mars. After my son closes the front door behind him, Dr. Lejeune asks, "Why do you speak English to him?"

"Because he is an American," I reply.

"But you are from Mali. Why don't you talk to him in Soninké or Bambara or even French?"

"Oh, it would have been too complicated to teach him those languages by myself. But now that he is old enough, he can learn them if he wants," I conclude.

The doctor finally approaches me and starts feeling my neck and looking inside my ears and mouth. He takes my temperature, asks me to lie down, and begins to press my stomach with his fingers.

"*C'est dommage*," he says, "because children learn languages more easily."

"I know," I agree with him. "I grew up speaking several languages myself." I really don't want to get into an argument with him.

The doctor puts his tools back in the black bag and pulls out a notepad to write down a prescription. He concurs that I have malaria and that it will go away quickly after I take the Savarrine pills that he prescribes for me. He says that my malaria is not a serious type. According to him, most people from my region in Mali are chronically infected with the malaria microorganism, which can trigger the disease when the weather changes or when the patient is fatigued.

"What do you do in America, Monsieur Diawara?" he asks me.

"I teach. I am a professor at a university in New York."

"What do you teach?"

"I teach literature and film."

"What type of literature?"

"I specialize in the novel and narratology. But I teach mostly African and African-American literature and culture."

"Madame Gerjbine told me that you are here with your son on leave for one year. I do not mean to meddle in your business, but may I ask what you're doing here?"

Madame Gerjbine is my landlady. She knows everyone, and everyone knows her in the Quartier Vavin. I am glad to have the opportunity to tell the doctor what I do in America, myself.

"Not at all," I respond. " I am on a sabbatical leave from my university to do research on African immigrants in France. I am also involved in other projects with Professor Pierre Bourdieu at the Collège de France."

"What is the nature of your research on immigration, if I may ask?"

"Well, let's say that I am interested in people's cultures, and how their attachment to their cultures contributes to their marginalization in developed societies; or how dominant societies use cultural difference as a reason to discriminate against others."

"As for me," Dr. Lejeune interrupts me, "I was one of the protesters in front of the Eglise Saint-Bernard. While the intellectuals were wasting time debating on television, I went and marched against the treatment of the *sans-papiers* in our country. I find it intolerable the way our government treats African immigrants in this country. I am ashamed of my government's policy toward foreigners; it is racist. Do you understand me?"

"Well, I am not just talking about Saint-Bernard," I answer. "In fact, I believe that the way the issue was covered in the media—Malian illegal immigrants take over a church, and are demanding permanent resident permits—provided the government with an excuse to make immigration a security issue and therefore to politicize it all over Europe. My research focuses on how African immigrants live in France and how they are treated here, which may lead to such dramatic situations and confrontations between the police and the *sans-papiers* as we have seen at Saint-Bernard."

"What do you mean?" asks Dr. Lejeune, as if taken aback by my answer.

"Well, first of all, let me tell you that I know Malians who are here legally and who were embarrassed by the behavior of the *sans-papiers* at Saint-Bernard. They gave the impression that all Malians are lawbreakers and that they have no pride in their country. The way the *sans-papiers* clung to France and refused to be sent back home showed how ashamed they were of their origins. Saint-Bernard was also an embarrassment to the French intellectuals who deny that there is racism in France. They wished that their government was more gentle in its treatment of foreigners in front of a worldwide press. Just as the Malians with permanent resident permits did not want to be confused with *sans-papiers,* the French intellectuals did not want to be associated with the racism of Le Pen's National Front and the human-rights violation of the French government. Both sides felt exposed through the media coverage of the clash between a mounting racism in France and so-called lawbreakers from Africa. But I believe that, instead of focusing on Jean-Marie Le Pen and his National Front as that which is wrong with France, we should look at the cultural symptoms that give rise to fascist sentiments in France."

"Meaning?" he asks me.

"My research shows that France is doing a poor job of assimilating its African immigrants."

"I don't understand you," the doctor says. "Do you mean to say that you still subscribe to those old ideas of assimilation developed by Leopold Sédar Sénghor?"

"Let's say that I believe in testing the strength of the republic in welcoming every individual who feels oppressed by a monarchy, a dictatorship, or abject poverty in his own country."

"But, Monsieur Diawara, let's put clichés aside for a moment. Don't you believe that assimilation into French culture robs Africans of their culture, their identity—I mean, of their very difference?"

"That is exactly my point, " I say, now feeling challenged to rise above my malaria. I have deliberately provoked the doctor into denouncing assimilation so that I can defend it. "Why erect walls between Africans and French people in the name of culture and difference? It is clear to me that Malians who do not succeed here are in the condition they are in less because they are culturally deprived and more because they lack access to the resources that the republic makes available to other people in France."

"Tell me, Monsieur Diawara, what do you mean by this abstract term *république*? I don't see your point."

"The French Revolution laid the groundwork for universal human rights and the emancipation of the individual from the Church and the tribe," I enjoin, looking him straight in the eyes. "It is therefore a contradiction for French people, who believe in individual rights, to treat Africans as a community with a singular culture that cannot be integrated into the larger France."

"Let me tell you something, Monsieur Diawara. It is clear that you have a romantic view of the republic. I do not agree with everything that the French Revolution did. Look at the Bretons and the Corsicans who are now demanding their cultural rights. I believe that the imposition of a universal French culture was far too violent here and in the colonies. And we are now paying the price for the rise of religious fundamentalism in Algeria and terrorism in Corsica. I am not sure, either, that it was a good thing to have imposed individualism on society. I would rather live under the Church than the violence and rampant consumerism that everywhere seems to be spreading from America. You see, for me, the United States is the logical conclusion of the French Revolution that you are preaching here.

I don't want us to get there. When I look at the future of France, I see America, and that represents a nightmare for me."

"I also see America as the future of Europe and Africa," I say, "particularly when I look at immigration and the emergence of ghettos here. But I am not as pessimistic as you are. Yes, modernity is bad, and yes, modernity is violent, but modernity is also good and unavoidable. That's what Africans and French people here have to understand beyond and above their attachment to cultural differences and customs. It's only after we have all entered modernity, after we all have modernity in common, that we can begin to combat the evil within. I do not want Africans to be excluded from that in the name of tradition. As for the French, I believe that retreating from the promises of the revolution is conservative and backward. It must also be that they are afraid of including Africans in the redefinition of the new France."

"Excuse my language, Monsieur Diawara, but I do think that you are being too abstract. If you come with me to the *foyer*, where there are real working-class people from Mali, you will see that they do not care about the republic or the revolution. For them, what matters is a good paycheck, so that they can send money home to support their families. For those people, caring for their families at home is more important than eating in restaurants and drinking in bars to prove that they are individuals. That's reality for me, and I don't care about the rest."

"Surely, Doctor, you're not telling me that French people are afraid of modern Africans who eat in restaurants and drink in bars?" I am now feeling that I have him, and he is going to pay for all the pain I have suffered from French racism and my malaria.

"I am not racist, Monsieur Diawara. I don't care if a person is black, yellow, or red. For me a person is a person, and that's all. What I am trying to tell you is that it serves no purpose to force people to conform to a culture that is not theirs. That's against nature; you cannot change overnight things that were done over the course of a thousand years. I love my French culture, and I would not want to give it up to become American, simply because doctors make more money there."

"You have a point there, Monsieur Lejeune," I concede, "but you are in a different position than the Africans who come here. You are educated, you are a doctor, and you have the choice to practice your profession in a modern and competitive country like France. That, for me, constitutes a positive attribute of the republic, and it has less to do with the uniqueness of French culture than with the desire of men and women to democratize education for the masses. Surely, Africans who come here to escape poverty in their own countries should not be encouraged in their belief that they are so radically different from the French that modernity and the emancipation of the individual from the community are bad for them."

"It's you who's being conservative now," the doctor says triumphantly. "You want everything to conform to your republic. I am telling you that man needs his culture, his God, and the foundational myths that support them. That's true everywhere, whether you are in America, France, or Africa. But, listen, Monsieur Diawara, I must leave you. I have other patients to see. It was really nice meeting you. We must have dinner one day, when you are feeling better. My wife, Aminata, who is from Mali, would be delighted to meet you. Maybe we can cook a *maffé* or a *yassa* and have you over. Meanwhile, give me the money for my visit and prescription, and I'll have somebody at the pharmacy deliver your medication. And don't worry; the worst is over. You'll get better once you start taking the medication."

Doctor Lejeune leaves me thinking about his last statement, "man needs his culture and his God everywhere." Certainly, if I had known that he was married to a Malian woman, I would have stated things somewhat differently. I like to provoke French people to see where they stand on immigration. If they support assimilation, I defend communitarianism to see their reaction. It was good that neither of us wanted to back away from his beliefs. We showed each other the limits of our respective positions. For him, we should let Africans live their cultures in France, even if such cultures go against our modern notions of human rights and the rights of individuals. What makes us better people, for him, is our ability to tolerate difference in others. We all have our cultures, and bad people are those who cannot stand difference. That's why Dr. Lejeune protested at the Saint-Bernard Church; that's also why he sees Le Pen and the National Front as aberrations of French culture instead of the conservative norm that has always been opposed to the idea of the revolution and the republic.

I, on the other hand, may have overstated my case against Africans who hide behind their cultures in France. But the point I was trying to make to the doctor is that tolerance by itself is not enough. People have to be willing to lose something, in every cultural encounter with the other, to have a real cultural coexistence. The notion of loss as a prerequisite for any intercultural understanding is important, because it helps us see beyond such notions as tolerance, difference, recognition, and sameness.

After living for decades in a multicultural society like America, I believe that recognition and tolerance of the other, while necessary, are not sufficient in and of themselves. For most people, recognizing the other person simply means admitting his or her right to exist with a degree of autonomy within the same nation state, or separately. For some, it is also a narcissistic way of seeing oneself in the other and therefore denying the other person an existence. Finally, recognition may signify being for the other. That is, you are what the other represents you as; you exist for the other. In practical terms, this can lead to a self-interested recognition of the other as irreconcilably different from oneself: I know that you exist as other, with a different civilization and culture than mine. My culture is Western, and yours is African; I am modern and you are my other, and that is the fundamental difference between us.

In the United States, identity politics relies on this form of recognition. Black people believe that their blackness is unique; white people think that whiteness is normative; and the others follow with the Asian-American identity, the gay identity, and the women's identity, and so forth. What identity politics does for these different groups is to allow them the right to be recognized as one of the legitimate communities within the nation and simultaneously to naturalize their cultural difference from the others. This is what my nephew, Komakan, had in mind when he criticized the quota system in the United States. When the politics of recognition is forced to find a common ground between different communities, it can only do so in a narcissistic manner: My community is the most deserving; my community holds the key to American authenticity, national identity, good manners, and citizenship.

Whereas before I felt compelled to defend the caricature of identity politics by Komakan, now I have to defend universal values and cultural hybridity against stable and absolutist identities to Dr. Lejeune. The notion that you can leave one culture and walk into another without contaminating it or being contaminated by it is erroneous. Cultures are no longer that different from each other; they have lost to each other, and they have gained from each other. Although at a surface level, there are differences marked by color and physical characteristics, which are still capable of activating prejudice, at a deeper level the desire for modernity has considerably reduced the differences between people. What people want everywhere today—whether they are dressed in dashikis or three-piece suits, whether they claim to be authentic Africans or Europeans—is the shortcut to things that only modernity can give them. There are Africans who have better access to so-called Western culture—knowledge of the classics, French culture, and savoir faire—than do some French people. Similarly, there are French people who know Africa better than do some native Africans. Furthermore, what we call African culture—the vernacular, the religion, the music, the dance, and the food—has been appropriated by world cultures. Africans, too, have embraced various aspects of other cultures of the world. In the process, Africa has lost some characteristics of its cultures, and gained some new ones. The same can be said about everywhere in the world today. Because of modernity, we can have anybody's culture at every corner of the world, and anybody can lose his or her own culture to a new one anyplace in the world.

This brings us to African immigrants in Paris. By insisting on their inalienable identity and culture, they forget the reason they have come to Paris in the first place—which is to make quick money to build modern houses at home and to buy new things that they will take home with them. By choosing to remain unconscious of this process of losing one culture and gaining another, they maintain a fantasy that there is a difference between themselves and French people. They insist that their sons and daughters learn their cultures in France to hold a patriarchal authority over them. In the name of customary law, they maintain patriarchal practices such as female excision and polygamy. French people, meanwhile, seize on this artificial difference to exclude them from French society. A simple understanding of the theory of gain and loss can help them realize how France and Africa have contaminated each other. The question, then, will be how to organize a new alliance to redefine the republic. After all, we all lose when the world gets smaller, and we all gain when we get together; that is the next step for identity politics.

Doctor Lejeune and his defense of African culture in France also reminds me of a poem I wrote a long time ago and have since lost. "The Stranger" was about a tall black man who walked toward his destination dragging a big suitcase and his left foot with it. The stranger startled the people whom he stopped to ask for directions. Some people shut their doors when they saw him coming, and others let their dogs loose to chase him away. The police suspected him of theft, and the immigration officer scrutinized his papers at every stop sign to make sure he entered the country legally. The stranger had a proud frown on his face. He seemed tired of all this hostility and lack of hospitality on the part of the people of the host country.

As I remember that poem now, I am a little embarrassed at how autobiographical and full of self-pity it was. I was crudely describing my experience as a young student in Washington and northern Virginia in the early 1970s. I was angry then at how inadequate white people made me feel in public spaces like restaurants, receptions, movie theaters, and buses. I was also frustrated by their only seeing me as a black man, a potential criminal, incapable of refinement, and bred without a religion. I was invisible to them, and I hated them for that. The suitcase the stranger dragged behind him in the poem was the symbol of the culture he carried with him from his country, which no one wanted to see in America.

Even though I never went back to that poem again—I hid it somewhere deep in my suitcase and eventually lost it as time went by and I moved from apartment to apartment—it was clear that writing it was a necessary step in my Americanization. It made me realize that America was a society divided between black and white, and that if I were to fit in, I had to choose one side, its culture, habitus, and prejudice against the other. My dilemma was particularly shared by many African students who were forced to take sides daily between the two societies—on the bus, in the school cafeteria, on the campus lawn, and even in the classroom. When an African student sat with whites in the cafeteria, it meant that he thought he was better than black Americans, whom he considered criminals and pathological. If the same student were to sit with blacks in the back on the bus, he would get a tutorial not only on how racist and oppressive American society was toward black people, but also on how superior black culture was to white culture.

Living in the black community of Washington, I became comfortable with being a black man, instead of a man *tout court*, and I saw white men as "white men" instead of men *tout court*. In fact, my access to black culture—which was primarily invented in America to oppose white supremacist culture— opened my eyes to oppression everywhere, including black people's oppression of other people.

I knew, though, that my choice of a camp in America had the potential of making a racist out of me. Not a day passed without my black friends and I mentioning "white people this . . ." or "white people that. . . . " I was concerned about the lack of racial harmony between black and white in America, and I was aware of the risk of losing my individuality in the conflict between black and white.

I am not saying that it is this kind of cultural ghetto that Dr. Lejeune and his likes are preparing for Africans in France. But if I am going back to my long-lost poem again, it is because I have seen the limits of both the American and the French systems of integration. The French contempt for even that which is positive about the communitarian system in America—group recognition, empowerment, and affirmative action—and their criminalization of the immigrant at the same time align them, ironically, with the most conservative and racist lawmakers in America. Paris is driving me crazy with its racism. Again I am being made to feel constantly bad in my skin—and this time, by the country that first established the principles of universal human rights; the country to which blacks used to run to escape racism in America; and finally, the country known for the abolition of slavery and the creation of the Société des Amis Des Noirs. Now, I yearn for America when I am in France, just as I used to miss France whenever I was confronted with American racism.

As Dr. Lejeune leaves, I think about these months I have spent in Paris. The French people I meet who know that I am originally from Mali are always surprised that I have chosen to live in America instead of France. Surely I must have been aware of racism in America, and as a citizen of a Francophone country, how could I have stood to live there? They always look at me with a mixture of pity and impatience. Pity, because of all that I must have been suffering in a country that considered black people as less than men. They would then invoke a litany of human-rights violations by America against black people: racial profiling by the police, the shooting of Amadou Diallo, the lynching of a black man in Texas, the death penalty in general, and the Mumia Abu-Jamal case in particular. How could I live in a country like that? Was money more important to me than the freedom to move around and to be an individual? How about all the poor and suffering black people around me?

As my conversation with the doctor showed, that is where French people also seem to lose their patience with me. My living in Paris for one whole year, in an expensive neighborhood, must mean that I am rich. People I have run into label me *Yankee*, *l'Américain*, or *le cowboy*. Once, I offered to pay for a group of friends with whom I was having lunch. One of them resisted timidly, but another said, *"Laisses-le, il est arrivé!"* ("Let it go, he has arrived!") In short, I am a *nouveau riche*, which is another way of expressing the illegitimacy of my money and my opinion.

It is clear to French people that I have not only betrayed them by moving to America, but also bought into American racism, and only see the world in black and white. To live in America is to betray France, because the two countries have two diametrically opposed systems: One is for human rights and the common humanity of all people, and the other is for the separation of the races. I run into this caricature of America everywhere I go in Paris, from the Collège de France to the cafés and salons. As seen in my reaction to Dr. Lejeune and my nephew Komakan, it has put me on the defensive more than once.

I am not one to deny the existence of racism in America to justify why I chose to live there. In fact, I put aside any argument I might have had in defense of America's greater openness to immigrants to contradict French people's image of their country as a hospitable place for black people. As if taking revenge on them, I reserve my comments for incidents of racism in France that are as humiliating as any in America.

Even before globalization became a catch phrase for describing everything the French people did not like, Africans were feeling the weight of racism in France. One no doubt has to be aware of the historical and cultural specificity of both America and France before comparing them ad hominem. As Pierre Bourdieu and Loïc Wacquant have pointed out, the American racial situation and model are different from those that obtain elsewhere. After so many months in Paris, however, what strikes me most is a strange feeling of déjà vu. Every encounter with a CRS policeman, an immigration officer, a racist cabdriver or café waiter, or a patronizing French intellectual at a reception or a dinner sends me back to my poem "The Stranger."

My own hypothesis about globalization is that French people have conveniently used it to excuse racism in their society. Because of the stringent requirements of the European Union (the Schengen Treaty, for example), French immigration laws have been amended several times. But clearly, such changes have also been internally driven, with French people blaming African immigrants for their failure to assimilate into French culture. Globalization has enabled the French to live out two contradictory fantasies. First, they maintain a heroic image in the world by protesting against America, the market economy, and the cheap homogenization of world cultures; second, they have found a reason to discriminate against North Africans and black Africans. They say that globalization causes mass immigration from south to north and creates a cultural disorder against which the French have had the obligation to protect themselves.

One often hears that French people do not say what they mean, and say what they do not mean. The French say that they do not like the American system in which the market dictates everything and where there is neither culture nor respect for human rights. But what the French want most today is to be like Americans. They measure everything in their own society by comparing it with its American counterpart. One cannot turn on the television or open a newspaper in France without hearing or seeing *les Américains ceci, les Américains celà* (Americans this, Americans that). The French emulation of the American way not only is limited to the restructuring of the economy (Euro-Disney, McDonald's, the Internet) and the media, but also finds its shape in the forms of French racism that have emerged since the mid-1970s, when the so-called Pasqua law on immigration emerged. The only difference is that although there is a general resistance to the so-called McDonaldization of French society, there is only a general denial of the existence of racism in France

I will tell one last anecdote to illustrate my point about this kind of hypocrisy. I once made a faux pas on the telephone by revealing my race to a French woman whose apartment I was hoping to rent for the summer. A white American colleague who had rented from her had given me her number. The apartment was situated near Palais-Royal in the first arrondissement of Paris. Knowing how exclusive that neighborhood was, I did not want to surprise the landlady by showing up without her knowing that I was a black man, not just a professor like my American colleague.

I was drawing upon my experiences with racial relations in America and proceeding on the fact that for the French, I was not an American all the way: I was coming back to France as an African disguised as an American. So I told her, *"Madame, je ne veux pas vous reserver de surprise. Je vous dis tout de suite que je suis un homme noir d'Afrique."* ("To avoid any surprise, I wanted you to know that I am a black man from Africa.") She did not miss a beat, as her answer seemed to have come automatically from the other end of the line: *"Monsieur, la couleur de la peau n'a aucune importance pour moi. Un homme est un homme, qu'importe son origine."* ("For me, the color of one's skin has no meaning. We're all human beings.") She had left me a bit embarrassed by my behavior. But a few weeks later, she called me back to inform me that her son and his family were coming back to Paris. She was deeply sorry that the apartment was no longer available.

The whole incident reminded me of "Telephone Conversation," a poem written by Wole Soyinka in the 1960s. The narrator was also an African looking for an apartment, albeit in London. It is not that French people are color blind; it is just that they believe in a philosophy of assimilation into their culture, which they call universal, and they do not think of Africans as capable of such an integration.

VIII

My Cousin Bintou

I STAY A LONG TIME on the couch in the living room, even after my medication is delivered, though I wish I could get up and lie down on the bed. I'm unable to do so. My mind has wandered around the world, visiting all the places I had sojourned, but it can't command my body to travel from the living room to the bedroom. Oh, if only my son were to come home and wake me up from this lethargy. I am tired of thinking; I want to stand up and go to the bedroom. My son, if only he were here. I think for a long time about what I have been doing in Paris for this sabbatical year. I have now been in Paris exactly six months, before visiting Bamako and coming back here with this malaria. I finally manage to reach for my bag without getting up, and open it to retrieve my notebook containing what I have written about my experience in Paris so far. Maybe reading it will give me more energy to get up and lie down in the bedroom.

The day we went for the drive with Rod Stewart, Diafode and I spent a long time at my apartment talking about our childhood in Bamako, immigration, and French racism. I brought up what my cousin Aicha had said when we were at Bintou's house. Every weekend, when I was in Paris, Diafode and I visited my cousin Bintou's house. It was always the usual story: My cousins—four women and one man—cooked a Malian dish (*maffé, tiebu-dien,* or couscous) for me, and we ate and drank Malian tea. We watched videotapes of weddings and naming ceremonies that took place in Bamako, in our village, or even in Paris. We also watched soccer games on television. My cousins always supported the French national team; Aicha said that during the World Cup final between France and Brazil, she had gone to see a marabout to help the French team win. Late in the evening, Bintou made a millet or corn porridge, which we drank before leaving her house.

Visitors dropped in at Bintou's all day long. They were ordinary people coming to say hello and spend the day in the company of Malians in order to defeat homesickness. They were dressed in the traditional Malian gowns and scarves, with a lot of gold jewelry for the women and boubous for the men. They always engaged in lengthy greetings and benedictions before they sat down. Among the visitors, there were also griots (men and women) who came to see Bintou and sang praises to her and the other visitors in return for gifts in cash or in kind.

Bintou and her sisters liked to introduce me as their brother who lived in America. Every weekend, my cousins took turns giving me the same advice in spite of our age difference (I was ten years older than Bintou, who was the oldest). The message was that I should build a house in Bamako to prepare for my return and the return of my children. All the people from Mali who had made it in exile had built big houses in Bamako. There was the house of so-and-so, built along the river on the road to Koulikoro. With a big yard and a swimming pool that took its source directly from the Niger River, the house resembled a castle. There was also the house of this guy who made his fortune from the diamond trade in Angola; it was like a big ranch and a plantation put together, with cows and sheep on one side and banana trees, guavas, and a vegetable garden on the other side.

My cousins would then stress to me that it did not matter so much whether my house was the biggest and most beautiful. To them, money in the bank in America or France was less important than a home. We had seen millionaires go bankrupt. A house, on the other hand, was permanent; it guaranteed that you had a place to go to when your exile was over. A house was also a safeguard for your children who would one day come home.

I never felt comfortable being at the center of this conversation in Bintou's house, so each time, I tried my best to redirect the topic away from me to another of my cousins. For example, I would ask Bintou how her day had gone. I knew that she had a difficult shift. In addition to her daytime job as a cashier in a minimarket, she had to get up every morning at 3:30 to go clean offices until six o'clock. She thus only had a few hours of rest before she went to her daytime work. Now that she was remarried, she also had to take care of her new husband's domestic needs. It was not as if she were not already busy in the house, what with cleaning every room and keeping it tidy, as well as cooking and serving as host to the many visitors. Her three sisters helped her in the kitchen and with the guests, but it was never enough.

When I asked Bintou about her day, she would stop in the middle of whatever she was doing—she was always in the middle of something—and say, *"Ça va, Manthia"* ("I am fine, Manthia"), with the kindest and most reassuring smile I had ever seen. Then she would ask if I wanted some more tea, or another kind of drink, or some fruit. And before I even had the time to answer, she would tell one of my other cousins to go to the kitchen and bring me some tea, water, or fruit.

So, to keep Bintou from thinking that I was in need of something else, I would ask the other cousins about their day. The youngest, Orokia, was a student at the Université de Créteil. Bintou had practically raised her along with her own son, Komakan, the oldest of the four children Bintou had had with her first husband. Komakan was also a student at the Université de Paris, Sorbonne. As the youngest of the four women, Orokia was always between the kitchen and the living room, serving tea to the guests or cleaning the table. After Bintou, she was the busiest. According to our Soninké custom, household chores were a woman's activity, and everybody delegated them to the youngest woman around. Bintou acted like a mother figure in the house, and Orokia was like a daughter to whom she had to teach the role of a housewife. When I asked Orokia about her day, she would simply say, "*Ça va.*" It was hard to get her to speak. She was shy, with a long and sad face. I used to press her to tell me about her school, and she always answered in short sentences, without interrupting her activities between the kitchen and the living room. School was fine. She was a history major. She was interested in African history. She would like to do a Ph.D. someday. The exam was OK. But she did not know the results.

My cousin Aicha—the second youngest after Orokia—was the most religious and the most bluntly spoken in the house. That day, when Diafode and I were visiting them, she said that if she were Bintou, she would have killed her ex-husband for the way he treated her. Aicha said that she was especially angry with him for marrying a second wife and putting Bintou's four children out in the living room in order to place his wife in their room. Bintou should not have tolerated that; she should have left him then and there. "Me, Aicha Diawara," she continued, "I'll never let a man treat me like that. I'll kill him first." But Bintou allowed him to take a third wife and to beat her up for no reason.

My cousin Aicha said that she herself had left her husband in South Africa for precisely that reason. He had made money smuggling diamonds from Angola to Johannesburg and came to Bamako to marry her. Once back in South Africa, he started staying out late with women. She knew that, but did not say anything to him. But the day he came to her with the news that he was going to marry a second wife, "I said, 'Not in my house! If you bring her here, I am leaving.'" The man called together the entire Malian community in Johannesburg to beg Aicha to let him take a second wife. After all, he said, it was the custom in Mali and in the Holy Quran—for the man who could afford it—to marry several wives. But my cousin Aicha refused to allow him to take the woman into her house as a legitimate second wife. They divorced, and Aicha went back to Mali. "Manthia, deh!" Aicha said, putting her arm on my shoulder to get my undivided attention. "I don't know how Bintou could have taken this for as long as she did."

Bintou was embarrassed by the way Aicha was bragging about herself. I could also see that she did not appreciate Aicha's opening up an old sore in public. "Listen, Aicha," she said, stopping and looking at her sister for a moment. "You don't know what I went through, and why I stayed married for as long as I did. But let me tell you one thing: I regret nothing, and I have nothing to be ashamed of. When I got married to this man, I was fourteen years old. I quit school in Bamako to join him in Paris. My mother and father told me to respect and obey him. Everything I went through, I did for them, and I am proud of myself. I have always worked since I set foot in France. I cleaned houses and offices for people. I have always received the minimum wage. But I never stole from anybody or prostituted myself. I am better off today than that man. I have this apartment, where we all are today. If he had been put out the way I was put out when we were divorced, he would be homeless now. It is not easy for a foreigner to find an apartment in France these days."

I knew then that I had to attempt to change the subject of the conversation. For as much as I wanted to know the details of my cousin Bintou's story, I did not want it revealed by Aicha in this inelegant way.

"Leave Bintou alone," I said. "Can't you see she's stronger than all of us here? She survived that marriage, and she is as kind and beautiful as ever." Bintou smiled and moved away toward the kitchen.

I asked Aicha how her week had gone, for I remained determined to change the conversation. I was tiptoeing around my cousins, as I had not seen them for a long time. In fact, when I left Bamako for the last time in 1973, they were all under ten years old, except for Bintou, who was about fourteen or fifteen. With me in America and them in France now, we were practically strangers to each other. As Bintou walked out of the living room, Aicha smiled and gave a sigh of mingled relief and defiance. But it was clear that she too was eager to turn to another subject.

"Manthia," she said, "so you haven't heard? They didn't tell you what happened to me a week ago on my way to work? Kadja, tell Manthia what happened to me, and what I saw on my way to work!"

Kadja was my other cousin, who came after Bintou in age. She was in Paris to give birth to her child in France and thus provide it with the chance to become a French citizen. Kadja was the wisest and most articulate of my cousins. Reserved, careful with her words, and sincere, she was different from the generous, warm, and jovial Bintou.

"You tell him yourself," Kadja retorted. "I don't think Manthia still believes in those things."

"But it's true," said Bubba, my other male cousin in Paris. "Hey, Manthia! You don't believe in demons? Everybody knows there are demons in France."

Bubba was about thirty years old. He had come to France a long time ago in the custody of Bintou and her ex-husband. He was a French citizen, as were Bintou's children, and he had even done his military service in the French army. Bubba spoke French by rolling his *r*'s like French people do. He considered himself an orthodox Muslim and behaved with authority in Bintou's house. Bubba was saving his money to go to Mali and get married in the village with a fifteen-year-old girl.

"Manthia! Why don't you believe in our customs?" he asked me defiantly. "Don't you know that even French people believe in demons? They also know that our marabouts can protect you against demons better than their doctors. Even Chirac has a marabout in Senegal. Didn't you know that?"

"OK, Bubba! Leave Chirac alone for the moment. I'm dying to hear Aicha's story," I said, a bit dismissive of my cousin.

"*Waala-hi*, Manthia!" ("Allah is my witness, Manthia!") said Aicha. "I am not lying. I saw a demon. It was about four o'clock in the morning, and I was on my way to work. The all-night bus had dropped me by a building complex that was a ten-minute walk from the offices I clean. I was passing by the building when I saw a young girl, about eight years old, walking toward me. She had long hair that glowed under the streetlight, and she was all by herself. I passed her without paying much attention at first. I was early for work and knew I would finish by a quarter to seven. But a second after leaving the girl behind, I started having goose bumps all over, and it was as if someone had poured ice water all over me. I decided to turn around— but what if she were no longer there? She was by herself with no mother or father in sight. I said my prayers and turned around. She was still there in plain sight. I walked toward her. She had on a white dress and her hair was very long. When I approached her, she stopped. 'Where are you going?' I asked. 'And where are your parents?'

"'I am looking for candies,' she said without raising her head and looking at me.

"'At this hour?!' I exclaimed. 'Where are your parents?'

"'I am looking for candies,' she said again, and walked away.

"I myself had to get to work, so I turned around to retrace my steps. Suddenly I felt very scared. My legs were quaking. The distance to my work seemed never-ending. I could hear my heart pounding, and every shadow I walked under weighed like a heavy load on my shoulders. To protect myself, I recited verses from the Quran all the way. When I got to work, I told the Antillean woman who cleaned the offices with me about my experience. She too was very scared. She said that she had to take me to the priestess who lived in her building and who knew how to handle things like this, as well as problems with men and money worries."

"Aicha, are you sure that the little girl was a demon?" I asked.

"OK, you tell me then, what was a child like that doing in the street all alone at four o'clock in the morning? She had long hair, and she did not look at me."

"Well, maybe she was a gypsy child, or maybe some man was visiting her mother and she had to put her outside," I ventured.

"Come on, Manthia, don't take me for a fool," Aicha countered. "I too know something about white people. They would not even let their dog go outside without a leash. Are you telling me that a woman would put her own child out at four o'clock in the morning? A white person would never do that."

"Look, Aicha," I said, "there are no demons. Maybe you were too tired, maybe you were momentarily asleep while you were walking to work. You could've had a dream, you know!"

"*Waala-hi*, Manthia, I saw her! She was standing in front of me as you are sitting here now. I was awake and I was not dreaming!"

"It's just that I don't think it is in your best interest to believe that there are demons," I said, trying to be more conciliatory this time.

"I told you that Manthia no longer believes in our customs," Kadja broke in. Turning toward me, she added, "But you know something? White people themselves believe that the devil exists!"

"I know, Kadja," I said. "However, we don't want Aicha to quit her job. That to me is the real demon she has to overcome in order to survive here."

"Aicha had to visit the marabout because there was another occurrence after that first incident," Kadja declared. "But she never saw the demon again once the marabout wrote down some verses with ink on a piece of paper, washed off the writing into a bottle for her to drink and to pour into her bath water."

"She saw another demon?" I asked incredulously.

"Yes," said Aicha, who was now enjoying being the center of everyone's attention. "I was walking on the same road to work when I saw lights flickering in a tree I always pass under. I had never seen lights in that tree before, and no lightning or fireworks were occurring at that time of night. There was no airplane passing over the tree, either. The amazing thing was, as soon as I passed the tree, I looked back and there were no lights."

"Aicha," I said, "didn't the marabout tell you that if you believe in God the devil cannot harm you?" I had decided to stop challenging her belief and to try to reason in a language she could understand. My friend Diafode, who had been silent all this time, joined in: "Manthia, what she's saying here is serious. It's not a joke. Many people in the immigrant community here see demons. They are not always bad, but they have driven some people crazy. They even hound some people to their death. You yourself read about the case of Traoré in *Le Monde*."

"*Waala-hi*, I saw it on television too. That poor man," Kadja intoned.

According to the French press, Amadou Traoré was an African serial killer who raped and killed more than five people—all by strangulation and stabbing. Traoré had been born in the suburbs of Paris to a West African couple. When his parents divorced, his father sent him home to his village. Traoré managed to escape and find his way back to the suburbs of Paris, where he was always in and out of prisons until he reached the age of twenty-one. Then he started killing the women with whom he came in contact. They were mostly prostitutes and go-betweens.

When Traoré was finally arrested, he told the police and the court that he was possessed by a demon that his own father had released on him. Traoré was sentenced to life in prison. The psychiatrist assigned to the case determined that Traoré's behavior was shaped by his people's belief in the supernatural, and he was therefore fit to stand trial. He was behaving according to cultural norms that differed from French law and customs, but his judgment was not impaired in terms of the norms of his own culture. He was fully aware of the crimes he had committed, even though he believed that the devil was responsible. For Traoré's universe in Africa, demons were as real as the ladies in blue who gave tickets for parking violations in the streets of Paris. French people and Africans had different cultural norms. Traoré was suffering from this cultural conflict, but that did not mean he was unaware of how serious his crimes were.

In fact, Traoré was feeling very bad about his crimes, which he had blamed on his father and the demon. He had said to his psychiatrist that he could not erase the image of the victims from his mind. In Traoré's culture, murder was a taboo that was punishable by the person's being cast out of the community while still alive and by having one's soul condemned permanently to hell after death. Finally, Traoré's psychiatrist conceded that his childhood was marked by constant uprooting and ruptures, which, combined with the abuse he suffered from his father's constant beatings, provoked two contradictory feelings in him: guilt and frustration, which might have led him to violent actions.

"We suffer too much here, Manthia," Bintou said, finally sitting down to finish the tea that Orokia had just handed her. "But what can we do? We have our families at home who need us. We who are lucky enough to be in France are their only hope of survival. Here too, we have children to support. So one has to work."

"Aicha was also lucky," Kadja said. "The demon she saw did not intend to harm her. Maybe it was intending to reveal to her the path to her happiness. That's why it was always on the same road."

"She's lucky," Diafode said as well, and left it at that.

"Oh yes," continued Kadja. "That's why the marabout told her to sacrifice a cow at home and to feed only three old ladies with the meat. I am sure that this year is going to be good for Aicha."

I knew that Aicha needed encouragement—for what would happen if she stopped working under all this pressure? I felt sorry for her having to wake up so early every morning to go and clean offices for French people. In fact, I feel sorry for all my cousins—whom I left behind as happy, innocent kids in Bamako—for having to face such a tough life in France to support the family in Bamako. I asked Aicha if she was afraid or discouraged. Was she sorry she came to France?

"Me?" she laughed, showing her white teeth. She was bigger than her sisters, with her flabby arms. She still had a very nice face and liked to put on makeup. "Discouraged, me? Never. I came here to work and to finish building my house in Bamako. I am already halfway finished. After building my house, I'll buy me a nice car and start a little business in Bamako. You see, Manthia, when you go to Bamako, you have to look rich. You have to have a nice car and nice clothes. Then people will respect you. In Bamako, if you do not dress nicely and look like you have some money, nobody will respect you. You can be a fifty-year-old sitting in a crowd, and they'll tell you to stand up to give your chair to a twenty-year-old who is dressed better than you and looks like he has money. So my plan is to land in Bamako with my new car and move around like I am loaded with money."

We all laughed. There was something about Aicha's dream that we all shared. I guessed that this dream was what kept my cousins and other immigrants going in France.

"You know, Manthia," Aicha said, looking at the ceiling with dreamy eyes, "what I want most now is my identity, my name back."

"What do you mean?" I asked.

"You see, I came here with someone else's papers, and I cannot rest easy until I have my own papers. You know, the person can denounce me any time. You know how selfish some people are. With me, even though the person is married in Bamako and has no intention of coming to France, she always asks me for money. The implication is that if I stop giving her that money, she'll denounce me."

"But how could you have gotten past the French police with someone else's papers?" I asked, surprised by her candor.

"I went to see my marabout. He assured me that I would be able to enter France without a single problem. If not, he would take no money from me. In fact, I did not pay him until I was safely here; then I sent him a thousand French francs."

"Your marabout told you that he could protect you from the French police?" I asked again, quite amused by now.

"*Waala-hi*, I am telling you the truth, Manthia," said Aicha, as serious as ever. "He told me that no policeman would dare stop me on my way to France. He even said that whoever dared to ask me questions would have a serious misfortune fall on his head. Sure enough, only one policeman asked me a question, and even before he finished his sentence, he came down with an upset stomach and had to go to the bathroom. Another policeman had to stamp my passport, and he did not ask me a single question. My marabout is not like the others. He does not take your money unless he can do the job. Heh! My marabout is not like the others!"

"Manthia, deh!" said Diafode. "What she said is true. There are good marabouts and bad ones. The good ones can tie you down without you or anyone else knowing about it. They can keep you from talking, and from remembering. So what she said is true."

"But Diafode," I protested, "how can the marabout's spell work on French policemen here? If he had that kind of power, how come we still need French people?" I felt that I had them in a corner this time.

"But Manthia," Kadja said with a kind smile, "French people themselves believe in marabouts. Chirac has his marabout in Senegal. Mitterand had his marabout, too. You should look into it yourself, Manthia; they'll make your wishes come true sooner. Look at what the marabouts did during the last World Cup. They tied up Ronaldo, and even the doctors could not find out what was the matter with him. He was sweating and shaking in the middle of the field like a malaria patient. Whoever heard of malaria in France? So there, that's the marabout's power." Kadja smiled triumphantly.

That brought our attention to the television, which had been on in the background all day long while we'd been talking. France had just scored against Portugal in the closing minutes of a European semifinal qualifying match. A black player on the French team had scored the winning goal. Everybody in Bintou's house jumped for joy. Aicha said, "I am even happier that a black person scored the goal than I am for the French victory."

"Oh, yeah? Why's that?" I asked eagerly. The ethnographer in me was again awakened by this information on black spectatorship of soccer games.

"*Waala-hi*, Manthia," Aicha said, smiling maliciously. "I feel very satisfied when a black person scores. You know, when we score, it's because we have worked twice as hard. The French people themselves do not like to make a sacrifice of their body to make the team win. They give up quickly. Black people, on the other hand, fight to the last drop. But when the team wins, they only talk about the white players, as if the black players did not exist. So every time a black person scores, it's a victory for me, even if the team loses. It shows that black is better."

IX

WE CAME HERE WITH OUR TEETH

My cousins did not live in the sixth arrondissement, where I had my apartment. Bintou's building was in the middle of several high-rises built by the government to house low-income workers and immigrants. The French acronym for these projects was HLM (for *habitation à loyer moyen*). Some kids had written graffiti on the entrance of Bintou's building: "*Tuer la police*" ("Kill the police").

Diafode said that all the suburbs were like this now. The children of immigrants, who felt neither French nor African, were running loose on the streets, selling drugs and stealing. As a frame of reference, they only had American ghettos and rap music. Diafode said that the police were afraid to come to some suburbs of Paris, where Arab and African immigrant children ruled by violence. I told him that I was pleased that Bintou's son Komakan was going to the university and staying out of trouble. Diafode said that it was really difficult for immigrants to raise kids in France. He had three children himself, and their future constituted his biggest worry.

Sitting in my Montparnasse apartment, I asked Diafode what he thought about what my cousin Aicha had said. He laughed and brushed his mustache as if looking for an answer. He no longer smoked, but out of habit, he still pushed his lips together and blew out the air. I liked Diafode's face because it was expressive and gentle. Sometimes it reminded me of a Baule mask.

"Manthia, deh!" he said, taking all his time until he had my full attention. "Having your own papers and working under your own name is the most important thing for the immigrant here. Do you see all these Africans around you in the suburbs? The majority, if not all of them, came without a legitimate work permit. They hide from the police and work under the table or with someone else's papers until they are able to receive their own *carte de séjour* with a permission to work."

What I actually had in mind when I asked Diafode what he thought about Aicha's statement was the story about seeing a demon. Now that we were by ourselves, just the two of us, I wanted to know what he really thought about my cousin's story. He had lived in more sophisticated circles than the other immigrants from Mali had, and I wanted to know if that had affected his views about religion, demons, and ghosts. But because I considered myself so removed from the African community and from French people, I wanted to rely on Diafode as my informant. His response to my question, however, revealed what he thought was more important for me to understand about immigrants in France. Maybe he was less interested in people's private beliefs than in what they faced every day from the French police. Maybe he did not even want me to question his own beliefs and had decided to talk about something else.

"Listen, Manthia. We all came here as students or tourists, or illegally, but with the intention to stay and work. All, all!" Diafode said, sweeping the air with his hand. "You see, people want to come here legally to work. But it is impossible to get a work visa from our countries. So what can we do? We know there are jobs here for us. We know that once you can get here, legally or not, you'll find work. That's why we come, and we'll continue to come as long as there are jobs here. There are no jobs in our own countries. Even if you work, the pay is nothing compared to the pay in the industrialized countries."

"So, Diafode, do you think that French people deliberately refuse to give work visas so that more Africans would come illegally to be even more exploited?" I asked.

"Manthia, deh! That's it. You've got it. There are jobs and they keep hiring Africans. The unemployment of French people is going down. At any rate, French people do not like to take the jobs we do for the most part—cleaning offices, sweeping streets, carrying loads, and construction. So why don't they give us visas to come and do those jobs?"

"Why don't they?" I asked.

"Aha! Because they want us to think that they don't need us. They want to play politics with us. They blame us for their job losses, and they would like to blame every evil in France on us. There are politicians who promise that if they are elected, they'll kick us out. There are, on the contrary, others—like Mitterand—who stated that if they were elected, they would resolve the illegal immigrant problem by giving everybody the carte de séjour. I think the solution for us is to organize ourselves into a community and defend our interests. Instead of that, each person, once he receives his work permit, stays in his corner. He wants to remain anonymous. He does not want to have anything to do with other immigrants; he thinks he has become a Frenchman. You see, now a few French intellectuals are talking about the African immigrants' right to vote in the municipal elections if they have a *carte de séjour*. Immigrants from the European Community already have the right to vote. If we too organize ourselves, we can demand our right to vote. We can use our vote to change the way visas are issued in our countries."

"I think also that the African countries can play a role in changing the visa policy," I said. "They should be able to put some pressure on France to treat their citizens with more respect. After all, there are multilateral and bilateral agreements between France and the African countries. French corporations benefit from these privileged relations by taking raw materials out of Africa."

"Hey, Manthia," Diafode responded, "*o to ye*" ("never mind that"). If our countries had any power, do you think that the scandal of the *sans-papiers* at the Saint-Bernard Church would have taken place? The police surrounded the Africans in that church for months. They were living there like animals in fear of being expelled from France. Not a single African leader raised even a little finger in protest. I'm telling you, we need to organize ourselves here and defend our rights. We pay taxes like everybody else. Therefore, we have rights like the others. That's the way it is in France."

"That also means, Diafode, that Africans have to change their ways. They'll have to become more democratic. They cannot go to meetings and leave the women behind, and maintain a caste system," I said.

I was referring to a meeting Diafode and I had attended at an immigrant hostel in Montreuil. One of Diafode's friends who had been in France since 1967 had passed away. The man was at work when he was suddenly overcome by a coughing fit and choked to death. They said that he had asthma and had had an attack at work. This was not the first time that Diafode was involved in making arrangements for the return of the body of one of his friends to Africa. It was not the first time, either, that someone had died on the job. Diafode said that the thing about France was that you worked and worked until you dropped dead.

After people passed away, their bodies were sent back to Africa because they had neither insurance nor money to be buried in France. The truth was also that nobody had planned to die in France. Everybody came here with the intention of returning home one day to retire to his or her own house. That was the reason why people sent all their money home to prepare for their return. When death came, it was always unexpected and a financial burden for those who came from the same country as the deceased. They had to collect money to pay for the necessary arrangements to send the body home.

When I asked Diafode why they did not bury people here in Paris or let their employers or the hospital deal with them, he replied that our customs were different from French people's. Aside from the lack of money to buy land on which to bury people properly, our religion did not recommend burying people here. Nobody wanted to be buried in the same cemetery with non-Muslims. This country was too far from home, and it was difficult for the soul to find its way home by itself. That was why they always sent the corpse home.

Listening to Diafode tell me about the travels of the soul, I could not help remembering a recurring dream I had when I was about nine or ten years old. I was in Quranic school, and after listening to my teacher's description of hell, I would always have the same nightmare at night. I was dead and it was Judgment Day. People were standing in two lines: one for hell and one for heaven. I was following the people going to hell when my mother came running and pulled me away. "You are in the wrong line," she yelled. "Come with me." Then I would wake up bathed in sweat, relieved that at the last minute, my mother had saved me from going to hell.

That weekend at the Foyer Baara in Montreuil, when I attended with Diafode the meeting to arrange to send his friend's corpse home, I was shocked by the behavior of some of the Muslim men. We were gathered in a big hall that the immigrants had transformed into a prayer room. It was not far from the kitchen, where the women cooked African dishes for a very reasonable price. Right outside, vendors sold fresh fruit from Africa, corn on the cob, brochettes, videocassettes, and African clothes.

Such meetings were usually only open to men. But since the deceased had been in France for a long time and was known for his popularity, open-mindedness, and womanizing, two of his female French friends were allowed to sit in on the meeting. One of the women was a former girlfriend who had remained loyal to him and continued to assist him financially from time to time. As I had said, the deceased was known to everyone as being very open-minded and not too bogged down by cultural boundaries and conservative attitudes. He had moved easily between cultures.

The meeting was really about practical matters, such as when to pick up the body from the morgue, how much money to collect from each person, who would volunteer to travel home with the body (as required by tradition), and what airline was the cheapest. The deceased's former girlfriend said that she had consulted her travel agent, who was willing to give two tickets on credit. She had left her credit-card number with the agent as a guarantee.

"What?! You booked two tickets and you did not even consult with us?" exclaimed a man who had appointed himself the leader of the meeting. Everybody in the hall—about fifty men and one other woman sitting in a circle—turned their heads toward the woman, whose face had gone completely red.

"I . . . I . . . but . . ." She tried to say something in her own defense.

"*Tu te tais!*" ("Shut up!") the man said. "This is a meeting for men. No women are allowed. You just shut up, or I'll throw you out. Funeral arrangements are a man's business. Just because we are here in France doesn't mean that we have to forget our traditions. Why do you Europeans think that your way is always better than ours?"

"I'm sorry, I didn't mean to . . ." the woman pleaded with tears in her eyes.

"No, I refuse to hear you," the man cut her off. "I am tired of taking lessons from everybody in France."

I was dumbfounded by the man's brutal manner toward the white woman, which had momentarily imposed a deadly silence on everyone. Diafode had gently put his hand over mine and pressed it to keep me from intervening. He must have sensed what I was feeling then, unless he had felt it himself. I was angry and humiliated by the man's behavior in the name of a so-called African tradition that had no place in this room of working-class Africans. I had also interpreted our silence in the room as evidence of our general cowardice. How else could we have condoned the man's behavior, approved of what he said, perversely enjoyed this violent treatment of the white woman? I had imagined each of us in the room as a hypocrite. How could we have invoked tradition in a group when none of us lived by it individually, when we were so far from home? There were probably other people in the room like me who were not bound by this so-called tradition and who believed in equality between men and women.

If this was so, then why were we afraid to speak up? I remembered what Diafode had said after the meeting: "Stay out of it! Everyone in the room knew what that was all about. This man and this woman had known each other for a long time. They were settling an old score." So that was it! Using an African tradition to settle a score with a white woman; using tradition as a force of resistance against white power. Was my cousin Aicha's vision of the demon also another form of resistance against white power? I had wished for a more rational, more direct way of confronting French racism and the alienating effect of work in France.

Now that Diafode was talking in my apartment about modern ways of organizing through taxation and representation, I was pushing him to see how far he would go in questioning African traditions in Europe.

"Manthia, deh!" Diafode said after a brief pause. "Not everything in our African tradition here is negative. On the contrary, it's what gives us our strength to keep on working; it's what keeps us from losing our sanity here. Look, now and then you see an African who's homeless and begging for money in the subway, or one who's an alcoholic and has forgotten where he came from. These are all individuals who thought that they could do without tradition and make it on their own, people who willingly detached themselves from the community. Now look at them: They have no attachments and no names. As long as you stay with the community, you are protected and you do not forget why you are here in France in the first place."

Diafode was also reminding me of an incident we had witnessed one night in an African restaurant called Le Petit Farafina. It was our weekend-night hangout on Rue Jean-Pierre Thimbaud, between Oberkampf and Parmentier in the eleventh arrondissement. We would meet there with my friends—African filmmakers, artists, writers, and some French colleagues I had met at the Ecole des Hautes Etudes en Sciences Sociales. I even took my American friends to Le Petit Farafina. The food was ordinary—*maffé, tiebu-dien, poulet braisé, poisson braisé, atiéké, aloko,* and *yassa.* But the atmosphere was great, with Sékou, the owner, playing the host and his Ivorian wife and her sister serving the food. There was a live band, with two regular musicians—Le Sultan, from Cameroon, and Vuku, from the Democratic Republic of Congo—that played soukous, classic Cuban hits, and Afro-pop. The musicians incorporated the names of the customers into their songs, and people danced in the small and crowded entrance. Late at night, African cabdrivers who were also musicians came and played with the band. With a little bit of encouragement and alcohol, some of my African filmmaker, writer, and artist friends picked up the mike and sang a song. Even superstars like Salif Keïta and the great *kora* player Soriba had dinner at Le Petit Farafina. However, the most satisfying evenings for me there were those when—around one or two in the morning—Sékou's sister-in-law finished washing the dishes and came on the stand to sing a song called "Premier Gau." She was about twenty-five years old, a black woman with short hair and wearing blue jeans. She had just arrived in Paris and must have been lured away in the prime of her life from Abidjan, where the song had just come out and had become a hit all over West Africa.

"Premier Gau" was about men who were easy prey for the big-city slickers. A *gau* was also someone easily manipulated by city women. To be a *gau* was to have been brokenhearted, to have been swindled out of something, or to be a dope, plain and simple. The refrain of the song went like this: *"Premier gau, n'est pas gau leh! / C'est deuxième gau qui est cacao."* ("First-time *gau* is not a *gau*; it's second-time *gau* who is cocoa.") In other words, the song explained in Ivorian French that the real dope was the one who could be had endlessly. He was always being cuckolded by the city slicker. "Premier Gau" provided a sentimental touch, even a sense of heroism, for those late-night owls whose most reliable companion at Le Petit Farafina was a bottle of wine. It was a song that identified with those who had had their hearts broken twice; the *gau, nyata o, cacao*, or cuckold. Seeing Sékou's sister-in-law sing "Premier Gau" at Le Petit Farafina—suddenly coming to life when she mentioned such Abidjan neighborhoods as Yopugon, Plateau, Adjame, Cocody, and Treichville—it was easy for us in the restaurant to imagine ourselves back in the steaming nights of Africa with her.

When Diafode reminded me of the perils of living in France as an individual, he was referring to one night at Le Petit Farafina when a man—already drunk and shabbily dressed—had wandered in and interrupted our conversation to beg for ten francs to go buy more alcohol. The bum had two tricks for extricating money from people. First, he feigned familiarity with Diafode, whom he had heard speaking in Bambara to Sékou and me. "Hey man, how are you?" he said to Diafode in Bambara. "It's been a long time since I saw you last! Were you traveling? No? And how are you? How about the family? I'm glad everyone's doing fine. *Ça va, Jo? Ça fait longtemps, n'est-ce pas?"*

Then the man overheard the conversation I was carrying on in English with the other people at the table—that night, I had invited an Africanist friend from the Ecole des Hautes Etudes and two black American visitors to Paris. "How are you, my friends? I am Konaté from Mali. I am the son of Mamadou Konaté, one of the pioneers of African decolonization, *n'est-ce pas?* My father traveled all the way to America during the time of segregation. He knew Martin Luther King, Jr. *N'est-ce pas?* Martin Luther King, who said, 'Do not judge me by the color of my skin, but by the content of my character.' *N'est-ce pas?* My friends, the man you see standing in front of you is a doctor of political science from *Sciences-Po.* You could not have guessed that, could you?"

We were impressed by the man's English and knowledge of black American history. He was jumping from one subject to another to keep us interested. I was on the verge of inviting him to join us—he was happy to see Diafode, an old friend, and he did not seem to be in a hurry. But at that moment, the man shocked me by asking Diafode for ten francs (about $1.50) so that he could go next door to buy a drink. Without changing his composure, Diafode said no. I put my hand in my pocket and handed the man ten francs. He left Le Petit Farafina in a hurry, promising to be back soon.

I asked Diafode who the man was, for I did not remember him as one of our childhood friends in Bamako or as someone I could have known here in France in the early 1970s before I left for the United States. Diafode answered that he did not know the man and had never seen him before tonight. I asked him if there were many African intellectuals like this one in the streets of Paris. He had said to me then that the only Africans like this were those who behaved like individuals from the time they arrived here. They thought they were white and treated their own people and customs with contempt.

"But Manthia, deh!" said Diafode in Bambara. "You do not know French people. They'll never accept a black man as one of their own. *Jamais!* No matter how many diplomas you have. *Jamais.*" Then, noticing the eyes of everyone around the table on him, he added in French that African traditions were an antidote to such behaviors, that there were very few Malians like this man because they lived in the *foyer* together and maintained their customs. France was very bad for those Africans who came from big cities like Dakar, Bamako, and Abidjan and thought of themselves as educated. Africans from the rural areas had a better chance of succeeding because they were more traditional, serious, and hardworking.

I then told Diafode and the rest of the people at the table that the man was also a victim of French racism. His problem was more than an alienation from an authentic African tradition that he, in all likelihood, might not have experienced growing up in the city of Bamako. One could argue that when he came to study in France, he had more in common culturally with French people at the university than with Africans in the suburbs. More than a detachment from the African tradition, French racism and rejection could have driven him to alcohol.

"That's what I am also saying," Diafode cut in. "If he had been proud of his African tradition, maybe he would have been protected from French racism and rejection. You understand me? We're talking about the same thing, deh!"

But I was not so sure about that. For Diafode, this man deserved his fate because he had chosen to live as an individual. I too felt like an individual, and that was why I felt compelled to defend the man against so-called African tradition and the reality of French racism. In Diafode's diagnosis of the man's problem, I had sensed that he was letting French racism and French people off the hook by putting all the blame on the man himself.

Clearly, I had seen in the man what I myself could have become had I stayed in France and studied. For having assimilated the French tradition of individualism, the man was entitled to what other French men and women of his qualifications had. His situation was therefore an indication of the French system's failure to guarantee *liberté*, *égalité*, and *fraternité* for all, rather than the man's rejection of his own culture and a failed attempt to assimilate another. Perhaps I was being less objective than Diafode, because my own situation was too close to the man's. African intellectuals like ourselves were thought of as bastards of two irreconcilable traditions: Both Africa and France despised us and considered us misfits. Perhaps it was that description of our condition as pathological that I was resisting that night at Le Petit Farafina.

Sitting in my Montparnasse apartment, Diafode and I had lost track of the time. It was like being in Bamako again. By now, the night was quiet outside, except for the occasional noise of people leaving the Irish pub on the Rue Bréa. Sometimes in the morning, on my way to the Café la Rotonde, I could see on the street the vomit of people who had gotten drunk the night before, as well as dog shit. That was before the African street-sweepers reached our block with hoses and brooms to clean the filth.

"Manthia, deh! *Les Français sont hypocrites.* The French person never really tells you what is on his mind. A black man is fooling himself if he thinks that French people will totally accept him. Our best bet here is our tradition. I am not talking about those people who exaggerate everything with their superstition, witchcraft, and abuse of power. But not everything in our tradition is bad. You understand me?" Diafode said, standing up because it was time for him to leave my apartment and go home.

I went downstairs with Diafode to accompany him to his car. It was half past two. Our little street, Rue Jules-Chaplain—which was no longer than five hundred feet—was quiet from one end to the other. The small movie theater, MK2, next to my building had shut its doors a long time ago. A big moon was still visible in the Paris sky, illuminating the street and casting our shadows in front of us. I could clearly read the posters of the films being shown at MK2. On one of the walls, graffiti read *"Sale Juif."* I said to Diafode that if this had happened in America, it would have caused a big scandal and the police would have done something about it. Diafode told me that graffiti calling people *sales nègres, bougnouls, sales juifs, étrangers, retournez chez vous* (filthy . . . foreigners, go home!) were commonplace in the suburbs.

When we reached Diafode's car, parked at the very end of my street, with its nose dipping into the cross street at Rue Nôtre-Dame-des-Champs, we stopped and leaned against the doors for a while. We were not sleepy, and it was a very pleasant night. I was feeling guilty, however, because I knew it was late and Diafode had to get home to his family. I really liked Diafode for his genuine simplicity—he was proud of being an African in Paris—and his generosity toward others, which was a sign of sophistication and a cosmopolitan temperament. I knew that he too enjoyed my company because we went to places in Paris to which he did not normally have access. Diafode was always happy to see that he could hold his own among my artist, professor, journalist, and writer friends. He gave the credit for his cosmopolitan behavior to our teenage years in Bamako—our rock and roll years, which taught us tolerance, self-confidence, and politics. Diafode also used to tell me that our generation was especially lucky to have had fathers who passed their tradition down to their children. Look at all these African children born in France. They did not know where they came from; nor did they care about the meanings behind their names.

"Manthia, deh!" said Diafode, placing his arm on my shoulder. "I prefer living in my dream of France over facing the real thing. Whenever you are here and we go out, I get closer to what I had dreamed Paris was like. I talk to people who appreciate me for my intelligence. I like that, because I had imagined French people to be liberal, tolerant of difference, and eager to work with intelligent people like themselves. When I found out otherwise, I did not want reality to spoil my dream. That's why I say that I prefer to live in my dream rather than reality."

Time was passing quickly, but neither Diafode nor I wanted to end the long and fun evening we had started at my cousin Bintou's house. I felt duty-bound to say, "Listen, man, it's almost morning, and you have to go to work today."

"Listen," he said, "never mind that. I want to tell you something."

Diafode fell silent for a moment. I looked up my street. There were two or three windows with their lights still on. Someone was going down the Rue Bréa toward Vavin, shouting insults. The noise he was making broke the silence of the night, interrupted our concentration for a moment, and must have also awakened some people in the neighborhood. We waited for the noise—now moving toward the Luxembourg Gardens—to die out so that Diafode could continue.

"François Mitterand gave me back my name," Diafode declared as the quiet night returned.

"What do you mean by that?" I asked him.

"I mean that all French people are not alike. There are some who cannot stomach our presence here. The Pasqua law and the Chévènement law are all revisions of the 1945 French Immigration Act in order to push us further into clandestinity, to stop those who are permanent residents from practicing their customs and cultures here, and to prevent people born here from getting French nationality.

"There are those like Laurent Fabius who characterize us as people coming from poor and miserable countries. We become pawns for them in their definitions of liberalism and humanism. They say that we are here because we were starving in our countries. They talk about us as if we were starving Ethiopians. The worst thing is, they call us the poorest people in the world, as if we were nothing without them. It hurts me to see liberals plead our case like this as if we were beggars, or as if we needed their pity. Why can't they see us as a working class trying to better our material conditions like everyone else? Like them, we came from places rich in culture, tradition, and human relations. All we need is work, not their pity.

"Of course, there's the National Front that tries to win votes on our backs. But at least with Le Pen and the National Front, you know what you're dealing with. They say they don't like Arabs and they don't like Africans, because we steal their jobs and take their social security and health insurance. They say their culture is different from ours, and if there are too many of us here, our culture will contaminate their own. I'll bet you, Manthia, that ninety percent of French people think like Le Pen and the National Front. But they are hypocrites.

"Manthia, deh!" Diafode continued, looking left and right in case somebody was within earshot. "I don't know what I would have done if Mitterand had lost the 1985 elections. Paris was hot in those days. There was no place to hide from the police. The CRS was hunting for *sans-papiers* everywhere, in the subway, in the streets, and at train stations. You should have seen the way they used to line up black people at subway stops. Those who did not have their *carte de séjour* were handcuffed together, beaten up, and loaded in police vans to go to jail. They got deported soon afterwards.

"At that time, I used to have someone else's papers, and I did not want to be caught by the police. I was ducking them every day on my way to work. Until Mitterand was reelected, I was working under a fake name, Amadou Diallo. Everybody at work knew me as Diallo, even my boss, who trusted me and was fond of me. At home, I was Diafode Sacko, but at work, I was Diallo. I got the papers from the brother of one of our friends who was a travel agent. You remember him, he used to work in the 1970s near the Foyer Baara in Montreuil. One day when I visited him, he said, 'Look, Diafode, somebody left this *carte de séjour* behind. Do you want it?' I took it and thanked him.

"For five years, I worked with Amadou Diallo's papers without any problem. I was careful not to get into trouble. But I was getting tired of being known under someone else's name. I had heard that Mitterand was promising to give amnesty to all the *sans-papiers* who arrived before 1983 if he got reelected. I started praying for his reelection. I wanted to get my name back.

"When Mitterand was reelected, I was very happy. But the most difficult thing was to tell my boss that I was not who I had said I was all this time. So I went into his office and said, 'Monsieur Pierre, I want to speak to you.'

"'What, again, Diallo?' he said, without raising his head. 'Aren't you happy here?'

"'It's not that,' I replied.

"'Then what? Do you want another raise?'

"'No,' I said.

"'Diallo!' he exclaimed, this time raising his head to look at me. 'What's wrong? Family problems?'

"'No, Monsieur Pierre. I want to tell you that I've been lying to you all this time. I am not Diallo. My name is Diafode Sacko.'

"'What? Oh, *merde alors!*' he exploded, standing up to face me. I looked him straight in the eye for more than fifteen seconds. Then he knew I was being serious.

"'Why did you lie? Who are you hiding from?' he asked.

"'No one. I did it to be able to work,' I answered.

"'What's gonna happen now? You've gotten all of us in trouble. Me for employing you illegally, and you for lying,' he said.

"'I heard that Mitterand has given amnesty to all the *sans-papiers* who arrived here before 1983. I am going to apply for amnesty.'

"I left Monsieur Pierre's office feeling sorry for him. He was visibly shocked by what I had told him. The next day, I went to the préfecture and filed for a *carte de séjour* under my own name. That was how I gained back my name, and I'll always be grateful to François Mitterand.

"Seven years later, when he died, I cried. He was the best French president. On the day of the memorial for him at the Place de la Bastille, it was raining in Paris. But I had to attend it. How could I miss it? I went there and stood in communion among thousands and thousands of people. He was a great man. Not like the others." Diafode's story had ended.

We said good-bye and set a date for the following weekend. I made sure that his car started before I walked back toward my building. The garbage trucks were already out collecting trash from building to building. The smell of fresh bread was coming out of the bakery on Rue Bréa. Paris was waking up. As I walked up the stairs to my fifth-floor apartment, the many stories evoked over the weekend were rushing past each other in my head.

I opened the door, went to the bathroom to brush my teeth, and lay awake on my bed. In a couple of hours, my son would be going to his school, and then I would be able to get some sleep if the telephone did not start ringing. Diafode had received his amnesty after Mitterand was reelected. How about my cousin Aicha: When would she get her amnesty; when would she get her name back? What was in a name, anyway? Wasn't being able to work the most important thing? Who cared about a name in a place like Paris? In today's technologically advanced societies, with computers and DNA methods of identification, people had been reduced to numbers. Why were Africans still clinging to their names? On the contrary, in these modern societies, wasn't it more important to have multiple identities so as not to be trapped in only one?

I remembered a long, long time ago, when I was in Guinea with my parents and my younger brothers. I was sent to school with the birth certificate belonging to one of my younger brothers because mine had been left behind in Mali. I attended school for three years under my brother's name until my family had to go back to Mali, where my mother established a new birth certificate for me. I was two years older than my brother, and it always used to bother me to be treated as if I were his age. Besides, my brother needed his own birth certificate to be able to go to school. I wondered what would have happened if we had stayed in Guinea, where one of us would have been without a birth certificate?

By reminding Diafode of his own story, and me of mine, Aicha's story revealed how immigration forced people to change their identity, and how they tried the rest of their lives to get their original name back. People were always trying to establish who they were, in order to be recognized and respected by others. Immigrants often made their breakthroughs when they were living under borrowed names. It was at that time that they identified most intimately with their work and behaved most like a working class—because they knew that only work could save them. But when the immigrant desired to come out of anonymity, to search for a name, he or she became alienated from the host country and from its working class.

African immigrants in France resist discrimination and exploitation by clinging to their names and their customs. Diafode and I were sitting with residents of the Foyer Baara in the public kitchen on the third floor, drinking the West African tea called Ataye. We often gathered there on weekends to talk about Mali, French politics, or sports. There were only men. On that particular day, a guy whom Diafode called "the Ambassador" because he always praised Malian culture and history, said that he had heard me interviewed on the radio. I was talking about my book *In Search of Africa* and about the necessity of questioning tradition, narratives of return, and the concept of the hero in the *Epic of Sunjata*. To my surprise, the Ambassador was proud of me for the way I had defended and celebrated our Malian tradition on French radio. He said that Malians were the best, most intelligent, and most civilized people in the world. French people did not know Malians as they should have. Unfortunately, there were only a few intellectuals from Africa who were capable of telling the truth to white people in the way I did—the truth about Sunjata, Mansa Musa, Ibn Batuta, and others. Mali had important empires, and everyone knew that; French people just did not want to acknowledge it. The Ambassador had then proceeded to compare me to Cheikh Anta Diop and other great African historians. But I explained to him that I was not a historian, but someone who wrote literature. I was more like an artist who liked to question people, history, and other things.

But the Ambassador was not someone to argue with when it came to Mali. He had said that we all had the responsibility to praise Mali abroad. We were underappreciated here because people did not know who we were, what our culture was, and what our religion meant. Look at the great French anthropologists who had studied the Dogon in Mali and the Bambara initiation ceremonies. The Dogon had discovered Sirius, a distant star, long before the European astronomers. The same anthropologists had also shown that in the past, the Bambara had their own system of writing.

"Diawara," the Ambassador had told me, "you know that in every African country there is a French cultural center, an American center, and a Goethe Institute. Here, we have no African cultural centers. It is therefore the responsibility of every Malian to represent a good image of Mali here, to be proud of being from Mali, and to celebrate Mali. That's why we wear our grand boubous and other traditional clothes in the streets, in the subway, and in other public places. You see, Diawara, every Malian in Paris is a cultural center. Every Malian has a duty to teach Malian culture to French people."

"*Ça suffit, Ambassadeur!*" said another guy who had just walked into the kitchen. "Enough of that Mali business. Now we are in France, and we don't want to hear about Mali."

"Kanté," the Ambassador snapped, "where are your manners? You walk in without even greeting people and jump into the middle of the conversation like that! Back then, in the time of Sunjata, I would have tied you up for your insolence. Isn't that right, Sacko?" The Ambassador was now addressing Diafode.

"*Akoni!*" ("You said it!") Diafode replied.

"Come on, Ambassadeur!" exclaimed the man who was making the tea. "If we go that far back, I would have many slaves here in this room: the Sacko, the Traoré, and the Diawara." He laughed, and we all did likewise.

What the Ambassador was talking about was known in Mali as the concept of *yere don*, or self-knowledge. To know oneself was to exhibit, wherever one was, the qualities of one's lineage: to show, during moments of duress, the nobility, heroism, and moral strength embedded in the history of one's family name—the clan, the empire, or the state. There was a Bambara saying that everybody was born with a griot to sing his name. It was the griot who told you about the meaning of your name, the history behind it, and the activities you had to engage in to do more honor to the name. Your family name depended on you to make it known the world over, and you were nothing without a name.

The name also represented social capital for the Malian society. People who had never seen you before trusted you because of your name. People could lend you money, give you their daughter in marriage, or confide their deepest secrets to you because of your name. One of the griots we met at my cousin Bintou's house had said that the reason everybody went there was not because she had gold, for gold could run out; not because she had money, for money too could be spent; not even because she was beautiful, for there were beautiful people whom no one wanted to see. Bintou was popular, for she knew who she was: France had not changed her; money had not spoiled her; and gold had not ruined her, because she had all of the foregoing qualities.

The griot had said that the measure of Bintou's self-knowledge could be seen in the rules that she had set for herself in France: Her door was always open to people who were hungry; her door was always open to people who were thirsty. She never lied, for her mother never lied and her father never lied. She never danced, for her mother never danced and her father never danced. Dancing was a display of emotions, and it was unfit for a noble person. Bintou's nobility came from her father, who never failed the griots. It came from her mother—may she rest in peace. Bintou herself had never failed griots. She carried her name well.

As I said, immigrants clung to their names to resist exclusion and dehumanization in industrialized societies. Even those immigrants who had been less concerned about their name before they had arrived in France were now greater advocates of self-knowledge, or *yere don*. When I first started visiting Bintou, I was surprised to find the Soninké more conservative in France than they were in Mali. People much younger than I were proclaiming the virtues of tradition to me. Even the women, who should have found emancipation in working-class culture here, were telling me how important it was to send the children who had been born here to Mali, so that they could see the village, meet their grandparents, and learn more about themselves. There was a saying that an African child born in France was neither your son nor your daughter: *Haransi den te den ye* (A French child is not a child). By this expression, the immigrants meant that this child had not been trained from the beginning to know himself or herself, to practice *yere don*. For such children, there were no taboos: They were not circumcised; they had not participated in traditional initiations; they had no shame; they were like white people. *Yere don*, therefore, constituted everything for the immigrant.

But as I saw it now, *yere don* also constituted a trap for the working-class immigrants in France. I was convinced that it was through the philosophy of *yere don* that the immigrants entered into complicity with those same French racists who prevented them from assimilating into French culture. First of all, on an economic level this philosophy bound Africans to their original homes, where they kept investing their meager incomes to buy land and support the reproduction of the system. In this sense, the immigrants who sent money home were more concerned about investing in their cultural capital at home and abroad—which was governed by the philosophy of *yere don*—than about investing in an economic capital, which would have been based on a knowledge of Mali as a safe and profitable place to put one's hard-earned money.

Clearly, during the military dictatorship—when people's human rights were constantly violated and their lands taken away from them—any investment in the society was helping to legitimize and maintain the then-current regime. Even today, under the current democratic government, the riskiness of investing in Mali and many other African countries, because of the constant threat of currency devaluation, did not deter immigrants from sending their funds there to seek recognition. Remarkably, the government did not even have to entice immigrants to invest in Mali with offers of cheaper land or tax exemptions.

But obviously, with *yere don*, the pleasure of self-knowledge and recognition, the enticement for people to invest in Mali was greater than any modern economic theory. People invested because they wanted others like them to know that they had done so—a factor that contributed to the building of their cultural capital. When one bought a home in Bamako or owned cattle, it was like providing the griot with a new motif for his praise song to you. In fact, the concept of *yere don*—or respect, as it is referred to among young men in U.S. ghettos—organized the lives of immigrants in France in a certain way. Because of *yere don*, the power struggles among them were more important than the struggles between them and the systems that oppressed them: their employers, the French police, the housing system, and so forth.

It was because of the competition among immigrants for recognition that my cousin Bintou and her sisters advised me to buy land in Mali and build a house. I would never forget what one of the Diawara potentates in Paris said to me on the day Bintou was remarried. He was actually a close relative, since our fathers were brothers. I still remembered him from the village when I was young and he was but a teenager. Now he was a kind of chief of the village of the Soninké in Paris. When he spoke at marriages like this, or at naming ceremonies and big Soninké holidays, he measured his voice, and the griot interpreted his speech to the people. On the day Bintou was remarried, people who had arrived from the other suburbs and the different provinces of France were surprised to see me there, too. They had heard that I was a professor in America, and some were curious about how well I was doing. But I soon found out what their expectations of me were when I was introduced to my relative, the potentate.

I was talking to Mamadou Baraji, the Soninké man who had his own travel agency on the Rue d'Avron, where I had once been stopped by the French police. Baraji had asked me if my esteemed relative had seen me, if he knew that I was here. I had told him that I was not sure, because there were so many people at Bintou's house that day. But just at that moment, he passed by Baraji and me in the hallway. "Look who's here," Baraji told him. "Don't you recognize your brother? He's Manthia from America."

The potentate stopped for a moment and considered Baraji without looking at me. Then he said, "I don't know that Manthia. Who is he? I do not have such a brother. People say that he had studied for the highest diplomas in America. Some even say that he teaches white people there. But what has he done in the village? What has he done in Bamako? There are people in Mali today who do not have half the education he has received, nor are they as noble as he is. But they are presidents and ministers. There are others here in France from casted clans. But they have used their contacts with white people to bring investments to their villages, to dig wells there, to bring electricity and hospitals. What is the use of Manthia's education if he can't do that? That's why I say that we do not know him. Baraji, I thank you for your good intentions. May Allah repay you. But I must go now."

He had left without looking at me. Baraji told me not to worry, as he was going to fix everything. The best way was to visit my relative one weekend and pay him our respects. Baraji would come with me, and we would bring along some kola nuts and some money to make peace. According to Baraji, my relative was hurt because I had not gone to visit him since I had been in Paris. Baraji concluded by saying that this was how our tradition was. You were nobody unless you had done something for the village.

Of course, I was shocked by the behavior of my relative and by other macho posturings at Bintou's wedding. I disagreed with my relative, who, like other Soninkés, took his focus of recognition away from France and placed it in Mali, into an archaic tradition that worked to trap them in France instead of linking them with other working-class men and women in the struggle for better living conditions. When one worked in France, but only thought of Mali, one could only lose sight of the reality in both places. As time went by—some immigrants had now been here for more than twenty-five years—Mali had changed, and so had France. Only the mind of the immigrants had remained static and at odds with their environment; they were strangers even to their own children born in France.

Diafode once told me that when he first arrived in France, he could not even buy a shirt without thinking about how it would look in Bamako. When winter arrived, he bought his first coat with as little an investment as possible because he knew it was worthless in Bamako. Such was the power of the ways of knowing oneself in Bamako that Diafode had difficulty recognizing himself in Paris. I felt the same way about the Ambassador and my potentate relative. By overstating their case for *yere don* in Paris, with clumsy, grand boubous in the streets and cafés, they were failing to recognize their true situation.

For me, the salvation of the African immigrants in France lay not in an ideology of *yere don* but in an identification with the French working class, which embodied the ideals of the French Revolution. But everything in France today pushed the immigrant to maintain his or her original culture, to engage in something like *yere don*. Those Africans who took advantage of the new resources made available to them—whether intellec-tually or by joining the working class—and introduced subver-sive elements into their habitus were castigated by the purists of *yere don* as lost people, as nonpersons. When Diafode talked about uniting to defend the rights of African immigrants, I wondered if the enemies of the democratic rights of immi-grants did not include both the French system that had excluded them and the purists of *yere don* who had maintained in France the casted clans and the subjugation of women.

Much had been said in the French press about the National Front and its obsession with French culture. But, contrary to the teachings of the French Revolution and the recent celebra-tion of *francophonie* (the cultural, political, and economic unity of people who use French as their national language), the deployment of expressions such as *franco-français* (French French), *français de souche* (French by origin), and *la specificité culturelle française* (French cultural specificity) went beyond the sole purview of the extreme right and persisted in the media as popular means to undermine the legitimacy and rights of immigrants in France. French liberals probably expressed these discriminatory terms as often as the National Front did.

One time, I had dinner with two French professors, an American colleague, and a French student of Moroccan descent. The subject of immigration and integration again came up. The French people at the table were more concerned about the misunderstood youth in the suburbs and their lack of cul-tural bearings. They were fascinated for a moment by the way in which immigrant youth had appropriated rap music and the dress style of American ghettos. We also talked about the *sans-papiers* and the right of African immigrants to vote like other immigrants from Europe. At that point, the student said that she had always been an outsider in school because the other students would not treat her as a real French person. They made fun of the way she dressed and of the scarf her parents made her wear to school. At the end, when no one forced her to, she continued to wear the scarf to defy her classmates and to make them angry at her. She also said that, at home, her parents constantly chastised her for not being a good Moroccan girl, for being too French.

I asked the student why immigrant children—who were born in France—did not follow the black American example and force the population to deal with them as French people, not as outsiders to French culture. But instead, one of the French professors responded to my question. He told me that the situation in America was very different, because in America, it was too easy to become an American. Anybody could do it. French culture, on the other hand, was very difficult to penetrate. Unlike other people, the French did not take their culture lightly. It took some people generations and generations to become French. It was not a matter of race, but of cultural specificity.

As I lie in my bed now—with the sunlight coming through my window and my son walking back and forth on the wood floor, getting ready for school—I ponder the Malian philosophy of *yere don* and the importance of cultural specificity as stated by the French doctor and professor. Was I being unduly insensitive to these positions in my attempt to create a space for the inclusion of African immigrants in the definition of French identity?

When the French soccer team won the European Cup in 2000—with more than half the players hailing from foreign backgrounds—Diafode's daughter ran to him saying, *"Papa, Papa, nous avons gagné, c'est super!"* ("Daddy, Daddy, we won, it's great!") She was coming from a *colonie de vacances* (a summer camp), which was fully paid for by the government and open to all the children of the municipality. Diafode's daughter, who was eleven, had been away for three weeks. "You know how French people are with their vacation!" Diafode had explained to me, laughing.

When his daughter jumped off the bus, ran toward him, and kissed him on the cheek saying, "Daddy, we won, it's great!" Diafode was proud and happy. The white schoolteachers were all standing by the bus and watching. It was late afternoon, and the weather was nice. Diafode replied to his daughter, loud enough for all the teachers to hear, *"Oui, chérie, nous avons gagné. Viens, je vais t'achêter de la glace."* ("Yes, sweetie, we won. Come on, let me buy you an ice cream.")

I wonder what was separating Diafode and those French teachers who took his child to summer camp. What invisible wall occupied the space between his car and their school bus, which his daughter could march through so easily whereas they could not? I suppose that the wall had been built on one side by the philosophy of *yere don* and on the other by the notion of the purity of French culture, which made a stranger out of anybody who was not a *français de souche*.

I turn on the radio. The French prime minister, Lionel Jospin, is talking about the republic as a *lieu commun* (a common space) for all the French people to reconcile their differences. He is addressing the controversial topic of the people of Corsica. But it is clear that some people also have in mind the way the republic is going to deal with the demands of the Bretons, the homosexuals, the women, and the immigrants.

X

Portrait of the Writer
by Himself

I finish reading what I have written so far on my cousin Bintou, my friend Diafode, and their experience in Paris. I am feeling better, enough to feel my muscles in different parts of my body. Reading always does that to me. It gives me strength to do things impulsively. I rise up to drink some water in the kitchen or to go to the bedroom. I am not thinking or planning my actions. All I know is that I am happy to stand up. But suddenly, I feel dizzy, with my head spinning and something pulling in my stomach. I lie back in the couch before I know it and decide not to move again until my son comes back. My mind starts wandering again. I think of the last letter I wrote to my friends in Bamako, when I was a young man in Paris in 1974. I was not too much older than my son is now. I was so angry at this city then, I had never thought that one day I would forgive it and come back to it. My Swedish girlfriend had left me, and I was completely disillusioned with life in France. The letter was written with red ink and it went as follows:

Paris, 21 June 1974

My Dear Friend Joe Cuba,

Your letter fills me with great joy. You cannot imagine how good it feels to receive a letter from Bamako, when one is lost in the desert that is Paris. Yes, indeed, my dear friend, my happiness is double because I have not heard from you for such a long time.

Your letter mentions Maï. My dear friend, I am not high on marijuana, but I can still see her. All I have to do is think about "Samson and Delilah," to see her standing in front of me. What a crazy generation we were. Maï loved life and did not want to be denied. Never! God was jealous of us. He has said, "Be afraid of me. I am the absolute master. If you forget me for one second, I will not be happy." We, the Rockers, the renegades, the sons of B. B. King, the cousins of John Mayall, the cursed ones, we ignored God's warning; and Maï paid for it.

No, let's be serious! Maï was a pioneer of a rising generation of rebels. I can compare her to Angela Davis; she was also a George Sand; and she was Mahalia Jackson's voice in "Imitation of Life." It is, of course, a loss for Watt; it is a loss for the Rockers. Her parents may feel unconsciously vindicated, but they too have lost. But Bamako has won with Maï's death. If the parents of other girls hear about Maï's death and its circumstances, then they will take a lesson from it. It's an example. It serves no purpose to lock up your daughter, or hate her because she does not listen to you. Just let her be. She will use her head. (Remember the song by Blind Faith.)

Yes, the stick no longer works as a disciplinary measure; it's the head that guides us. Once our parents have a girl in the family, they dream of millions of guests at the poor child's marriage. So they take away her freedom; in short, they kill her. Yes, I am accusing the parents of murder and infanticide. Now, Maï's death (Maï has sacrificed herself) marks the beginning of sexual education in Bamako. That is why I say that Bamako has won. I am telling you that Maï has sacrificed herself, because the shut ears needed someone to die in order to begin hearing again. I am sad. There is nothing I can do. But let me tell you that I am boiling with rage, revolt. I feel like screaming: "Almost cut my hair" (Crosby, Stills, Nash & Young).

Dear friends, let us resign ourselves to the situation. It is our role to witness and to participate in the evolution of our country. We are paying dearly for it. Maï's death is one example. But we will be heard. I am not saying that I am for the sacrifice. Far from it. I am too selfish to sacrifice myself. What's the logic anyway? You sacrifice yourself for your son, and he sacrifices himself for his son. What does it all rime to? It's better to live your life instead.

The important thing for us now is to support Watt in his loss. You must admit that his star has not brought him good luck for the last three years. Let's hope that he will soon have a reprieve. Macumba, the romantic, would paraphrase Musset like this: "Man is an apprentice; pain is his master. And no one is wiser, until he has suffered. It is a hard and sad law, but a natural law." Manthia, the skeptic, would say: "And why not someone else in Watt's place; why not Sly, or Diafode, or Douss, or Crosby, or Johnny Hallyday?" Do you remember one day when I was high, I started reciting these lines from Sartre: "The important thing is not to succeed in life, but to live successfully." We are getting old already; that's why we're thinking so much about death. So, let's change the subject.

My dear friend, I am surprised and pleased to read your long letter without hearing you once mention your desire to come to France. I must confess that it is a victory for you to have forgotten France. Yes, frankly speaking, it is a hell of a country. There is no mercy here; you must earn everything you have. I will say, without any irony intended, that I envy you. You've got girls, and you've got your own apartment you pay for. I must conclude that Bamako is not hell for you. As a piece of advice between friends, this is what I deduce from all that: forget France! Of course, you may think I am selfish. When I was in Africa, I used to think of people who told me not to come to France as selfish.

But here is the sad truth: as you must already know, capitalists are not stupid. They trap us here. They know that black people are big and strong, and as docile as trained animals. They do not use their heads (Blind Faith again). So the scenario goes as follows: I come to France, and when I realize that I have fallen into the capitalist trap, I find out that it is too late to go back. So instead of revealing this truth to my friends, I keep sending them letters to attract them into the same trap. Sometimes, I even go on vacation, with nice clothes and record albums to impress them with. That is the future of 99% of Africans here. Only 0.025 of them succeed here. But you will never know this reality from Africa. That's why I have had enough of this. I can no longer take it. I feel like pulling my hair out.

My friend, know that I too will be coming this year on vacation. I will be part of those invading Bamako this summer. I am escaping the vultures for a little while. I am working hard to buy a ticket. Times are very hard for me at this moment, because as soon as I get back from Bamako, I will only have fifteen days in Paris before moving to the United

States. I would have liked to bring you lots of records, but I must save my money. I must save myself from the wolf's trap. I will see if the friends here can give me some records for you. I can only bring two albums for the whole group. Please send me the names of three of your favorite records, so I can ask the friends to buy them for you.

Guy, you'll see me as soon as I make the full price of my ticket. You'll see me on the third of August.

Kiss your girlfriend, Awa Magassa, for me. She is so beautiful.

P.S. My last girl has left me. It's just as well. I don't think I will look for one again.

I remember the last year in Paris before I moved to America, and the August vacation in Bamako. My girlfriend from Sweden had left. She had been spending a year as a nanny in Paris to learn French. I had been looking for someone with whom to practice my English in preparation for going to America, and she had wanted to practice her French. We also had music in common. The Rolling Stones had just released a new album with the hit song "Angie," and she knew the lyrics by heart. When we were at Café Saint-Michel, she would insert a coin in the jukebox to play the song and start singing along with Mick Jagger. I used to love listening to her sing "Angie" and know that she was my girl. She was also the first person to take me to museums in Paris. On weekends, she would bring her Paris guidebook and take me to the Musée du Jeu de Paume and the Picasso Museum, before ending at Montmartre, where we would have a late lunch in the same cafés frequented by the artists whose works we had just visited. Sometimes, we would go out with a group of her Swedish friends. We would see movies or eat in Vietnamese restaurants in the Latin Quarter.

We often went back to Shakespeare and Co., where I first met her, to listen to poetry readings or just to browse for books by Solzhenitsyn and Steinbeck, or plain English dictionaries.

The day I met her at Shakespeare and Co., I was wearing a mudcloth dashiki shirt, a pair of New Man jeans I had just bought on Boulevard Saint-Germain, with my hair combed in an Afro like the Chambers Brothers. The advertisement in the *Village Voice* newspaper had said that the hipster poet Ted Joans was reading that evening at eight. In those days, I was crazy about America. I already knew the music, the movies, and the literature and was dreaming of discovering the country itself. I also knew that at a reading at Shakespeare and Co., there would be many women. So I wanted to look as American as possible. I had not heard about the evening's poet, Joans, before. He looked like LeRoi Jones, but that was not the attraction. In fact, the poetry reading itself did not matter much, because I was going to meet people and look at the pictures of my favorite writers on the walls.

At that time, I lived at 56 Rue Monçeau. My apartment was a maid's room on the sixth floor, rented to me by an English couple who worked for an international organization in Paris. At first, they didn't want me as a tenant, but when I told them I was a writer from Africa, they became more interested in me, as if I were an exotic animal, and let me have the place. It used to impress people then to hear that I lived in the eighth arrondissement near the Parc Monçeau. The eighth, like the seventh and sixteenth, is known as a bourgeois neighborhood, and people thought that my parents in Africa must be rich. My landlords, on the other hand, had their own obsession: When they were not concerned about their rent's being paid in cash and on time—they did not accept payment by checks—they were curious about what I was writing about, or if I was taking good care of the room. Then I would tell them all kinds of stories about Africa, just to get them off my back. The only reason I had told them that I was a writer was so that they would let me rent their *chambre de bonne* on the sixth floor. I knew that they would not rent to a working-class African, or even to a student.

In those days, I did not know what I was. I was working at a factory called Arena, which assembled radios and televisions for Thompson. My job description was a *magasinier*, which meant that I assembled the pieces from the warehouse for the electronic engineers who were working on the radios and televisions. It was my best job in Paris, as well as the easiest and the one that paid the most. On the other hand, I was enrolled at the Université de Paris, Vincennes, which I never attended the last year, except to get my student ID. So I did not really know what to call myself: a foreign student or an immigrant worker, like all the other Malians in France. Taking on a third identity as an African writer in Paris had its advantages. People looked at me differently in cafés and bookstores like Shakespeare and Co., even when they found out that I did not have much money to spend. Everybody seemed to want to come to your aid, to be there when you were in need. No doubt my English landlords had fallen for that myth of having rented their room to an unknown African writer. Maybe one day I would be like Wole Soyinka or Sembène Ousmane.

That Saturday, I left my place as early as five P.M. and walked to the Métro Miromesnil, which took me to Strasbourg Saint-Denis. There, I transferred to the Porte d'Orléans and Porte de Clignancourt line for the Saint-Michel stop. Once above ground, I lingered for a while by the Saint-Michel Fountain, where some young boys and girls in long hair and jeans were hanging out, playing old Bob Dylan tunes with a guitar and a harmonica. First they sang "Blowin' in the Wind," and by the time they got to "Like a Rolling Stone," a large crowd had surrounded them. When they had finished, I put five francs in the hat one of them was passing around, amid loud applause and screams from the crowd. The smell of marijuana smoke was rising in the air as I crossed the street to the Gilbert Jeune book and record store. I stopped in front of the store to look at posters of Hollywood idols, from James Dean to Marilyn Monroe. As I was looking at a poster of Jimi Hendrix, I was distracted by an African man chasing a white woman into the subway, repeating, *"Madame, moi je vous aime!"* Everybody was looking bemusedly at the scene. I felt embarrassed.

I went into the store and climbed the stairs to the second floor, to hide myself among the books of fiction. I passed the sections of F. Scott Fitzgerald, André Gide, Victor Hugo, and James Joyce, ending all the way in the back with Jean-Paul Sartre, Richard Wright, and Marquis de Sade. In the background, as if the books on the shelves were singing to me, I could hear Aretha Franklin's voice, "You make me feel like a natural woman." That put me in a good mood, and I picked up *East of Eden*, by John Steinbeck. Some sections of Paris, like the Saint-Michel Fountain, where I had just listened to live music, and this bookstore, had the effect of making me happy and spend money like it was nothing. It was at once a feeling of anonymity and self-validation. I was like everyone else in these places, an equal figure in the crowd, but also significant to its composition.

I left the Gilbert Jeune with my new pocket-sized edition of *East of Eden* and walked down the small alleys that linked Saint-Michel to the Rue du Petit Pont like arteries. There were small Greek restaurants, souvenir and antique stores, and vendors all along the alleys. At one point, I came to a circle where a clown was eating fire and blowing it out in the air toward the crowd around him. I finally reached the rue du Petit Pont, where I turned left to enter the Café Nôtre Dame at the corner. The café faced a small park on the other side of the street, behind which the Shakespeare and Co. Bookstore was located, on a small street called Rue de Bucherie. I sat down and ordered a *croque monsieur* in the café while watching tourists go in and out of its namesake, the Cathédrale Nôtre Dame, behind the Seine. It was now 7:30 P.M.; time for me to go across the street and through the park to Shakespeare and Co.

The bookstore was a small world unto itself. There were shelves against the wall outside, with oversized books, old issues of *National Geographic*, travel books, and adventure and mystery novels. On the door and windows were flyers announcing tonight's reading and forthcoming ones. There were also want ads for rooms, used bicycles, clothes, and typewriters. Behind the glass windows sat books on display by such authors as Fitzgerald, Hemingway, Paul Bowles, Gertrude Stein, Poe, and Steinbeck. This display alone attracted many people to the front of the store. They spoke to each other in English, as if they were in London or New York. I remember that I used to eavesdrop on such conversations to see how good my English was. I would also look at the want ads for a long time, pretending to be somebody who had just arrived from the United States.

In the store, a dusty, bookish-looking man with long hair sat behind a desk facing the door. Piles of mail were on the desk, and beside him, stacks of newly arrived books. People coming in or out asked questions that the man often answered without even taking his eyes off the work on the desk. I heard somebody ask for Ted Joans, and the man simply pointed his hand in the direction of what looked like an antechamber ahead. Shakespeare and Co. is a house converted into a bookstore. The building had several small rooms, a second floor, where some of the readings took place, and what seemed like a basement that was off-limits to visitors. I learned later that the building had a secret underground passageway that led to the Seine and that was used by the Resistance army during the war. The first floor was full of stories about the American writers known as the Lost Generation—mainly Hemingway and Fitzgerald—but also people like Langston Hughes and Joyce. There were photographs and memorabilia in every small corner of the rooms. Each room gave you the impression that you were in some important writer's private study, a writer you had really touched, in such a way that you too knew what it felt like to be a writer.

I went upstairs, where women were already gathered around a black man whom I took to be Ted Joans. He had a salt-and-pepper beard, a Hausa Kufi hat, a green vest over a long Indian shirt that came down to his knees, and white Indian pants to match the shirt. The room was small and not very well lit. Just when I was getting ready to join the group, I heard Joans telling everybody to wait downstairs, where tonight's reading would be taking place. He was speaking in heavily accented French, even though all the people in the room were speaking English to each other. I took the same stairs back to the first floor, feeling a bit put off by the way Joans had dismissed everybody just when I was arriving.

Downstairs, people had already taken their places, and there remained only a few standing-room spots that would not block anybody's view. I leaned against a bookshelf somewhere where I knew I would have a good look at Joans in the middle of the room, surrounded by more than forty people and books everywhere. Not long after that, Joans himself arrived amid applause with a bagful of his own books, which he placed on the floor in front of him, before greeting the audience in French, Arabic, Swahili, Mossi, and English. He then told a few stories about Shakespeare and Co., the writers he had met here, and something about bebop jazz and poetry. Of this last discussion, I could only understand the sound of famous names: Hughes, Breton, Charlie Parker, Allen Ginsberg, Bob Kaufman, and LeRoi Jones. Then he started reading from the books he had spread on the floor. One particular volume he picked had a back-cover photograph of him posing stark naked except for a cowrie-shell belt he had around his waist, and leaning backward with his hands behind him so that the camera could show him frontally. He told a story about the photograph and his mother, which I didn't understand. But I smiled when the audience laughed. He also talked about surrealism and African art for a long time before opening the book. But the audience seemed to be with him, enjoying the whole thing. I also pretended to be appreciating this show, nodding my head from time to time and smiling.

Then the reading began. Joans read like the African bards who recite the Sunjata epic. That meant that he read as many words together as possible, and came to a sudden stop-time pause. In this staccato manner, his poetry was like a jazz song, and one could almost predict where the lines began and where they ended. I could hear words like Ouagadougou, Timbuktu, Nairobi, and Nefertiti, but the rest of the words were coming at me too fast to understand. But it did not matter, for Joans made poetry sound like music and therefore universal. I gave up trying to understand the words and started marking the beat by stamping my foot and occasionally snapping my fingers and nodding my head. But somewhere in the back of my head, I was wondering what it would be like to have been a black American, listening to Joans's poetry and understanding every word.

My biggest surprise, therefore—at the end of the reading and after the applause—was when Joans pointed at me, with all the heads turning in my direction, and said, "When I was reading my poems, I could feel the guy standing over there. He was with me, and I could feel it. If you are a poet, you know what I'm talking about. Ya dig?"

Everybody was looking enviously at me, and I did not know what to do myself. I knew they were all aspiring writers like me, hoping to have their names added to the list of icons on the walls of Shakespeare and Co. They were dying for recognition in everything they were involved in, and they did not care to give anybody credit for anything. For Joans to have anointed me in a crowd like that was meant to put me in a difficult situation. I knew that whereas I had instant admirers among the women, the guys were jealous of me. I was surrounded by a group of women from Sweden who wanted to know where I was from, what kind of writer I was, and how I liked Paris. Meanwhile, Joans himself had returned to his work, signing books, exchanging addresses, and pocketing money. He had gotten me into this trouble, and there was no one to come to my rescue.

I had to lie a little bit, saying that I had written a few short stories and that I was now working on my first novel about an African in Paris. I had said nothing about my work during the daytime, or how difficult it was for me to be both a student and a worker at the same time. I had also told them that I had been to America and lived in San Francisco and New York, and was getting ready to go back there as soon as I had finished my novel. In fact, I would have told them more stories if Joans had not invited everybody at that moment to join him at the Café le Rouquet, right above Café Flore on Saint-Germain. I left Shakespeare and Co. with the group of Swedish girls, who had offered to take me to le Rouquet. They said that they had attended parties there with Joans, and that the parties were lots of fun. We walked together on the Quai Montebello to the Boulevard Saint-Michel; there, we took a small street, Saint-André des Arts, which meandered through different street names, all the way to the Boulevard Saint-Germain. It was past ten o'clock, but all the stores, movie theaters, and cafés on Saint-André des Arts were open. We found Joans waiting with his group on one block, pointing to an apartment where he said Picasso used to live. He also showed the group where Richard Wright had lived, and continued the history of literary Paris past the Café Deux Magots and Café Flore, until we arrived at the Café le Rouquet, which had become his headquarters. He said that he did not like the two famous cafés—Deux Magots and Flore—because they were always too crowded with tourists and people pretending to be famous writers. Joans, for his part, was going to make le Rouquet famous.

I attended Joans's party that evening in the company of my new Swedish friends. Joans was the center of attraction; he mesmerized us with stories about riding camels in Egypt and canoes on the Nile, being hosted by the Moro Naba in Ouagadougou, buying a house in Timbuktu, and crossing the desert from Mali to Morocco to visit his friends Ginsberg and Bowles in Tangiers. He also told us about his experiences in Paris with the surrealist writers and painters, the Présence Africaine circle with Aimé Césaire, Alioune Diop, and Léopold Sédar Senghor. He winked at me a couple of times when he mentioned Africa or African writers in Paris. That too added to my legitimacy in the eyes of my friends. But what fascinated all of us more were

Joans's adventures with jazz musicians in Greenwich Village in the 1950s. He used to go listen to such great musicians as Thelonious Monk, Parker, and John Coltrane in the New York clubs, saying that that was how he, Kaufman, Ginsberg, and Jones developed bebop poetry. His own particular style was influenced by surrealism and African art and the vernacular. He loved to imitate the sound of African languages in his poetry, and juxtaposed contradictory imageries to shock the reader. Joans had also been a well-trained painter before he even started writing poetry. He said that he used to hang out with the great painter Bob Thompson in Greenwich Village in the 1950s. All at the same time, Joans was pulling out of his bag the books and drawings that he autographed to sell to our group.

The evening came to an end when Joans realized that he had told us all the stories he wanted to and had sold all the books and drawings he could. He called over the lady he was with at the time, and she paid their bill and started helping him pack his things. Joans winked at me again, shaking my hand to say good-bye, and told me to come by the Café le Rouquet or Shakespeare and Co. if I wanted to see him again. I stayed behind with the Swedish girls, and that was how I met my girl-friend. She was the one I was talking about in my letter to Joe Cuba. One weekend, she had gone skiing with her host family and met another man there.

Thinking back on that evening with Joans—I should be calling him Ted now, for as you will see, our paths crossed several times after that night, and we became more than friends, more like brothers—I was both excited by the life of a writer and worried about how much I did not know. Since I had been in Paris, I had not even set foot in Présence Africaine. Moreover, the only reason I had gone to Ted's reading that night was to meet foreign women, because I was tired of Parisians. Could

Ted have known my intentions? Did he know I was not a real writer, that I was a fraud among these people? If that were the case, was Ted laughing at me when he pointed me out as someone who really understood his poetry? Or was he covering for me, because we were the only two black people there for the whole evening, and he had wanted to make me look good? That night, my ignorance of all the things Ted was talking about had really frightened me. Would I have to know all the writers he had mentioned—along with all the musicians, the painters, and places around the world—to become a famous writer? At Shakespeare and Co., I also found out that the writers I admired most—Hemingway, Hughes, and Wright—had traveled around the world and written about the world outside their own environment. How much did I have to know to write a book? Could one be a good writer while being locked in one's own culture?

The other thing about Ted that had impressed me that evening was how comfortable he was with himself and with his audience, which he had kept mesmerized at all times. Right away, Ted fit the image of my ideal black American in Paris. Everybody admired him, unlike the situation with African men, who were despised in Paris; he was welcomed everywhere—whether at Shakespeare and Co. or at le Rouquet—and all he had to do was open his mouth and speak American English to have everybody fall at his feet. People romanticized him as a poet, a jazz musician, and someone who had withstood American Jim Crow racism and survived. In a word, he did not have to prove anything in Paris; he was accepted right away. But to his credit, Ted was a cosmopolitan. He was more than just an American—black or white—in Paris. He had traveled everywhere in the world, spoke several languages, had a cool style of dress, spoke in black English, and used hand gestures that made you want to be in his company. His friendship automatically legitimized you as a sophisticated person, a connoisseur of jazz, art, and literature.

How much did I have to know, to be like Ted? Besides never having visited Présence Africaine, I knew nothing about museums or even jazz to be able to talk like Ted. In one evening, Ted had opened a whole new world to me and shattered my own. How could my knowledge of rock and roll and literature measure up to his masterful display of all the world's cultures in one? How was I to find my voice to prove to Ted and the world that I was a writer? That evening, I realized that I was lacking many references that someone like me interested in literature ought to have known. The Swedish group I was with were talking about what one had to visit while in Paris— the Louvre to see the *Mona Lisa*, the architecture, Picasso, Rodin, the Place des Vosges, Giacometti, the Musée du Quai d'Orsay, and the Luxembourg Gardens. They also talked about opera, theater, and classical music, in addition to jazz at the Duc des Lombardes. I had not been interested in any of these before, had not even heard of some of them before tonight. For me, Paris was the rock music concerts and the boulevards— Strasbourg Saint-Denis, Saint-Michel, and Châtelet—where I could meet new friends, sit in cafés, or shop in stores. From that night on, I decided to learn more about that world, too. I had already made a rendezvous with one of the Swedish girls—the one who would later become my girlfriend—at the Musée Rodin in the fifteenth arrondissement, not far from the Maison du Japon. If I still had time in the afternoon, I would go to Présence Africaine.

The next time I saw Ted was at the Café Select on Montparnasse. There was a jazz festival at the American Center on Boulevard Raspail, after which the crowd walked over to Café

Select. This café too had its share of fame in Paris, because Hemingway and other American writers used to hang out there. It even had a nickname, "le Café Américain," and much of its clientele were aspiring writers and artists.

"There's your friend," my girlfriend said.

"Who?"

"Ted Joans, the poet," she replied to my surprised inquiry.

As we approached Ted's table, he stood up to greet us. "Hey, *mon ami. Comment ça va? Tu as trouvé une copine*, yeah?" ("Hey, my friend, how are you? I see you found yourself a girlfriend, yeah?") he grinned, speaking in heavily accented French.

"Yes, Mr. Joans, this is Ulla Britt, she is from . . . "

"Sweden, I know," Ted interrupted. "Sit down, sit down and have a drink with us," he added, calling the garçon over.

We had our drinks, and Ted introduced me to more people as a young, up-and-coming African writer. Again, he made me feel as if I belonged to the group of expatriate writers. He was one of the famous writers there, and if he had accepted me, the others had no choice but to do the same. I had a good time with that, but I kept wondering about the way Ted had smiled when he saw me with my girlfriend. As for Ted, he soon forgot me and settled into his usual role of master of ceremonies and virtuoso storyteller. Every once in a while, he would wink at me, with a big smile that showed all his teeth, but that was it.

I kept showing up at Ted's readings with my girlfriend, until she decided to leave me for somebody older and more experienced in life. I asked her who the man was. Did I know him? Was he an African or an American? She said that I did not know the person, but that it did not matter, anyhow. She had met somebody who went skiing with her and liked some of the same things she did. And that was all that mattered. She still liked me as a friend, but no longer as a lover.

My girlfriend's departure left a big void in my life. I no longer wanted to see places in Paris that we used to visit together. Soon it was Paris itself I was tired of. I did not like the Parc Monçeau, where we used to sit and eat our sandwiches. I hated opening my window, because during the wintertime she used to leave our milk and cheese outside the window. I was feeling that everything and everybody had rejected me, and I did not want to see my friends, who at the time also had Swedish girlfriends. I wanted to disappear from Paris, to go to another country, to leave all this behind me.

Around this time, Ted was having one of his readings at Shakespeare and Co. again. I debated with myself whether to go. There was a possibility I would meet Ulla there, and in the company of someone else. It had been three months since she had left me, but I suddenly had a strong urge not to miss the opportunity to see her. I had bought nice new clothes since I last saw her, and my Afro was longer and wavy. I wanted to know if she had no regrets and if she could resist me now. But I also had to prepare myself for an unpleasant surprise, what- ever that might be. So on the appointed evening, I had more than two glasses of wine and one beer before walking into Shakespeare and Co.

Ulla was not there when I arrived. During the reading, I spent all my time looking at the door to see her when she walked in. Every time somebody entered, my heart pounded. More than once I imagined her walking hand-in-hand with another guy, just as we used to do. It felt so real that I had to shake my head to wake up from it. But she never showed up.

As usual, Ted ended the evening at le Rouquet, where a group of friends followed him. When we got there, even before we sat down, Ted came over to me and said, "Manthia, I want to talk to you later, so don't leave." Then he got down to business, telling stories and selling books and drawings.

I spent the whole evening at le Rouquet, wondering what Ted was going to tell me. Had I done something wrong during his reading? Or was it about Ulla? What did he have to do with it? My stomach was in knots, but Ted kept me waiting until the last customer had left. His girlfriend was there to help him pack his stuff before we were able to leave.

"Manthia?"

"Yes?" I said.

"Manthia," said Ted again, as if he had not heard me, "I want to have a talk with you. I have been watching you, and I know what you're trying to do. But I want you to know something: You don't have the talent to be like me. That takes a lot of perfecting of craft and genius." Ted paused and cleared his throat. I guessed that he wanted me to feel the entire weight of what he'd just told me. But I just remained silent, listening to the sound of our footsteps in a partially lit, small Parisian street near the Rue Mouffetard, where Ted lived. The three of us were walking side by side, with Ted in the middle. It was about three o'clock, and there was no one else in the street, not even a passing car. I was listening to Ted as I would have listened to the scolding of a bigger brother, or a father in Africa. There was no question, therefore, of interrupting or arguing with him.

"Listen, Manthia, come upstairs with me," he resumed. "I want to give you something."

I followed him, not knowing what to expect. Was that what he had wanted to talk to me about? To brag to me about his talent, and about how much I did not know? As if I were unaware of that and had not thought about it myself? I followed him and his lady upstairs to his apartment, which was on the third floor. The lady—a white Canadian woman with long hair and wearing a long skirt—had not said a word since we left the café. Ted's apartment had a living room—cluttered with African masks, books, and paintings—and a hallway to the left that led to the bedroom, kitchen, and bathroom. Ted and his lady went back there for a moment while I waited in the living room, looking at the arrangement of the different objects. When Ted came back, he was holding a black note-book, and he was soon followed by his lady, who had now taken off her jacket and looked much younger with her white cotton blouse and a large belt around her waist. I was looking at an ashtray with strange-looking lipsticks on it.

"Manthia, do you know the origin of the *rouge* that women put on their lips?" Ted asked.

I just looked at him, waiting for him to get to the point of why we were here in the first place.

"It originates in Egypt. The Egyptians, in the time of the pharaohs, used to insist that women put on lipstick before per-forming fellatio. You know?! Most people do not know that that is the origin of lipstick," he said, laughing. His lady laughed too, and I joined in, albeit politely.

"Manthia," Ted said, sitting down by the light and inviting me to come closer. "You want to go to America, and I think that you should go. In fact, I am telling you that you should go. You can't stay here. Don't stay here unless you want to end up like all those Africans you meet in bars, running after women on Saint-Germain. They have been here twenty, thirty years with-out finishing school. They can't get a job here, and they can't go home, either. If you stay here, that's your future. You won't be a writer or anything else here. They don't love your kind here. That's why I say to you that you should go to America. There, you can go to school and work like so many Nigerian and Ghanaian students have been doing. They like Africans better in the States than they do black Americans. That's why I am here. I can't stand it there. Go there, and you'll have a chance of succeeding. Don't stay here.

"Here are some addresses and information I'm going to write down for you. The information has to do with a charter flight they have been advertising for some time now. It's a Tower Air flight from Amsterdam to New York that's leaving in three months' time. The ticket only costs a hundred dollars. That's very cheap. I mean dirt cheap. I was going to take it myself, but we will be in Istanbul by that time. Save your money and don't miss it. I'm telling you, it's your best chance. You'll be traveling with all those Americans who ran away from the draft because they didn't want to go to 'Nam. You know what I mean? Now that the war is over, they're going home, and they don't have the money to buy tickets. Some charity is paying for a bunch of them.

"The names and addresses I'm giving you are those of my friends from the days of bebop and the Black Arts Movement. They are artists and writers between New York and Washington, D.C., and they include Amiri Baraka, formerly known as LeRoi Jones, Toni Cade Bambara, Jayne Cortez, Mel Edwards, Charles Saunders, Lois Mailou Jones, and others. They are all very important people. They can help you with school, or with your writing.

"That's what I had to tell you. So long," Ted concluded, handing me the piece of paper.

I said good-bye to him and his companion and walked from the Rue Mouffetard across the Seine all the way to the Place de Châtelet, where I took an all-night bus to my apartment.

That was the last time I saw Ted for ten years. And I never saw my last girlfriend in Paris again. When I next saw Ted, in

1985 at Shakespeare and Co., he still looked the same. The bookstore and its clientele hadn't changed, either. I had completed my Ph.D. in literature and had my first job as assistant professor at the University of California, Santa Barbara. I was also married with two children—my son, here with me now in Paris, was barely one year old at the time. I had come to Paris to do research for a book I was writing on African cinema, and thought I'd stop by the bookstore to see if I could find out news about Ted Joans. I found the same dusty, old, bearded, long-haired man there, and I asked him if Joans was in Paris. He told me that I was in luck, because Ted was coming by in a couple of hours to pick up some mail. I hung around for old times' sake, looked at memorabilia and photographs of Henry Miller, Hemingway, and the rest of the gang. Everything still looked the same, and the place was getting ready for a poetry reading that night.

By two o'clock, Ted walked in, wearing one of his favorite khaki vests with several pockets and the same knapsack strapped on his back. When told by the man at the door that I was looking for him, Ted put on his glasses to size me up, as if I were a bill collector.

"Hi, Ted," I said, reaching out my hand to shake his.

"Am I supposed to know you?" he asked, shaking my hand and still looking me up and down from head to toe.

"Manthia," I said. "Don't you remember? You told me to leave Paris and go to America."

"Oh yeah? Did I tell you that?" Ted asked.

"Yes, you did, and I am now a professor at the University of California, Santa Barbara."

"Oh yeah? Let's go to lunch and talk about it. It's your treat."

"It'll be my pleasure, Ted. Let's go wherever you want to go, and it will be my treat."

"In that case, we'll go to the Procope. Do you know the Procope on Rue de l'Ancienne Comédie? It's the first restaurant in Paris. Molière and all the writers used to eat there," Ted said, winking at the bookstore manager, who had followed the whole scene.

"It'll be my pleasure to treat you at the Procope, Ted. Let's go," I said.

When we were outside, Ted asked me to forgive him for not remembering me right away. He had given the same advice to many Africans, because he was tired of seeing the way French people treated them here. Then he asked me about the Swedish girlfriend I had picked up at one of his readings. I told him that the relationship had ended even before he took me to his apartment to give me his advice. I reminded him of the story of the lipstick. Then he remembered the whole thing, blushing somewhat, and we laughed. It was like old times again for me.

After we had eaten at the Procope, Ted took me back to Shakespeare and Co. and introduced me to everybody as the young man he had told to go to America. "Now he's a Ph.D. and a professor at the University of California, Santa Barbara. A Ph.D., you see what I mean? We ate at the Procope, and he paid for it. He's now a fancy professor at the University of California. And I told him to go to America. I knew it! Ha, ha, ha!"

After that, Ted and I went out, because he had something else he wanted to show me, this time in a small park on Rue des Ecoles. We walked past the Présence Africaine bookstore and arrived at the park. There, Ted showed me a street name and number on a wall at a dead end. It looked like there used to be a door there.

"You see this address, Manthia?" Ted pointed at the dead end. "That's what I give to young people in America who want to visit me in Paris." We both laughed and gave each other a "five" handshake.

Ted and I are still very good friends, more like brothers. Whenever he visits New York, I invite him to give a reading at my university and introduce him with a shorter version of this story. The truth is that we both have our own versions of the story, and it keeps getting longer and longer.

XI

Me and Mrs. Jones

My son returns from school earlier than usual, saying that he is worried about me. I give him money to go buy a roast chicken and fries at the butcher's on Rue Bréa. I have a craving for chicken and Dijon mustard and feel that I am getting better, although I am still dizzy even after taking another two pills of my prescription. My son and I eat everything on the plate before I move into the bedroom and go back to bed. I reassure him that I am getting better, but the truth is that I am still tired. I could not have imagined in 1974 that one day I would be in my apartment in Paris with a son tall enough to remind me of myself then. I had been so obsessed with myself at that time and interested only in one thing: to go to America. For me, going to America was like the sweet taste of revenge I was taking on France and on all the people who had ignored me, rejected me, and refused to hear me.

The year was 1974. I was standing in line at the Bourget Airport, along with many American men in torn jeans, long hair, and thick beards, to go to Amsterdam, where we would connect with our Tower Air flight to America. A Frenchman, who had thought I was in the wrong line, approached me to ask where I was going. When I said America, he asked me, for what? To study, I replied. He was very impressed. Even French people knew then that America had become number one. France had nothing more to offer.

I wondered how much better off I would be in America than in Paris, where I had lived for the last three years. Africans who had been to America had told stories of a land of wealth and prosperity, where even the poorest had toilets, showers, and bathtubs in their ghetto houses. They had televisions, refrigerators, telephones, and even cars. I had also heard that— in spite of all the news reports we had been hearing in France about racism in America—the black person was more respected in America than in any other democracy in the world. In Paris, where I used to work, the whites never took the trouble to learn the Africans' names. They'd call me "Bon Bulah" or "Dis-donc" or simply "Mamadou." If the wrong person answered their call, they would simply reply, "Not you, the other Mamadou." People who had visited America said that no such thing could happen there, after the time of Malcolm X, the Black Panthers, and the Black Muslims. Whenever the waiters ignored us in restaurants in Paris, we would tell ourselves the story of a black American whom a waiter had mistaken for an African. He was in a restaurant in Saint-Michel— in some versions, it was Maxim's in the eighth arrondissement, and in others it was a café in Place de la République—where the waiters passed him over several times to take white people's orders. He had a big Afro hairdo, wore a dashiki, and had gris-gris around his neck and bracelets on his wrists. Finally, when he saw a waiter pass by him to wait on a couple who had just walked in, he got angry. He stood up, shouting epithets in American English, and started smashing the dishes on the floor and breaking the tables. All the people in the restaurant were shaking with fear. He just walked away, like those actors in the movies.

Thinking about that story, I wondered what I would be like ten years from now. With my high-school English, I could already read American magazines on movie stars and rock singers. In Paris, I could also communicate in English with foreigners from Sweden, Denmark, and even Canada and America. So ten years from now, speaking English like a native son, wearing Levi's jeans and sporting an Afro hairdo, I would be all set to make a spectacular comeback in Bamako. I would have my diplomas and all the American know-how. I smiled at the thought of seeing myself at the Bamako airport in ten years, just as I was standing here at Bourget now. My relatives and friends would be there as I exited the plane. I would wave back at them with a Black Panther salute, just as the black athletes had done at the Olympics in Mexico. I would call them "brothers and sisters" and say, "Right on." When my friends, who would have been educated in France, tried to mystify people with French ways, I would cut them short by telling them that France itself looked to America for new trends.

I continued brooding over my new vision of myself as the plane taking me to America traversed cloudy blue skies. My imagination often took me down paths as full of mystery and surprise as the small roads I saw from the plane window, winding their way to mountain tops. I wondered what was behind the doors America would open for me. What would it feel like to meet real American women after all the movies I had seen and novels I had read? What would it be like to meet a woman like Mary Dalton in Wright's *Native Son*—those blonde, blue-eyed ladies who lived on the rich side of town, drank a lot of liquor, and loved black men? (I remembered that *Native Son* was the first novel I had read from cover to cover. It was thus a natural transition for me to the novels of Emile Zola, Dostoyevsky, Balzac, and Hugo's *Les Misérables*.) What would it be like to meet an American woman like someone out of *The Great Gatsby*—so innocent and so beautiful as to be irresistible, even with her excessive drinking, lying, and cheating?

I wondered about all those American women on magazine covers—they looked so beautiful. Some were black, yet they had long hair falling to their shoulders, like white women. Some were more than forty years old, yet they looked so young and virginal. I said to myself that God did not make American women. God had simply made the black woman, the white woman, the Chinese, and the Indian. America had completed God's job by making them all perfect. In America, a black woman could transform herself into white, Chinese, or Indian if she liked. It was like a story we had in Africa, "The Perfect Gentleman," about a girl who wanted only to marry a man who was perfect in everything and every way. So to win her, one man went around borrowing a perfect leg here, a perfect arm there, until he was able to fool her. After the marriage, he had to return to different people the parts he had borrowed from them. A lot of time passed as I sat on the plane, reading articles in one magazine after another and thinking about the *Woman:* made in America—so permanent, so strong, and just looking so innocent and untouched by time.

When I first arrived in the United States, I could not get over how nice everybody was and how easy everything was— particularly school and work. People said "Hi!" (meaning hello or good-bye) when passing you and when they encountered you in the street, even if they had never seen you before. Could you imagine that happening in France, where everybody was always sad? The Americans also called you "buddy" or "partner" when you met them for the first time, and they said "excuse me" for everything. At first I was surprised when somebody I didn't even know called me "buddy" or "partner." I would also think there was something wrong with me, or that people were afraid of me, when they said "excuse me," just because they had touched me in the crowd. As for black Americans, they called me "brother" or "blood" or "dude" whenever I ran into one. They also said, "Peace!" "What's up?" or "Salaam Aleikum!" At first I felt so welcome in America that I thought I was special. Coming from France, where people were so rude in the sub- way, on sidewalks, and in restaurants, I could not believe how nice Americans were. When I went to stores or restaurants, people always said to me, "Can I help you?" "Thank you for shopping at . . . " "Please come again," and so forth. No kidding, I said to myself, thinking that they were humoring me. But it was like that in every store and every restaurant.

It took me a while to realize that behind the politeness of Americans, there was an unstated law that required that shop owners be courteous to their customers, that citizens greet each other as part of their civic duties, and even that the police kindly inform presumed criminals of their rights. I said to myself that French people could benefit from some of these American legal and social contracts of civility. Black people, especially, would feel more comfortable going to public spaces in France if there were a law requiring restaurants and café owners to be courteous, instead of assuming that French civi- lization naturally and universally predisposed them to be cour- teous to each other and to foreigners.

As for school and work's being easier in America than in France and Africa, I found out that my first impression was deceptive. For someone coming from France or Francophone Africa with a high school degree, the first two years of university in America seemed like a review of what one had learned in high school. The introductory classes in the history of Europe or ancient Greece and Egypt, the math and philosophy classes—all these seemed like child's play. In America, students studied a small fragment of things, for a period of three or four months, instead of being required to know everything about a subject in a year—for example, learning in one year about philosophy from the Greeks to the French to the Germans and back to the French. In France, one was used to playing with an idea—for example, "What is reality?" or "What is 'being'?"—and tracing the theories of that idea from Plato, Aristotle, Descartes, Rousseau, Hegel, Kant, Nietzsche, Heidegger, Merleau-Ponty, Wittgenstein, and Sartre. In America, instead of studying the idea or the theory, they simply spent the semester or the quarter on the philosophy of a person or a school.

Deceptively, the beginning of each class in America was always easier for us, the Francophone students, because we were more familiar with the generalities and the history of the ideas behind the subject of study. And this had the effect of making us lazy and unable to take our homework seriously. We would therefore receive poor grades on tests and in our overall class grades. I remember being upset with my professors for dumbing down the level of the classes for the benefit of American students, for basing the grades on test scores instead of what the students really knew about the subject, and for giving too much significance to the particular school or philosopher instead of the universal importance of the theory. I then realized that if I wanted to get good grades—which were necessary to earn tuition remission—I had to take the classes seriously, and as they were being taught by the professors. From that point on, I no longer thought that American education was easier than the French. I had to work hard to get good results.

Working in America was based on the same principle: getting results, achieving goals. Coming from France, where one depended on the unions for every form of security and protection one got from the workplace and the employers, work in America seemed easier. The employers left you alone to do your work, and they did not dare steal hours from you. In America, since everybody was terrorized by the prospect of lawsuits, the employers did not expose you to unsafe working conditions. Nor did they discriminate against you. Everybody at work had to be concerned about breaking the law, because the customers could sue, the employees could sue, the government could sue for tax evasion, and the owner could file for bankruptcy. As an employee, I initially felt good in a world where my supervisor did not bother me at work, even without the protection of a union. Then I began to feel alienated by a system so devoid of personal relations and so dependent on lawsuits for justice. Finally, I said to myself that work was not easy in America, either, because you always had to bring results, and you could get fired for not performing well. What's more, there were no unions in the restaurants where I worked to protect us from getting fired or to help us raise our salaries beyond the minimum-wage level.

The interesting thing I had come to learn quickly about America was that life got more complicated and therefore more difficult by the day. When you first landed, everything seemed so much easier than where you had come from—no matter where in the world that was. There seemed to be more freedom, and people acted nicer than you were used to. Everything appeared brighter and merrier in America, as long as you remained innocent and the laws were invisible to you. But once you had become aware of the different laws, how easy it was to break them, and the consequences of breaking them, then you would begin to wish sometimes that you were back home. It was like being caught in a spider web of legal maneuvers. The laws also invariably seemed to work against those with less education and less money. In other words, laws could be bought in America.

Life was beautiful in those Washington, D.C., days when I was young. They used to call it Chocolate City then. Even though I had enrolled to take classes at American University on Massachusetts Avenue—in a white neighborhood past George-town—Washington for me was Federal City College on E Street, where most of my Malian and African colleagues went; Howard University, home of Miss Black America, on Georgia Avenue; the Dupont Circle; Columbia Road; Mount Pleasant Street; Sixteenth Street; Florida Avenue; U Street; and Four-teenth Street. This was my first experience in a black city—as modern as Paris—that was run by a black mayor and where there were eight women to every man. My fortune had sud-denly changed from being an African, exotic, and marginalized man in Paris to a black man among many in Washington. For sure, I was exotic here, too, but it was because of my accent, and the "authentic" dashikis and trade-bead necklaces from Mali I was wearing. Being an "authentic" African and a black man who spoke French also added to my exotic capital. In Washington, I had to get used to women telling me that I was handsome and they liked my deep voice, or that I was cute, whereas in Paris, I was devalued because of my origins and the color of my skin.

What I liked most about D.C. in those days was that every black man I encountered inspired me to improve myself. I would compare myself to them, and if they had a better Afro hairdo than I, then I would go to the barbershop to fix mine. If I dug a pair of Florsheim platform shoes that someone was wearing, or a little leather bag—bags for men were all the rage in the 1970s—then I would try to get one. If I heard them speak English in a particular manner, I would use that style to make my pitch to the women. In Paris, I knew I had potential that I could not realize because I was African. In D.C., I discovered myself as an individual in a large black community. I had found my Africa in America. I could compete with some people, could imitate others, and had a chance to excel. In D.C., as long as I lived in the black community, I found out that every song James Brown sang, every move Dr. J made in basketball, every speech Stokely Carmichael made, every word Toni Morrison wrote, every play Ntozake Shange staged, was also about me. I was just another black American in Chocolate City . . . or was I?

I soon found a girlfriend who made me forget the last one in Paris. When I first arrived in D.C., two Malians I had already known from Bamako acted as my hosts. Just as I would send Johnny his immigration papers later, Mamadou Diaoune and Né Dicko ("James") had corresponded with me and sent me school applications so that I could obtain a student visa at the U.S. embassy in Paris. At the time of my arrival, both Diaoune and James had their own cars. They came to pick me up at Union Station—where I had come on the train from New York—in James's Mustang. I would learn later that Mustangs were very fashionable cars in America in those days. We stopped by a Safeway store on Columbia Road to pick up some food before going to James's apartment on Mount Pleasant Street, where I would be staying. I remember being impressed by the size of that supermarket and the order in which the merchandise was organized. The produce stands were gigantic, and the fruits were the freshest I had ever seen. The floor was so clean and shiny that I could see my reflection in it. There were mirrors on the ceiling at the end of every aisle, enabling the security guard to see everything that was going on. I remembered telling James and Diaoune that I had never seen anything like that in France.

We went to James's place. I was expecting a small room on the sixth or seventh floor like the *chambre de bonne* I had in Paris. I was again surprised to walk into a large living room on the second floor of a four-story building. There was a long couch against the wall, surrounded by chairs in the middle, a double window to the right, and a dining table in front of the window. The bedroom was in the back to the left, and there was also an adjoining kitchen and a bathroom. The kitchen had a refrigerator and a stove, and the bathroom had a bathtub, a shower, a basin, and a toilet. As I took a look around, I thought to myself that only rich people in Paris could afford this kind of standard of living: an apartment on the second floor, a kitchen with a refrigerator and a stove, and a bathroom with a bathtub.

Diaoune was staying in a house with an American who had been a Peace Corps volunteer in Mali and who was now a lawyer on Capitol Hill. He had offered Diaoune free lodging for all the time he was going to school in Washington. We said that Diaoune was a lucky man, because he did not have to pay rent and therefore did not have to work in restaurants like the rest of us. We also said that Americans were nicer than French people, because a Frenchman would never take an African into his house for free. I remember that the way America had impressed me in the beginning had also led me and my friends at that time to make easy generalizations about France and America. But as time went by, some things about America would make me nostalgic for Paris and Bamako.

Every weekend, I would go out with James to a nightclub called the French Underground, a new discotheque near Dupont Circle. Diaoune could not come with us, because he was afraid of coming home late and waking up his host. In fact, as time went by, we would see less and less of Diaoune, who would find new associates on Capitol Hill, while we were mixing with the black community of northwest D.C. Every so often, I would meet Diaoune on Capitol Hill in a bar called Mr. Henry's on Pennsylvania Avenue. That place had some of the best hamburgers I had ever had. Mr. Henry's was also special for the jazz on the second floor. It was there that I saw Roberta Flack live for the first time, singing "Killing Me Softly."

It was also at Mr. Henry's that I met my first American girlfriend, Bea Jones. She was sitting at the bar across from us, with her back against a window. Diaoune had seen her first, and was threatening to go talk to her. I remembered that our eyes met and she smiled back at me, and so I got to her first.

She was sitting at the bar, a soft light falling on her smiling face, looking like a beautiful color picture in a magazine. I began to see images in my head. First I saw Diana Ross, then Beverly Johnson, Lola Falana, and Cicely Tyson. But she was more beautiful than all those beautiful black women. There was also a sweetness and confidence in her face that reminded me of Minnie Riperton and Roberta Flack. All this finally convinced me of her beauty. She wore a cottony white dress that spread over the chair, barely leaving room to reveal her white boots. A white headband surrounded her long black hair, which fell on her shoulders and made her look like an Indian woman. Her dangling gold earrings reflected the light from the bar. They were made in the shape of Africa and matched the gold pendant resting on her chest. Her skin was the color of ebony, and it radiated under the soft light like a river absorbing the sunlight at dusk. In fact, under the milk-white dress and the makeup she was wearing on her lips, cheeks, and eyelids, her complexion looked like brown sugar and reminded me of the women in Jean Toomer's *Cane*. Leaning slightly over the bar with a glass in her hand, smiling as I came toward her, she looked like a Chi Wara mask.

I looked back to make sure she was not smiling at someone else. I did not want to be like Charlie Chaplin in *The Goldrush*, in which he had returned a woman's smile and walked toward her without realizing she had been looking at another man coming up behind him. When I reached her, I asked her if I could sit down and buy her a drink. She said yes, and to my surprise, started a conversation with me.

"I am Bea Jones, that is, Mrs. Jones. How are you?" she asked.

"So your husband is married, I see," I answered, imitating a black American expression I had heard recently. "My name is Manthia Diawara, and I am from Mali. *Enchanté!*"

"You must like Roberta Flack," Bea observed. "I was watching you as she sang. Her song seemed to have transported you to another place. Am I wrong?"

"I don't understand. Speak slowly. Do you speak French?" I entreated her.

"*Un petit peu seulement*," she said with hand gestures. "I said that you like Roberta Flack's music. It makes you dream of home."

"Ah, I understand now. You look at me when she sings? I love her. She and Minnie Riperton are my favorites. When she sings, I hold my breath," I said, placing my hand on my heart.

"Yes, you do indeed. I mean, *oui, oui, vous aimez beaucoup sa chanson.*"

"No, no," I objected, putting my hand on hers, "'*Tu aimes,*' not '*Vous aimez.*' I am your friend, and you must say '*tu*' when you are talking to your friend."

That was how I met Mrs. Jones. I corrected her French, and she corrected my English. We laughed at our mistakes and congratulated each other when we got it right. Laughing, we touched each other's hands and shoulders, and it was as if we were made for each other. As if she were reading my mind at that time, Bea took my hand, put it on her chest, and said, "*Appelles-moi Bea.*"

"And you can call me Manthia." I imitated her by putting her hand on my chest.

"*Tu es très charmant, Manthia. Tu aimes beaucoup la musique.* How's that for French?"

"Excellent. Your French has gotten as perfect as you yourself. Bea, you are the most beautiful girl here; I like your beautiful eyes; your dress is very nice; I like your necklace, your . . ."

"Hold it!" she exclaimed, laughing and putting her hand on my mouth to stop me. "Not so fast, Manthia. Lay it on me one at a time, slowly. I am in no hurry. Now, what did you say about my eyes?"

"I said that your eyes are as limpid as a stream," I told her, remembering a line of nineteen-century French Romantic poetry.

"Oh come on, you're jiving me. What's so beautiful about these brown eyes?" she teased me.

"What does 'jiving me' mean?" I asked.

"It means that you are not telling the truth."

"Me? I swear to God that I am telling you the truth. I only speak from my heart. Your eyes are big, white, and beautiful.

They match your beautiful dress, your headband, your white teeth when you smile, and, and . . . "

"You've got to be jiving me. And I thought you African brothers were more serious than the ones here."

"Who, me?" I protested, beginning to feel offended. "You don't believe me, when I said that you are the most beautiful woman here. Everybody is envious of me here. My friend over there wanted to come to you first. And there are many others looking. I beat all of them. I am the luckiest man."

She kept on teasing me, and I kept complimenting her on her looks. At the end of the evening, I managed to get her telephone number and to invite her to come with James and me that weekend to the French Underground.

The French Underground was located on Twenty-first and Q Streets, in northwest Washington. The name, besides connoting a recent blockbuster film, *The French Connection*, also had a sexy sound to it that was related to everything French in America. I found the French presence in America quite important. People were impressed by French things like perfume, clothing, restaurants, pastry, and movies. I also noticed that more people were impressed with those of us who were from Mali and Senegal than with those from Anglophone Africa, simply because we spoke French. We were therefore supposed to have culture, and to be sexier. I even had an extra advantage over the other guys from my country because I had lived in Paris before coming to America. All this, instead of making me happy and contented, left me wondering at times. Why were the Americans feeling such an inferiority complex vis-à-vis the French? Why weren't they as impressed by my African origins as they were with my French experience? If France had been so good to me, then why had I left it for America?

The discotheque was packed when I arrived with Bea, James, and Khaled, a friend from Algeria I had first met in Paris. The clientele was predominantly black. There were some whites here and there, and Africans like us, who were mostly gathered around the bar area, sitting with girls in the dark corners of the room. The black Americans were on the dance floor or standing around and watching the dancers. They reminded me of traditional dances in Africa, where people gathered around the dancers to clap their hands, admire the dancers, or steal a dance step from them.

In the club, it was also remarkable that black Americans could be recognized and distinguished from the Africans and others by the way they stood—with their waists cocked as if to show that the lower and upper parts of the body were detachable—and the way they danced and dressed. They wore silk shirts, dashikis, or T-shirts with prints or images on them; slacks; and necklaces, wristbands, or gris-gris. Even though I was dressed that evening in the best suit I had brought from France, it dawned on me that this was the black style I had been looking for all my life in Bamako and Paris. This was where I had always wanted to be: hairstyles with their own languages, shirts that were symbols of some political struggles, and bodies that were modern enough to rival machines. They looked defiant and rebellious. Just looking at them brought out in me some deep feelings of Africanness that had been repressed by Islam and French colonization.

While I was lost in admiration for the people around me, the voice of the disk jockey took over the room: "And now, brothers and sisters, give me 'Hey!' for Baltimore! Those from Philly, say 'Ha!' From New York, say 'Ho!' And from Chocolate City, say 'Yo!' And don't forget, Thursday is Ladies' Night.

Now, let's give it up for our brothers and sisters from California, Sly and the Family Stone, 'Stand'!"

I looked at the women as they moved on the dance floor, some with men and others by themselves. They had braided hair with trade-beads in the braids, Afro hair, short hair, long hair falling over their shoulders, and shaved heads. They had on see-through Indian silk or linen shirts, pants that revealed their curves, skin-tight, or big dresses or skirts to mask their large sizes. Other sisters wore hot pants and short tops that revealed their navels. They danced gracefully, some ecstatically, and others moved back and forth with their partners, singing along with Sly Stone.

I looked at Bea, and she smiled back at me.

"You wanna dance?" she asked.

"Yes," I answered simply, taking her hand and moving toward the dance floor from the corner of the club where we were sitting. At that moment, I had forgotten I was different from black Americans. I was enjoying myself and feeling on top of the world. By the time we had reached the dance floor, a new song had started: "Lady Marmelade," by Labelle. It had become a hit in France before I left. So Bea and I danced to it as to a familiar song we had always danced to together. First we did the bump: We bumped against each other from the sides, the back, and the front. Then Bea started moving forward with her long legs and arms, gesturing in rhythm with of the song "Voulez-vous-coucher-avec-moi-ce-soir?" We both laughed and continued to demonstrate more dance steps, until we were interrupted by a slow song: "Let's Get It On," by Marvin Gaye.

That was the first time I held Bea, the first American girl, in my arms. Back home, I knew and loved Marvin Gaye's music. We had thought his ancestors came from Senegal because of his last name—which was common in Senegal—and because of his dark complexion and elegant manners. I danced with Bea, my body against hers, as Marvin sang, "Baby, you don't have to worry / let your feelings flow / let's get it on." Time stopped as I abandoned myself to the music and to Bea, and in my mind, Africa and America became one.

When we returned to our seats, Khaled and James were still there. Ignoring Bea's presence, Khaled started speaking French to James and me.

"Tu sais," he turned to me, *"les Américains noirs sont des racists."* ("You know something, black Americans are racist.")

"Hum!" I said, paying attention to what he was saying, but without much interest.

"Do you know why I say that?" Khaled asked. "Because they only dance among themselves. They don't even like to see other people on the dance floor. And the only ones who dance with foreigners are prostitutes."

"Come on, Khaled," James interrupted, "you always lose your manners after a little drink. What's wrong with you?"

"No, no!" said Khaled. "I am not drunk. I am telling the truth. Black Americans are racist, and they don't like Africans. That's the truth!"

"Listen, Khaled," James said, "it's always the same. You are jealous because no one dances with you. That does not mean that black Americans don't like Africans. You by yourself do not represent all of Africa."

"You just don't want to see the reality in front of you. But I am not talking to you. I am talking to Manthia. I am trying to warn him before he makes a fatal mistake."

"But Khaled," I finally said, "how do the women in here know who is African and who is a black American?" I was trying to pacify him.

"Oh, *mon cher*," Khaled answered, "don't be naïve. A black American can recognize an African a mile away in the dark." He laughed bitterly, and we all laughed as well, to change the conversation.

However, I took Bea to the dance floor again, because I did not want to give Khaled a chance for a comeback.

Then came the time to go home. The dimmers were raised, so we could see more vacant tables around us. Busboys had already started cleaning and closing down some sections. And luckily for me, Khaled had left earlier, because he had to go to work on Sunday morning. I was therefore left with Bea and James, who offered to give Bea a ride in his Mustang whenever we were ready. But I told James to go without me. I wanted to walk Bea to a cab before walking home myself.

A fresh breeze greeted us as we walked out of the French Underground. The weather was nice enough for me to leave my jacket off and hang it on my left shoulder. I covered Bea's shoulder with my right arm. The streets were empty, except for a few taxis passing by. The traffic lights were flashing yellow, and there was an occasional light coming out of the windows of some buildings. I felt romantic, like Diana Ross and Billy Dee Williams in *Mahogany*. "Manthia and Bea," I thought to myself as we crossed the street to Dupont Circle.

We sat on a bench in the park, facing the fountain. We had passed benches where homeless people were sleeping. We also had seen some people sitting and having a conversation in front of us. From where we were sitting, we could see the end of Connecticut Avenue, where the White House and the Washington Monument were located. Below us, Krammer Bookstore was to the right, and a movie theater to the left, right above R Street. It was around three o'clock in the morning. I had put my jacket over Bea's shoulders to keep her warm as we started talking.

"Manthia," Bea said, gently putting her arm on my lap, "may I ask you something?"

"Sure," I said, not knowing what to expect.

"Why did you come to America?"

I remembered being somewhat disappointed by the question. But given the seriousness with which she had asked it and the way she looked at me, I had to give her question serious consideration. I had to think of the best ways I could make my answer sound romantic enough to appeal to her.

"Well," I began, "I wanted to read black American books, from *Native Son* to *Soul on Ice*. I admired Malcolm X, the Black Panthers, and Muhammad Ali. One day, I met a black American poet by the name of Ted Joans at a bookstore called Shakespeare and Company. We became really good friends; in fact, he treated me more like a brother. It was he who advised me to come to America. He knew Langston Hughes personally, and he is friends with many writers and artists here. To make a long story short, he told me that, given my desire to become a writer, I had better chances of succeeding in America than in France. He gave me the example of Kwame Nkrumah, who had gone to Lincoln University here. When I was leaving France, he gave me a winter coat, and I gave him a boubou from home. I had always considered black Americans as my brothers."

"But why didn't you stay in Africa?" asked Bea in her quiet, controlled voice. "I mean, couldn't you get your education there?"

"Why didn't I stay in Africa? I'll tell you why," I said, rolling up my sleeves as if ready to defend myself. "Because every boy's and girl's dream there is to go to Europe or America. This is because everything is from those countries. The clothes we wear are from there; the education we receive is from there;

the music and even the food are from there. Everything good we know is from there; even God is from there. So we come ourselves to see where all these good things are coming from, to be part of the West ourselves. Of course, now that I am here myself, after being in France, I see some things differently. The racism of the West has turned me into a black nationalist."

"Then why don't you go back and help your people to over-come their self-hatred and destroy the myth of white supremacy?" Bea asked.

"I need a degree from here to make my people listen to me; otherwise, they would think I am a failure, just like the rest of them."

"That's what they all say: 'I need a degree, then I'll go back to change things.' Why don't you just admit it, Manthia? You love it here. And your friend, what's his name again?"

"Khaled."

"Yeah, whatever. What amazes me about Africans is how you all love white people, you get along perfectly with them, and now you hate us for being in the way. I mean, you Africans come here, drive cabs, and take whatever jobs you can get from us, and your friend has the nerve to call us racist. I bet he didn't think I understood French."

"Khaled's really not a bad guy when you get to know him. It's just that he's had some bad luck lately. A black guy asked him for a quarter, and when he gave it to him, the guy asked for more. He said no, and the guy started beating him up. And his girlfriend, a black American, has just left him for a diplomat from Senegal. So he is using his personal experience to pass judgment on all black Americans."

"Oh yeah? It seems to me there's more to it than that. I mean, you guys adapt so well to this country, you think this country belongs to you, forgetting all the sacrifices we made so that this goddamned country could open its doors to other people like you. Look at what's happening now: Even our streetwalkers are being replaced by Ethiopian girls on Fourteenth Street. Y'all wanna run us out of D.C."

"Bea, you are speaking as if I am here to conspire against you. I came here, in the first place, because I admired Malcolm X, and the way the black American struggle made every black person around the world proud."

"That's another thing you get wrong from the outside," said Bea, now pointing a finger at me. "You make heroes out of all them Black Nationalists—the Panthers and the Muslims. But they have all sold out. Look at what they did to Malcolm. Listen, Manthia, I was here when all that bullshit was taking place. I believed everything they said. And what did I get out of it? A husband in a federal prison in Virginia, two unemployed brothers, and several dead comrades. I know what the image of defiant blacks did for you in Africa and Europe. But here, all we have left are drugs in our communities, black-on-black crime, and brothers and sisters in jail.

"Did you say your husband is in jail?" I asked.

"Yeah," she said simply, looking at me with her big eyes.

"What happened?"

"He's a political prisoner. He was like the rest of us, a member of the Black Power Party."

"Why is he in jail?"

"He was framed by the FBI. They accused him of being part of an armed robbery, and they came in the middle of the night to snatch him away from our bedroom."

"I am sorry," I said, putting my hand on her lap.

"Oh, that's OK. As I said, he is a political prisoner. They let me see him one Sunday out of every two months. In fact, I have to go there today."

"How selfish of me! I kept you up all this time," I apologized.

"It's because I wanted you to. I like you. I wanted to know you, if we were going to be friends. And we're gonna be friends, right?" she asked me pleadingly, putting her hand over mine, which was still on her lap.

"But what about your husband?" I asked with great concern.

"Oh, he wants me to. He knows that the chances of him getting out are very small. He wants me to start my life over. He's been pushing me to get divorced from him and be free to marry again. I'm the one who's against it."

"But what about us?" I objected. "We can't do that to him!"

"Do what to him? My husband is my problem, not yours or anybody else's. I insist on wearing this ring and on being called Mrs. Jones, because I want white people at work to remember that he is a political prisoner. But what I do in my private life is my business. Besides, we're not doing anything behind his back, or to him. If we become friends, that's our responsibility."

It was five o'clock when I put Bea in a cab home. As I walked down Connecticut Avenue toward Columbia Road to go home to Mount Pleasant Street, I thought to myself that I had never been presented with as important an ethical and political dilemma as now, because of the love I was feeling for Bea. I had never been with a married woman, let alone one whose husband was unjustly jailed. I remember saying to myself, "Here is a man who was fighting for civil rights for all black people, and the FBI threw him in jail." How could I do that to him; how could I go out with his wife? I remembered what Bea had told me, that we were not doing it to him, but to ourselves. She had also said that he wanted her to start her life over. So in a sense, I was taking his place, just as in Africa, where a man took his brother's wife when she was a widow. Or was I stealing a civil-rights combatant's wife? Was I cheating on another man? Bea said that Africans wanted to run black Americans out of D.C., take their place, and make white people forget about the crimes they had committed against black people in America. How could I show her that I was different, that I wanted to continue the struggle in which her husband was involved? How could I prove to her that I was a man like her husband?

Down Columbia Road, near Eighteenth Street, I passed a Latin American restaurant to the right. A large red banner bearing the word *Pueblo* waved above the door. Later in my career as a writer in training, I would come to this place and many others on Columbia Road and Eighteenth Street to listen to poetry and fiction from Central and South America. It was in these places, for example, that I was introduced to the works of Manuel Puig, Gabriel García Márquez, and Carlos Fuentes. Next to the restaurants, or on the second floor of the houses, there were antique shops, traditional-clothing stores, and jewelry stores selling merchandise from Peru, Colombia, and Mexico, as well as bookstores. Political leaflets were everywhere in the restaurants, bookstores, and shops, calling for the liberation of El Salvador or announcing marches against the CIA's role in Guatemala, Colombia, El Salvador, and Cuba.

I passed the McDonald's on Eighteenth Street, where I had had my first hamburger and french fries and my first American coffee. This place too would become a regular spot for me in my early days in D.C. I did my homework there before going to my English-as-second-language (ESL) classes on Connecticut Avenue. Next door, I bought rock magazines like *Hit Parade* and read them while drinking McDonald's coffee. Sometimes, I simply sat down and watched people and cars go by as I dreamed.

I kept walking down Columbia Road until I got to Sixteenth Street and turned left on Mount Pleasant Road, where James and I had our apartment. I was completely awake, even as I pulled out the couch to make my bed in the living room. It was six o'clock, and some people had already woken up and were going about their business on the streets.

The truth was that meeting Bea was the beginning of a political and intellectual experience that would change my life forever. Coming from Paris, my political awareness was limited to watching people marching on the boulevards against the war in Vietnam, the emergence of postcolonial dictatorships in Africa, and some people's desire to recreate the climate of May 1968 in Paris. In other words, since I got most of my politics from rock and roll, what the rock stars did not talk about was invisible to me. The American expatriates I encountered at Shakespeare and Co.—including Ted Joans—were mostly interested in art, as far as I could see.

In those days in D.C., most of the art I was exposed to was connected to politics. The black Americans were talking about an authentic black art, black music, and black nationalism. The Central and South Americans were lobbying in D.C. against dictatorship in their countries, and artists were using their art as a weapon for liberation. Through Bea, I met activists, poets, and journalists like Stokely Carmichael, Ron Dellums, Carl Rowan, and Sterling Brown at Howard University. I did not have a full understanding of everything that was going on then in D.C. I liked Bea, so I followed her wherever she went. She liked revolutionaries, and I guessed that she wanted to make me into one. I had thought at first that her own husband was a famous political prisoner, like Angela Davis or George Jackson. I therefore used to feel important knowing that I had taken his place. As for Bea, she related to me as one would to a revolutionary hero, until the end of our affair. Even then, she had said that she was leaving out of her sense of duty; there was a chance that her husband would be retried, and she wanted to devote herself to him again. Even though I never found out if the husband eventually came out of prison—or even if he existed in the first place—I remember my time with Bea as the most mature and political moment I had lived through since leaving Bamako. I was forced to grow up from a high-school boy to a conscious black man in the world. My relationship with Bea and my life in Chocolate City in general also made me more aware of race than my life in Paris ever had.

XII

⬩▽⬩

There Must Be
Some Way Out of Here

I wake up with my heart pounding. This time it is not from the usual fever or dehydration, but from a fear that I have missed something, that something tragic and unpreventable has happened, and that I was therefore exposed to shame. I go over my dreams during the night, wondering whether it was something I had done in the past—to Johnny, to my uncle, to Macky, to Bea's husband, to Ted, or to anyone else I could not remember—or if I have done somebody wrong in the present. Or perhaps my feeling of fear and guilt grows from a neglect of my work in the past few days. Then I realize that I dreamed that I missed the day of my appointment to receive my *carte de séjour* at the *préfecture de Cité*. In my dream, when I go there the next day, they tell me that it is too late, that I am no longer eligible for a residency permit in France, and that I have forty-eight hours to leave France. It was at that moment that I woke up with my heart pounding. The uncanny and the scariest part is that the French official in my dream was the same person as the American official who interviewed me for my citizenship. He denied me my right to become a U.S. citizen because I was from Mali and they told me that I could not appeal his decision.

I get up to go to the kitchen for a glass of water. I am definitely beginning to shake off the malaria. But I smile and say to myself that it must be that Johnny's story is still haunting me. It is four o'clock in the morning, and I go back to bed. The garbage trucks are beginning to come out again to collect the trash. But I know that when I go to la Rotonde in the morning to get my café au lait and croissant, there will be fresh dog shit in the street.

The restaurant days in D.C. are fast coming back to me even before I fall asleep again. It was three o'clock in the afternoon when I boarded the M bus on Mount Pleasant Street to go to my new job at Chez Dominique. I would get off on Connecticut at K Street and walk the rest of the way to Pennsylvania Avenue, where the restaurant was located. I had been really lucky to get my job at Chez Dominique. People said that I was the first African that he had hired at the post of the pantry. The owner, Dominique, was a mean guy, and he did not think that Africans were smart enough to make a salad or a crème caramel. That was the reason why he never promoted any African from dishwasher to cook, or waiter, or pantry man. Some people also believed that Dominique was not a real Frenchman, but was a southern Italian who had emigrated to France before coming to America. That was supposedly why he lacked real French culture and was brutal with his employees, starting with the Africans.

But, as I have said, I was lucky to get my new job, because it paid well and was easy enough. I had Jean-Pierre to thank for that. The pay was $175 a week, almost $200, compared to the $75 I was making as a dishwasher. Now I could buy a car, like the rest of my friends, and get to school faster and easier. My grade point average was above 3.5, which also had qualified me for a tuition reduction. I could therefore save the rest of my money and send some to my uncle in Bamako.

My new job was relatively easy. At the Bagatelle, I had to stay after the kitchen was closed to clean the stove, the refrigerators, and the pantry table before mopping the floor and throwing out the trash. Here, I was finished as soon as I shut down the pantry section. I left the restaurant around 11:30 P.M. on weekdays and 1:30 A.M., at the latest, on weekends. I had therefore enough time to finish my homework before going to sleep or to hang out with my friends. Nor was the pantry work as physically difficult as the dishwasher work, which took its toll on your muscles and kept you sweating all night—not to say anything about all the toxic soaps, roach killers, disinfectant, and fumes that you were exposed to.

In those days, most restaurants associated the service of cold dishes (chocolate mousse, vichyssoise, crème caramel, salad) with femininity, and hot dishes with masculinity. Many African and Latin American men stayed away from the pantry—preferring to be promoted instead to assistant cooks or to remain in their positions as dishwashers—because it was implicitly understood that the cold section of the restaurant was reserved for women or homosexuals or *maricon*, as I would later be called by my co-workers from Latin America. To be honest, I had my doubts about becoming a pantry man myself. I was worried about my image and my name reaching Bamako as a person who was making his living by preparing salad in America. What would people in Bamako think? That I had become so desperate in America that I had had a change of sex to survive making salad for American men? Or would they make up stories about me being a homosexual?

Immigrants like us were more worried about our image at home than in the country of immigration. Six months after I had moved to Chez Dominique, I had bought a car, a Grand Torino, and taken my picture in it to send to my friends in Bamako. A rumor soon had spread that I was homeless in America and living with all my belongings in a car. I did not know how that rumor got started, but it was clear that I had not intended to give such an impression of myself in any of the letters I had written to my friends in Bamako. We all were very careful to send only positive images—even slightly exaggerated on the positive side—of ourselves in America. Our intention was to make people in Bamako believe that we had come to conquer America; we hid from them all the compromises that we had accepted here. Working as a pantry man was one of those compromises that would have looked bad on my résumé in Bamako.

Although we did not get much into the discussion of homosexuality as a taboo when I was growing up, masculinity was an important issue for us. We called homosexuals in Bambara *gor-jigen* (a word borrowed from Wolof, meaning "man-woman"), *jege* (fish), or *jaa* (shadow). The most negative and contemptible term used to designate a homosexual was the French word *pedet*, which signified for us a person who let other men penetrate him in the anus. Such a person was also considered to be less courageous in fights. Like the Wolof term *gor-jigen*, a *pedet* was in our minds someone who was woman-ish, not strong, always ready to suck up to real men out of cowardice. A *gor-jigen* was someone who walked like a woman, talked like a woman, cooked for men like real women did, and fell in love just like a woman. A *gor-jigen*, unlike the French *pedet*, however, was not someone for whom we reserved hatred or animosity. On the contrary, we tolerated their presence in our midst because they flattered us, enhanced our masculinity by behaving like women, and entertained us sometimes in their homes, where we listened to music, read magazines, and drank tea. We laughed at *gor-jigens* and sometimes laughed with them. The *pedet*, on the other hand, was usually a French or Lebanese man or their prostitute African male. The contempt we reserved for them was derived from detective novels and movies like *Casablanca*.

I guessed that the terms *jege* and *jaa*, which were used to designate homosexuals, were the slang of the moment intended to brag about our own masculinity by emphasizing the lack of a fixed sexuality in the other. Both *jege* and *jaa* connoted for us an androgynous aspect and a tendency to be present and absent at the same time. For us, therefore, they were not men who shined by their omnipresence, their strength, and their courage.

Because we were concerned about our image as real men in Bamako, everything we did was intended to reveal an aspect of our masculinity. This was the reason I was at first hesitant to become a pantry man at Chez Dominique. Again, it was Jean-Pierre who told me that a job did not have a gender or race written into it. He said that it was wrong to believe that a job was beneath you, provided that it was an honest way of earning a living and the highest-paying job available to you. For Jean-Pierre, a real man was one who was willing to do any job in order to take care of his own, instead of stealing, or selling drugs, or depending on other people. He said that if he were to lose his job as a chef today, he would not hesitate to start over again as a dishwasher and work his way up.

I took Jean-Pierre's advice to heart and decided that I was a modern man and that, in the modern world, the important thing was making money quickly and honestly, not labeling employment masculine, feminine, or homosexual. The pantry job was the highest-paying job I could get at the time, and it left me with plenty of time to do my homework and get better grades. So not only was I going to accept it, I would learn everything about it and be proud of being a pantry man.

I remember that it was about then that I discovered a gay bookstore called Lambda Rising, on Nineteenth and S Streets, and decided to write a paper on it for my writing class. The owner of the bookstore had a lover, and they wanted to get married just like a heterosexual couple. That made me very curious about homosexuality, and I wanted to find out more about it. When the owner found out that I was from Africa and that I was interested in discovering more about gay life, he too became very interested in me. He asked me if there were gays where I came from.

"Yes," I said, "but we do not call them homosexual or gay, as you do here. We call them *gor-jigen*, or 'man-woman.' And there is no gay movement there as you have here."

"But why?" he asked, looking at me as if he were feeling sorry for me. "Aren't gays and lesbians denied their rights there? Don't they have to remain in the closet?"

"What do you mean? I don't understand."

"I mean, can you be openly gay in your country? Aren't people afraid to live their gayness openly?"

"Well we don't call them gay or homosexual there. We believe that those are from Europe, and that they have a bad influence on our youth. That's why we tolerate the *gor-jigen*, or men-women, but we don't like what you call gays here."

"But what's the difference?" he asked me this time with a puzzled look.

"Well, you see, the people there reject what you call gay, but accept what they call a man-woman. They also have no problem with men who live in the shadow and entertain young men in their houses."

"But," he said, "they're all people who like the same sex, aren't they?"

"Yes," I said. "They are more afraid of homosexuals there than they are of the man-woman. That's why they say that homosexuality did not exist in Africa, that it was white people who brought it there."

"How about you?" he asked. "What do you think?"

"Well, for me it is different. I grew up with friends who were men-women; I also visited men in the shadow, to listen to music, eat meat brochettes, and drink tea. So, for me, it's different."

"So, why don't you go back and start a gay liberation movement? You don't even have to be gay to do that. You believe in freedom and equality, don't you?"

"Yes," I said, "but I think that the priority now in Africa is to free us from neocolonialism and imperialism. We'll see what comes later."

I remembered my interview with the owner of Lambda Rising bookstore, or rather, his many questions put to me, for one particular reason: the look of sorrow the man had cast on me. Throughout the discussion, he had seemed to feel pity for me, while at the same time accusing me of being part of a homophobic society. Even though he had not asked me, I also had the impression that he believed me to be a closet gay. Why else would a straight person be interested in writing a paper on a gay bookstore?

I wrote my paper, however, focusing on the love story between the two men and their dream of becoming the New

American Couple. The writing professor liked my paper so much that she read it aloud to the class.

It was a Saturday at Chez Dominique, around five o'clock in the evening, and Dominique himself had rushed into the kitchen with news that the night was going to be special. He had just taken a reservation from Henry Kissinger, Elizabeth Taylor, Robert Redford, and the ambassador of Iran.

"I want everything clean and perfect," he had said, looking at every section and the people in it, one by one. "Do you hear me? I don't want no screw up tonight!"

Then he kept running back and forth, like a little boy, between the restaurant and the kitchen. His behavior made everybody in the restaurant nervous, including the chef and the headwaiter. We knew that on evenings like this, when there were important customers in the restaurant, Dominique was unable to handle the pressure and would be taking it out on one of us. Our French co-workers who had said that Dominique was not a real Frenchman but was Italian used his nationality to explain why he behaved the way he did under pressure. Johnny and I had also noticed that whenever Dominique was angry, he spoke French with a heavy accent that sounded like Italian or Portuguese.

By the time that Dominique had first run into the kitchen with the news of our famous guests, I had already finished preparing the crème caramel, which was cooking in a *bain-marie* (water bath) in the oven. I always did that first, when I started work at four P.M., because the crème caramel took the longest to make in the pantry. To make it, I had to beat egg yolks with milk, sugar, and a drop of Grand Marnier liqueur on one side, while the sugar that was needed to make the caramel sauce was cooking on the other side on the stove. Then I put the caramel in small cups, poured my egg yoke cream on top, and placed the cups in the *bain-marie* to bake in the oven. After the crème caramel was cooked, I took it out to cool it to room temperature first, before placing the cups in the refrigerator. The whole thing could take more than four hours, unlike the chocolate mousse, which only took me about thirty minutes to make. While the crème caramel was baking, I also washed the lettuce, cleaned the asparagus and endive; made potato salad, gazpacho, and vichyssoise; and chopped the parsley. We had cheesecake from the Watergate Bakery, and the chef made the strawberry cake and the different seasonal fruit tarts. But, as the pantry man, I was responsible for the service of all the cold appetizers and desserts. I had therefore to make sure that we had everything in stock and ready to serve before the kitchen opened.

The hot desserts, like the baked Alaska or the soufflé, were made on order, and the waiters had to inform me ahead of time. That night, as I said, Dominique had lost control of himself because of the important guests in the house. He would come to the kitchen every other minute to check if parsley was nicely sprinkled on a rack of lamb or to see if a bowl of vichyssoise was properly filled. He would say, "This is dirty" or "That's not how you serve *baba au rhum*. Put the Chantilly here and there, and place the cherry here. Do you know whom we have here tonight? Elizabeth Taylor. Do you realize that? Oh, never mind, you imbecile! That's not how you serve cold asparagus. Give me this, I'll show you. Oh, *merde!* The asparagus is overcooked. I told you it should be al dente! Can you get that through your head? You are fired the next time I see the asparagus mushy like this. Ah, yah yah! Where did you come from? The crème caramel is burnt. *Nom de Dieu, mama mia,* I swear I'm gonna send you back to Idi Amin. Eh, ho! Where are you taking that chateaubriand? I told you to always put it upside down. Otherwise, how do you know the . . . the . . . *cuisson*, how it is medium or rare? Wipe the plates and put them under the heat before putting the food on them. Tony, make sure the champagne is properly chilled, and the towel has to be spotless. I have to do everything myself! This is Chez Dominique; it is not your grandmother's kitchen in Bolivia. Come here, come here! Did you hear me? Listen to me when I am speaking. It's like working with children. I have to explain everything a zillion times."

And so, Dominique went on all night until eleven o'clock. As I worked in my section, with my head full of music and the songs changing as the orders increased, I wondered how long I was going to take Dominique's insane rantings before I threw one of the towels, still green with parsley dye, in his face and left forever. It was then that Tony, the Bolivian, ordered a chocolate soufflé from me. Like a spoiled child crying and pulling his mother's dress while she was busy with a boiling pot on the stove, Dominique entered my section, with a cigarette between his lips, the smoke from which forced him to close one eye and keep the other half open.

"*Allez, vite!*" he said. "It's for an important customer, and I want the soufflé perfect. Do you hear me?"

I managed to utter a yes under my breath, while breaking the eggs and beating the yokes to mix with sugar, a little cream, and the special chocolate from Zurich. But Dominique did not go away. He stood by the counter and the pantry refrigerator and watched my every move. When the orders came for other items, he would take a towel to clean a plate after me, or rearrange the way I had placed the cakes for a profiterole. He kept talking all the while, insulting me, insulting Africa, and blaming himself for hiring a bunch of inept people in his restaurant. I told myself to ignore him and to sing more songs in my head: "Crosstown Traffic," "Gimme Shelter," and "Blowin' in the Wind." I took two warm bowls out of the oven and rubbed butter inside them before filling them with the chocolate mix and placing them back in the oven.

Fifteen minutes later, Dominique, who had momentarily gone inside the restaurant, came back screaming, "Where's the chocolate soufflé, damn it?!"

I went and took them out of the oven and was getting ready to sprinkle some powdered sugar on top of them when Dominique said that they were not good. They did not rise high enough, and as he had said, he wanted them perfect. I looked him straight in the eye, hoping that he would see how angry I was and let it go, but he refused to back down. He dumped my soufflés in the garbage and took off his jacket, cursing me all along.

"I'll make the soufflé myself. I'll show you what a soufflé is. It is something that was invented in France, and we cannot have any other kind of soufflé here. This is Chez Dominique. *Nom de Dieu.* I have in my restaurant Elizabeth Taylor, Henry Kissinger, Robert Redford, and all the important people who rule this world. And you call this a soufflé? Do you want to ruin me? *Merde!* I'll show you what a soufflé is. With these people, I have to do everything myself. *Nom de Dieu!*"

With that, Dominique finished preparing his soufflé and put the bowls in the oven. When he came back to retrieve them, the whole kitchen was looking at him. They were flatter than the ones I had made. I kept working and pretended not to see anything but my work. The songs I was hearing then were "Knock on Wood," "Young, Black and Gifted," and "Say It Loud." Dominique blamed his misfortune on the oven and accused the chef of not putting it on the right temperature.

Before I knew it, he was taking his frustration out on a waiter who had forgotten to leave the cork of the wine bottle on the guests' table. Then it was Johnny's turn. The dishes were dirty; a wine glass was wet; he was lazy; people did not build America by sleeping on the job; Africa deserved Idi Amin; you need a person like that or nothing doing.

I woke up Sunday morning still in a bad mood from the night at Chez Dominique. It was true that, as immigrants, we did our best to ignore our employers' racism, abuse, and stupidities. We were different from black Americans, who would have done something about a guy like Dominique right away. That was another reason, besides the low wages, why they did not work in French and Italian restaurants. Yet, at moments like last night, I wished that I were a black American so that I could teach Dominique a lesson. I bet that restaurant owners like him took advantage of our illegal working status to treat us as they did. They knew that we would not fight back for fear of getting into trouble with the immigration services. They also got away with their despicable behavior largely because most immigrants from Latin America and Africa feared and respected them as their employers and as authority figures.

As for me, I had to keep focused on the important thing, my education. I did not want, therefore, to lose my cool while I still needed the job to support my education. I had to pretend that I believed—as most of my co-workers did—that Dominique was a fool and that therefore his words did not hurt. I had to pretend that humiliation at the workplace in America did not count, anyway, because no one here knew our names or where we had come from. I had to tell myself that only at home did honor, truth, self-respect, and one's image in public count. But what Dominique had done last night was too much to bear, too much to take, even for make-believe. I decided therefore to wait for the first opportunity to quit. I would look for another job and leave on the busiest night, without a warning.

On Monday, at eleven o'clock, I was still smarting over the soufflé incident and Dominique on my way to school. My first class that day was on African literature, taught by Charles Larson, who had quickly become my friend and confidant. I decided that I would probably talk to him about Dominique at the end of the class. Meanwhile, I had to stop by the Mali embassy at 2130 R Street to check my mail, before catching the bus on Twenty-first and Massachusetts Avenue to American University. We used 2130 R Street as our mailing address, first, because we moved a lot in those days and, second, because we did not want the immigration officials to come to our apartments in case they were looking for us.

At the embassy, I found a letter from my uncle waiting for me. I said to myself that I'd wait till I was on the bus to read it; then I would not mind the bus ride to school or think about Dominique.

> Bamako, May 28, 1975
> Mody Diawara
> Gérant Station Shell
> Bamako, Mali

> Dear Son,
> I have received your letter and the money you sent. May Allah grant you a long life; may he protect you from evil where you are. Everybody is fine here. Praise be to Allah, the merciful. You have the greetings of your mothers: Sokhona and Nana. Your brothers are fine. They greet you. Your sisters too. Everybody in Mali is doing well. *Tabari K' Allah* [Praise

the Lord]. All of Mali greets you and your friends. Give them my greetings. I greet your teachers, your hosts in America, and your workmates. Tell them we are doing fine, and there is nothing but peace here.

My dear son, don't forget yourself; always remember who you are. Remember our proverb "No matter how long a piece of wood stays in the river, it will not change into a crocodile." So remember that you will always remain a Soninké from Mali. When you are successful in America, you belong to Mali. But when you also fail, you will still belong to your fatherland. So don't forget yourself, always remember who you are. That's what I have to tell you on the question of who you are. You will never be an American, but always a Soninké from Mali.

As regards your ancestors and your discovery of their glorious past, and hence your new identity, let me tell you that you are mistaken. There is nothing to be proud of because your ancestors were idolaters and fought against the spread of Islam. Forget about them; your true identity is in Islam; your true community is among the Moslems of the world; your true kingdom is the Kingdom of Allah whose only prophet is the Prophet Mahomet, peace be with him.

Son, do not let yourself be tempted by the devil in America. You cannot go back to your ancestors' way of life, because they did not know Islam. And I do not recommend that you participate in anything that goes against Allah's path. To put it simply, the Bambara king, the Soninké king, all the way up to Sunjata, King of Mande, were all idolaters. They were lost souls, and there is nothing to admire about them. On the contrary, you should pray for their souls.

If Black people in America want to go back in history to reclaim your ancestors, that is their business. If they want to glorify idolaters as the source of their identity, let them do so. But I do not recommend that you have anything to do with them. The reward of Allah's Heaven is ten times greater than anything in this world. By returning to your ancestors' way of life, this is what you will be denying yourself.

My son, it has been almost two years since now when I gave you my permission to go to America. I told you to go study and bring us back knowledge or work and bring us wealth. If it were knowledge of your ancestors we had wanted, we would not have sent you to America for that. I want you to study something that will make us proud of you, something to make the whole Mali take note of you. I want you to remember your mission and leave aside American distractions. Stay away from all those people who do not believe in Allah. Do not forget your daily prayers and give to the poor.

My son, the rest of the news here is fine. I bought cereal with the money you sent and the moneys I received from Paris to send to the village. Life is very hard in the village because it did not rain much, and people have run out of provisions. In Bamako, everything is fine. Your sister Bintou Diawara had married Jambere Kamissoko, and they have gone together to Paris where he works. He is a very good man; everybody liked him here. Don't forget to visit them when you go to Paris. Your brother Mamadou Diawara has dropped out of school. We are now getting him a passport so he can go to Paris and work.

My son, I pray that this letter will find you in good health. I pray for you night and day. Again, don't forget us, and don't forget yourself.

Your father,
Mody Diawara

I reread my uncle's letter. The bus was passing by Massa-chusetts and Wisconsin Avenues. We were now in the rich res-idential areas of D.C., with big green lawns, expensive cars parked in the lanes, and only white residents. I felt so lonely in the world now. How could my uncle interpret my letter in this way? How could he reject my view without knowing the con-text in which I had written my letter? Couldn't he see that the black Americans were on our side? Looking out the window, as the bus passed by the world, I felt as if no one understood me. My uncle believed that African Americans were lost souls; Bea thought that all that Africans wanted was to take the black Americans' place among white people; Dominique treated all Africans and Spanish-speaking employees like small children; Khaled, my friend from Algeria, thought the same way my uncle did about black America; and my white professors also believed that Africans had nothing in common with blacks here, as if all Africans were the same.

My uncle's letter had left me with no other choice but to find my own way in life, to choose my own politics and my own system of beliefs. I would always respect him as my father and behave as his son, but it had become clear to me that we saw differently in religion and politics. Why could he not understand that the reason black Americans were resurrecting ancient African kingdoms was less against Islam and more to put black people into a historical context? Why did he have to see everything through religion? What I had said in my letter to him was not an attack on Islam, but a celebration of my ancestors.

I did not understand such behavior coming from my uncle, unless he was influenced by the person who read my letter to him. My uncle had never been to school; he had therefore needed to rely on my cousins and nephews in the house to read and write his letters. I myself did it for him when I was in Bamako. When a letter reader or writer did not understand something, the reader interpreted it in his or her own words. Similarly, if the person reading my letter did not like me, the reader could put words in my uncle's mouth and so on. Somebody must have said something, therefore, to push my uncle to write me in this tone.

I was still feeling lonely, even as I tried to understand the reasons behind my uncle's letter. From that moment on, I realized that life was going to be a struggle to explain myself to Africa and to America. Because of my exposure to American culture, I could no longer speak my mind freely and expect my uncle and other people in Bamako to understand me. And my identification with my uncle and the values with which he had raised me also required that I preface my views to Americans with an anthropological explanation. My loneliness was coming from my realization that my uncle's letter had shown that no one in Africa or America agreed with me.

But, just as Dominique's behavior the night before had led me to ask myself why I was still working in his restaurant, this letter too was forcing me to make some choices by myself. That meant that from now on, I would have to live in a world whose values and politics I would have to hide from my uncle, lest he reject me as a bad Muslim. I would have to adopt a double consciousness vis-à-vis him and America. Oh, how I had wished that I could stay in his confidence forever, come running to him every time I had done something right, every time I had learned something new, every time I had won a victory. Now I had to build a world apart from him: a secular world where Allah did not intervene every time, a modern world where the heroes were called Martin Luther King, Jr., Malcolm X, Angela Davis, and Richard Wright—all names that my uncle had never heard about. I decided, therefore, that if loneliness was the price for my exile and my political consciousness, I had better learn to like it.

It was four o'clock at Chez Dominique, on a Friday afternoon. I was chopping parsley as part of the routine in my daily preparation. Johnny was peeling English potatoes for the chef, who was busy cooking different sauces for the evening. There were other assistants in the kitchen: some cleaning fish, some arranging pots and skillets for cooking different dishes, some cutting onions for onion soup and *coq au vin* sauce, and some bringing the big *boeuf bourguignonne* pot out of the refrigerator. As we worked, we made jokes. Johnny and I ganged up on our Hispanic co-workers, who outnumbered us by at least eight, without counting the waiters.

"Come on, Moreno," one of them said. "Where's the soufflé? Give me my soufflé, or I'll call Dominique."

Everybody laughed, and I with them, without interrupting our work.

"Come on, compadre," I said soon after the laughter began to quiet down. "Who's the most afraid of Dominique, you or I? As soon as he enters the kitchen, you begin to tremble. Isn't that right, Johnny?"

"Yeah, Dominique is his boyfriend," said Johnny. Everybody laughed again. The smell of chopped onion now filled the restaurant. Some people were laughing with tears in their eyes—leaving me to wonder for a second whether the tears were caused by the laughter or the burn from chopped onions.

It was at that moment that Tony—from Bolivia—came running into the kitchen and screaming, "Immigration, immigration! They coming, immigration, they coming!"

At first, we thought that he was trying to fool us with a bad joke. But as the other waiters and busboys came running behind him, some of us began to panic too and run in different directions. I was frozen in my place, standing with two long parsley-chopping knives in my hands, between the counter and the pantry refrigerator. I saw some people running into the cold room for a hiding place, some into the toilets, some behind the dishwasher racks, and some jumping into the hamper to cover themselves with dirty linen. Some tried to exit through the kitchen door that led to Nineteenth Street, but seeing the immigration officers waiting there, they ran back into the kitchen. Some went through the door leading to the basement and to the storage room, where they could escape by taking an elevator to Pennsylvania Avenue. But it seemed that those exits too were guarded by the immigration officers. The chase went on for a long time, while I was still standing in the same place, with the knives in my hands, wondering what to do.

My whole life flashed in front of me. Why didn't I run like all the others and try to escape? Now it was too late. The events of the other night, when Dominique had humiliated me in front of everybody, should have been a clear signal. Why hadn't I quit then? And my uncle's letter. Why hadn't I listened to all these warnings? My left eye had been twitching all day. Weren't all those signals enough warning? Now it was too late. Now I had lost everything for taking too much risk, for failing to read the real meaning in my uncle's letter, for ignoring the twitching of my left eye, which would have been enough of a sign for anybody else in Mali. Now it was too late. They will put my name in their books, and I could not return here again. How about my school: Was this the end of it all? Was I going back to Bamako without a diploma? That was worse than death; it was better to die than to have everyone laughing at you, everyone treating you like a failure, as the guy who was expelled from America, as the guy who did not finish his studies.

I was still paralyzed by my thoughts when a woman came near me, with a black leather bag strapped over her shoulder.

"Excuse me," she said, "can you please put away those knives?"

"Me?" I asked, suddenly waking up from one nightmare into another. I was now wondering what the woman had in her black bag.

"Yes, you." She was now standing behind the counter near me. "Put away the knives. They are dangerous weapons, and you can never tell what people will do in desperate moments."

"You're right," I said calmly, putting the knives, still full of parsley, in the drawer and closing it again.

"Thank you!" she said. "You know, people are different. Some of these people prefer to die than to be sent back home. They can harm somebody or harm themselves, if they have to."

She looked at me in the eyes for some time, before moving away to look around the rest of the kitchen. I remember trying to hide my hands from her because they were shaking and trying hard to look back at her to hide my guilt. But, just as I was trying to recollect myself, who should enter the kitchen but Macky Tall.

"*Bonjour*, Manthia," he greeted me maliciously. "I heard that immigration is visiting you today."

"Macky," I pleaded with him, "why are you speaking in French to me? Do you want to get me in trouble with them?"

"Don't worry, Manthia; they've already rounded up their people."

"Please, Macky, can you go away? They're coming."

"OK. So long, man!" he said, moving toward the door.

"So long," I repeated, making a peace sign with two fingers.

Still standing behind my counter, I saw a line of my comrades in handcuffs, and framed on either side by immigration officers, pass by me.

"*¡Adios, Amigo!*"

"*¡Adios!*"

"*¡Hasta luego, Amigo!*"

"*¡Adios!*"

"*¡Adios, Moreno!*"

"*¡Adios!*"

And so it went on until Johnny was eye level with me. He did not say *"au revoir"* or *"¡adios!"* or "so long." He just winked at me, and I winked back, forcing back my tears. They had all left, and the restaurant was empty. I threw away my apron and quit Chez Dominique. That was how Johnny was deported. It could have happened to me, too.

When I wake up in the morning, my son has already left for school and my malaria is completely gone. I say to myself that I have to go to la Rotonde and resume writing my book on African immigration in France.

Fin